THE SPELL OF CHINA

A Chinese Street Scene

The Spell of China

Archie Bell

with many photographs by
E. M. Newman

Orchid Press

THE SPELL OF CHINA
Archie Bell

First edition, The Page Company, Boston 1917
Second edition, Orchid Press, Bangkok 2018

Orchid Press
P.O. Box 19,
Yuttitham Post Office,
Bangkok 10907 Thailand

www.orchidbooks.com

Copyright © Orchid Press 2018
Protected by copyright under the terms of the International Copyright Union: all rights reserved. No part of this publication may be reproduced in any form or by any means, electronic or mechanical, including photocopying, recording, or by any information storage or retrieval system without prior permission in writing from the publisher.

ISBN: 978-974-524-208-1

To

E. M. NEWMAN

AND

CHAS. D'EMERY
MASTER TRAVEL TALKER AND MASTER CAMERAMAN,
COMPANIONS OF THIS PLEASANT JAUNT INTO OLD CATHAY

CONTENTS

Foreword x
   I   A City of Terraces 1
   II   Canton the Incredible 16
   II   The Widows of Ah Cum 32
   III The Celestial Riviera 39
   V   "Paris of the Far East" 50
   VI   City of Heaven by Houseboat 77
   VII "Son of the Ocean" 105
  VIII China's Triple Heart 122
   IX   Burying a President 137
   X   Imperial Purple Metropolis 147
   XI   In Forbidden Palaces 171
   XII On Royal Bypaths 195
  XIII An Oriental Berlin 206
  XIV China's Little Sister 216

Bibliography 240
Index 242

LIST OF ILLUSTRATIONS

A Chinese Street Scene ii
Map of China .... xii & xiii
Hongkong, from the Peak 7
Peak Railway, Hongkong 11
Li Hung-chang 13
Boat-dwellers, near Canton 19
Pearl River, Canton 23
An Old Coolie 25
Wa-Tap Pagoda, Canton 27
Interior of Temple of the five hundred Genu, Canton 29
Sedan Chairs 31
Waterfront, Macao 41
Opium Smoking 45
Street Scene, Shanghai 53
The "Mandarin's Tea House" 57
Chinaman with bird-cage 61
Market-place, Shanghai 65
Cha Pih-yung 69
A Manchu Woman 73
A Chinese Canal 83
Watching the Canal Boats Pass 87
An Ancient Bridge, Hangchow 91
West Lake, Hangchow 95
A Garden in Hangchow 101
A Typical Chinese Village 109

A Chinese Junk	117
Hankow	125
Coolies, Hankow	133
The Late Yuan Shih-k'ai	141
Beyond the Walls, Peking	149
Chinese Priests at Prayer	151
Lama Temple, Peking	153
White Jade and Gold Buddha, Peking	157
Arch in Temple of Confucius, Peking	159
The Temple of Heaven, Peking	163
Brazier at Altar of Heaven	165
The Altar of Heaven	169
The Pavilion, Summer Palace	177
The Lake, Summer Palace	179
Marble Boat, Summer Palace	183
Marble Bridge, Summer Palace	187
The Kettler Pai-lou	189
Residence of the Late Yuan Shih-k'ai	193
Stone Animals at Ming Tombs	199
Boys at Great Wall	203
The Great Wall	205
Street Scene, Tientsin	213
Yang-ban, Seoul	219
A Korean Beauty	221
A General View of Seoul	223
Korean Farmers	227
A Typical Korean Gentleman	231
Man in Mourning, Korea	233
A Gateway in Seoul	235
The *Keikairo*, North Palace	237

FOREWORD

"I like to read books of travel," an old lady remarked to me, as she held a copy of "The Spell of the Holy Land" in her hand. "I can read them and imagine that I am visiting the countries written about. But there is one fault that I have to find with all of them; they tell you about the trip from New York to Jerusalem, Zanzibar or Patagonia, but they never tell how much the trip costs. Why, I was thirty years old before I knew that it was possible to spend the summer in Europe without a small fortune."

Within the quarter-hour another asked me: "Did you find it expensive traveling in China?" Half an hour later: "Does it cost more to travel in China than in the United States?"

Perhaps the old lady was right. The important matter of what a trip costs may have been omitted in most cases. It may have been done purposely. The singer does not wear a placard to blazon the fact that she spent five thousand dollars having her voice trained. Nor does the painter say: "It cost me five thousand dollars for instruction before I produced that canvas." Writers may have considered it as unnecessary to enumerate the steamer, railway or hotel fares that enabled them to see what they described.

A question in regard to the expense of a trip to and through China is pardonable, however, because, until recently, it was not undertaken by the casual tourist, and the excursion offers so many joys for the amount demanded in payment the number of travelers from America to the Celestial Republic is increasing so rapidly and is so easily accomplished that it is advisable to pass the good news along. Traveling is not expensive in China; no more so than in the United States. The average man or woman, who is satisfied with a comfortable hotel room and who does not demand a suite of rooms as a shelter for the night, and the one who keeps his requirements in the daytime to about what they would be in an American city, will find it possible to cover the long itinerary sketched in this volume for an amount ranging between fifteen hundred and two thousand dollars, granting that about five months elapses between sailing from an American Pacific port and returning.

One should not go to China expecting to remain less than three months, and the fascinating novelty of the Orient might begin to fade after a six months' tour. Between the two extremes is the length of time recommended by one who believes that a quarter year holiday in this ancient land of the pagoda is one of the most enjoyable jaunts afield now available to the Western tripper.

ARCHIE BELL.

Map of China

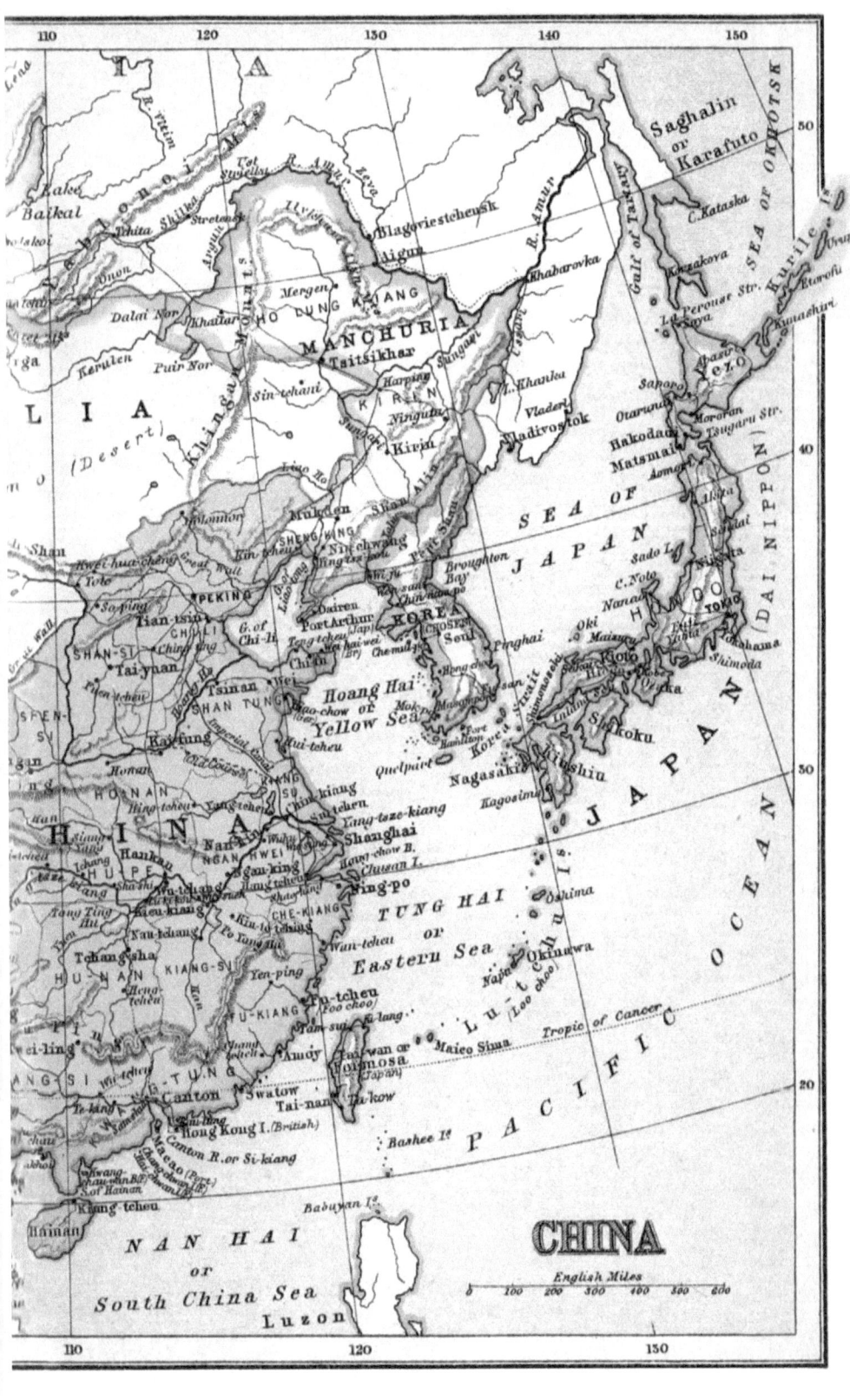

CHAPTER I

A CITY OF TERRACES

NAPOLEON BONAPARTE said: "When old China begins to move, she will surprise the world," and thus proved himself to be a good prophet. China has not only begun to move, causing the world to look on in amazement, but she has continued to move, and the world is more surprised than it was when the tremendous and ancient dragon raised herself for the first real attempt to rouse from a sleep that endured for so many centuries that she was blinded by the light of day, befogged and barely knew which way to turn. Perhaps her first impression was that it might have been better to remain asleep. The comatose condition had not been without its pleasant sensations. Like the dreams of one of her own opium-smokers, the rainbow centuries had passed and left her in the mauve vapor of unreality. She declined to admit the real, even when her eyes were open. Sleep and dreams were preferable, and although she had been awakened several times within a thousand years by the abominable clatter of young nations, their encroachments, claims and demands, she merely blinked her eyes fretfully and resumed her slumber, apparently leaving strict orders that she was not to be "called" until the beginning of the Twentieth Century, A.D., as the children among the nations reckon time. And then, when the time arrived, she awakened without a call from the outside. Old China awakened from within. She heard her own voice calling her to be up and stirring. And in this, probably Napoleon Bonaparte would be surprised. It was more than even a good prophet would have ventured. China is moving, and, in some respects, she is causing greater surprise by the celerity of her movements than by the fact that she decided to move at all.

Like a peevish grandparent, she is obliged to admit that she has been asleep, but she excuses herself by explaining that, in her life, a few centuries were nothing more than a brief spell of drowsiness. She is awake now, as she was awake in those days when she felt that she could go out and conquer the world. The seat of her central government is to China the center of the universe. While she slumbered, some of the children and upstarts among foreign nations tried to convince themselves that this was not true. But the dragon is stirring again and the world may well be surprised. Nothing more unexpected has occurred since the fall of Babylon, Athens, or Rome. Yes, a few things have happened since China went to sleep; America has been discovered and a great nation has resulted, political power has shifted in Europe from Spain to other countries; Japan, a troublesome little group of islands near her coastline, has shown remarkable vigor, and the heir to the imperial throne of her ancient sister, Korea, is a prisoner in his palace. The huge dragon realizes all of these things—none better than she—and the world wonders what is about to happen. The great French emperor said that China's awakening would change the face of the globe. Lord Wolseley added: "They are the most remarkable race on earth and I have always thought and still believe them to be the coming rulers of the world."

Aware of these things which are now common knowledge, I knew that one who had postponed his tour of China until the last Manchu emperor was lying in his tomb and Yuan Shi-k'ai ruled the country as an unpopular president, having unsuccessfully attempted to declare himself emperor and to found a new dynasty, must feel as one passing through Dante's gate and "abandon hope" of seeing China as she was in the days before the awakening. Probably, in the rather lengthy days of the Pacific voyage, I imagined that China in transition could not be so fascinating to the Westerner as in the older day when the Son of Heaven sat on his throne and any abortive attempt to change the ancient customs and manners was speedily answered by the sending of the silken cord, or decapitation. But the preconceived notions were quickly dissipated after arriving on Chinese soil.

One of the first things that attracted my attention was a big, stalwart Chinese blacksmith at his forge, swinging a sledge hammer. Stripped to the waist and wearing only bathing-trunks, his great bronze body was picturesque, as he stood only a couple of feet beyond the entrance of his shop on the public thoroughfare. And this powerful blacksmith at his forge wore a wrist-watch! At least in his own mind, he was very modern. He had adopted Western notions; at least he had adapted them to his own requirements. At the moment he merely caused a smile, but, as the days passed, he became not only typical of Hongkong, where I saw him, of Southern China, where the great revolutionary movements originate, but also of the vast republic.

I thought of him when visiting great commercial establishments, factories, hotels and even in the palaces of China's rulers. He was a veritable symbol of the great republic of four hundred millions of people, Orientals at heart and by heredity and training, who are popularly supposed to be adopting the civilization of the West, but who, in reality, are absorbing much of it and adapting it to their own requirements. A wrist-watch on a half-naked Chinese blacksmith! At the moment it was funny, but six weeks later it was no funnier than when I sat at table with a Chinese statesman and observed him wrestling with the intricacies of a knife and fork and attempting to swallow bread and butter without a word of disgust for the things that Westerners eat and the awkward implements employed in the process.

But this combination of knives, forks and chopsticks, or that of the undressed blacksmith and the wrist-watch, and thousands or tens of thousands of combinations of the ancient and modern, the unmistakable evidences of the "awakening" of China, should not discourage the prospective tourist. He should not draw upon his imagination, after reading of progress in China, fearing that everything has changed and that human eyes are no longer privileged to see the splendid or sordid sides of the amazing country which many serious writers have put down as the "hope of humanity." There is also the reverse side of the picture. There is much in China that can never change, much that it will take centuries to change; and, as before hinted, the veneer of Western civilization, the adaptation or misappropriation of occidental borrowings leaves the country as fascinating to the tourist as ever before, and the means of communication, hotels, railroads, even the attitude of the people towards the stranger have changed only for the better, and contribute a comfort, even a luxury, to Chinese travel and sight-seeing that were unheard of when the Son of Heaven sat on his throne.

Less than twenty years ago, even enthusiastic travelers who approached China's shores soon lost their enthusiasm and confined their visits to the larger coast cities, unless being specially desirous of reaching some inland point they pressed on and usually had tales of hardship to relate afterwards, inevitably ending with advice to others to profit by their misfortunes. Even the globe-trotters who ventured into the great ports usually were satisfied to "do" China in a few hours from a rikisha or sedan chair. As late as the year 1900 a well-informed writer said: "Nobody travels in China for pleasure," yet, for centuries, every traveler who put pen to paper, after penetrating beyond the outer crust of China, the principal port cities, scarcely found his vocabulary sufficient to communicate his impressions of the magnificent enigma. It was all a colossal contradiction, quite appropriate to the subject, for China was and is the supreme paradox of the earth. The so-called "Riddle of the Sphinx" is a problem for children by comparison. China is incomprehensible to the Western mind, just as it was when the first "paleface" arrived in the country. As it has been often repeated, the Westerner who attempts to understand is either a sublime egotist or a fool. But this eternal paradox and contradiction, even the well-meant advice of early travelers have had only one effect, and that has been to arouse curiosity and to attract attention to China. Perhaps it was true, in a measure, that travelers did not go to the celestial empire for pleasure twenty years ago. It is not true of the celestial republic today The world's steamers discharge thousands of passengers on Chinese soil every year, and what was once a "forbidden country," now attracts hordes of pleasure-seekers. Perhaps Americans are in the lead numerically, as the hotel lobbies swarm with them, the English language being heard more frequently than any other, excepting the countless dialects of China itself. China has become a favorite playground for sight-seers. Many of them are sophisticated travelers who find that the most novel sights on earth are among earth's oldest people.

I entered China by her great southern gateway, Hongkong; and for many reasons would recommend this route to others. Hongkong is the Asiatic terminus of many steamship lines that girdle the globe. It seems to be the great Chinese point of communication with everywhere. Something similar exists in New York as a gateway to the eastern part of the United States. Just as there is a Boston and Philadelphia, so there is a Shanghai and Tientsin in China. The city of Hankow is located on the Yangtze-Kiang inland, but approachable by steamer, as if Chicago were in the headwaters of the Mississippi. Travelers having a distinct destination may select other ports and find it a saving of time and a convenience, but for one who goes to China to see as much of the country as possible in a given time, Hongkong is the preferable gateway and more easily reached than any of the others, because it seems to have direct communication by steamers with all the other great ports of the world, as one readily realizes upon consulting the sailing lists of the world's steamship lines.

I admit that my first impression of China was not wholly up to anticipations, but China was not to blame, neither were the Chinese. A heavy tropical rain was falling and heavy clouds hung over the hills that surround the "Gibraltar of the Orient," looked upon by many strategists as important to Great Britain as the colossal granite gateway to the Mediterranean. A few Chinese junks,

A City of Terraces

with batwing sails, floated close to the ship as we came to anchor in the bay. Naked yellow sailors, and men with long capes made of palm-leaves came close by—men and sails dripping wet. And to the depressing scene was added the rather ridiculous examination by the British officials, who seemed to suspect that every comparatively innocent tourist who needed a change of clothing, necessarily placed in a box for the convenience of traveling, was a terrible spy of the enemy with designs upon Hongkong and carrying enough bombs in a small handbag to blow the place to atoms. But these were days of unusual excitement at home, and Englishmen in Colonial possessions were, perhaps, over-zealous in watchfulness. Hongkong is a free port, and the world's people usually come and go with less restraint or red tape inquiry and investigation than is commonly met with in other great ports of the world. Even the inconvenience of registering at the police office of Hongkong on arrival and departure was easily overlooked in after days when many pleasant memories of the place crowded for recognition in recollections of the visit.

Hongkong, contrary to popular impression, is not a city, but an island, the capital of which is Victoria, named after England's beloved queen. "Hongkong," however, usually means the city, and one rarely speaks of Victoria, or hears the word spoken. It is as if New York City were called "Manhattan," the name of the island on which it is located. The vast harbor covers a water area of about ten square miles, with different channel entrances for ships from Australia, the Philippines, or Straits Settlements, and those which come from the northern coast, Japan and North America. Perhaps there is a more beautiful harbor on earth, the distinction having been claimed for Nagasaki, Naples, Algiers and Rio Janeiro. The last mentioned I have not visited, but I have been on ships that poked their noses into the other waters, and excepting that "pearl surrounded by emeralds," Algiers, I have no hesitancy in casting a vote for Hongkong. It seems an exalted Mediterranean port, a gigantic replica of those beautiful bays along the French Riviera that have long prompted the admiration of the world. It seems land-locked, the beautiful hills rising in all directions around the azure waters of the bay. The steamer that floats into the harbor and passes an island or two, seems hopelessly "trapped" to the stranger. Only the experienced traveler will be able to see by which channel the ships enter from Pacific waters. And just as Venice is a never-to-be-forgotten marvel, if approached at sunrise, as the beautiful bride of the Adriatic seems to be rising from the waves, so there is a weird distinction to this city of granite which, as Longfellow said of

Amalfi, seems to be dipping her toes in the sea, and then rising by staircase streets far off to the top of the hill known as the "Peak," a height of only twelve hundred feet, but seeming to be much higher, either when the bay is viewed from the heights, or when the mountainside first comes to sight from the deck of an incoming steamer.

But it was raining in Hongkong; it was the "rainy season." Now, everyone who has traveled to tropical and semi-tropical countries, feels that he has seen rain. The American is obliged to go no further from home than Panama or other Central American States to see the sky open, drenching the earth with great torrents that seem to threaten the older interpretation of the Biblical rainbow. But it is safe to venture the opinion that one who has not been in Hongkong in the "rainy season" has never seen rain. In many other districts famous for their precipitation, the rain comes in showers. Thus, in Panama it rains many times a day at certain seasons of the year. In Hongkong it rains ceaselessly for twenty-four hours a day "in season," and frequently the waterfall continues for many days, even weeks. Fortunately, the city of Victoria nestles against the verdant hillside and the streets have wide stone gutters that carry the torrents to the harbor. Men and women in any corner of the earth seem to adapt themselves to physical conditions. Caspar Whitney relates that no dinner in a Broadway cafe has seemed more appetizing to him than did chunks of walrus blubber when he was in the frozen fields on the trail of the muskox. The camel is utilized as man's beast of burden in one country, the reindeer serves the same purpose elsewhere, and so does the llama in Peru, caribou in the Philippines and sheep in Madeira. The Westerner, who would consider staying indoors during a gentle rain at home, soon becomes accustomed to the terrific rainfall of Hongkong. Waterproof clothing becomes a necessary part of his wardrobe, and he ventures forth with no more thought than he would give to the tropical sunshine that suggests the advisability of a helmet and umbrella.

Hongkong is not typically Chinese; technically speaking, it is not Chinese at all, being a British possession, where a large part of the population of about one-half million is Mongolian. The island was first occupied by the British in 1839, when they hurriedly left Canton, Macao and other cities further south, as a result of the opium disputes. It is likely that the name is derived from the Chinese "Heung-kong" which means "Fragrant Streams," an appellation arising from the fact that the ships of the East India Company came there for water from the hillsides before starting on return voyages. Previous to 1839, the island was inhabited by

Hongkong, from the Peak.

not more than four thousand natives, most of whom, like the natives of Yokohama, Japan, previous to the coming of the white man, were engaged in deep-sea fishing, a trade of vast importance in a country where fish forms one of the principal articles of food. Hongkong was established as a crown colony in 1843. The peninsula of Kowloon, which stretches out near to the island, had been occupied for some time as a sanitarium by the British, for in the earlier days of occupation, terrible pestilences like cholera and fever had swept over the place; and in 1898, by the terms of a convention at Peking, Kowloon and several islands, most of which were desired for purposes of defense, about four hundred square miles in all, were leased to Great Britain for ninety-nine years.

I had not been many hours in Hongkong, however, before I absorbed enough "atmosphere" to know that I was in China, for although I heard an Englishman say that "one white man is worth a thousand Chinks," and the proportion of population, even in Hongkong, seems to the stranger to be almost at that figure, my eyes were on the Chinese rather than the British, who came to the hotel for the inevitable tea as punctually as when their country was not en-aged in warfare. England always impresses foreign colonies with three of her institutions: tea in the afternoon, handkerchiefs pushed up the sleeves and "dress" for dinner. They are the same everywhere. Nobody who comes into contact with them expects anything else. An American who has done a business running as high as twenty thousand dollars in one year with an English manufacturer in the Far East, told me that he had broken off formerly pleasant relations on account of the "tea habit." Having but a few hours, while his ship was in port, he called upon the dealer to place his order, but the Englishman said: "You will pardon me, please, but you have called exactly at my tea-hour," whereupon he put on his hat and started to go out. The American said: "I will not only pardon you, but I shall never see you again," and the Englishman lost his customer. Put him on a cocoanut island in the middle of the ocean, and you will find that he is the same; tea, handkerchief and "mess jacket" for dinner. Perhaps these things are innocent amusements in themselves, but the trouble lies in the fact that they impress themselves upon the "natives," who adopt them because they want to be "like white men." These things thrive in Egypt and other colonies, if the English have been there long, but I have never seen them carried to such a ridiculous extent as in Hongkong The climate is usually hot and the natives dress for the weather, most of them, so it is rather absurd to see a "Chino" wearing European clothes in an effort to be "English."

A City of Terraces

But this commingling of East and West may be a part of the charm of Hongkong. It is a great city and magnificently situated seaport, populated chiefly by people who seem to be neither oriental nor occidental. Although they would not admit it, the English of long residence have absorbed much of the East, doing it unconsciously. One who entertained me at dinner at his home, served soup in the place of dessert, in the oriental fashion. But the occidental is not a natural or good imitator; the oriental is.

On the second or third day, I took the cable railway that runs up to the Peak, which lies back of the city on the mountaintop. The city is really in three stories. Business houses of the better sort are on the waterfront, where the sun sizzles. The natives dwell in crowded streets on the middle terrace. The Europeans, principally the English, dwell on the top shelf.

On the Peak, where the cable railway discharges its passengers every fifteen minutes, one might fancy himself in England, were it not for the fact that every white man or woman is carried around the streets in a sedan chair or on the shoulders of coolies. Troupes of Chinese servants fill the streets, attending to the business of their masters' households. Servants are so cheap that the white man of diminutive income can stock his house with half a dozen of them without feeling the financial strain. White men soon become lazy and demand much waiting upon in this climate. It is argued that this fact is one of the "inducements" that keeps men of moderate means in the East. On every hand one hears from the natives and foreigners alike that there are "too many people." Enough survive the plagues and pestilences, infant deaths and typhoons (one typhoon caused the death of ten thousand persons a few years ago) to keep the great country swarming with population. It is not so much a question how to preserve the human race in China as it is how to find something for the people to do. When skilled embroiderers and makers of artistic objects average from eleven cents to fifteen cents a day for work from sunrise until sunset, it is not surprising that servants are glad to accept even the ridiculous amounts offered to them to act as domestic or personal servants.

Hongkong is so damp that clothing is wet when put on in the morning, and still wet when it is taken off at night. Thick mildew covers shoes in a single night. It is advisable to take everything from one's trunk and closets and give things a good "airing," at least every three or four days. Merchants wrap everything excepting food in oiled paper, so that the dampness will not ruin it if it is left unwrapped for three or four days. Verily, one who enters China by this port, and leaves it after a few days—or weeks—after living in the Anglicized hotels, as so many American tourists are said to do, gains a very inadequate and very inaccurate picture of China or the Chinese. Even a peep at the beautiful city is better than not to have come at all, but conditions have changed, and one should no more remain at Hongkong and think he has seen South China than he would visit Marseilles and think that he has seen France.

English residents have made it quite "incorrect" and socially forbidden to be seen talking with Chinese, or to be seen in the Chinese quarters of the city. When I told an Englishman that I would like to be presented to a famous Chinese authoress, he replied: "I could arrange for you to go and see her all right, and I presume it would be all right for you to go because you are a stranger; but really you'll have to excuse me, I couldn't be seen at the house of a Chino." Then I mentioned a famous Chinese official whose name is well known in the United States and asked if he were obliged to submit to any of this snobbery.

"When one of the boys is invited to this Chink's house to dinner, he usually comes to the club, explains that he must go to the Chino's house and we laugh it off, knowing his obligations. But, really, such things are not done. One would not care to be caught conversing about anything but business with a Chinese."

Perhaps the British officials know the "native city," but the civilians do not. It would not be "good form" to be aware of its existence even, and as most tourists burden themselves with that foolish old custom of trying to behave as the Romans do in Rome, usually making a botch of it, which would mean to try and be "English" in Hongkong, comparatively few strangers see the real life of the native city.

On the second shelf of the mountainside Hongkong is delightful. A big native theater flourishes with nightly change of bill. The hall is so large that it seats probably three thousand persons, yet I found it necessary, after paying a premium to a ticket speculator for the first night, to obtain admission at all to speak for seats a day in advance on all subsequent occasions There are scores, perhaps hundreds of mammoth restaurants always filled to overflowing at midnight, and the streets have a distinctive native flavor long after the sun has set and England in China is at its club or at home in bed. This side of Hongkong life is not disappointing and is worthy of a close inspection by strangers. Sir Walter Scott's advice: "Be aye stickin' in a tree," has been followed by the foreigners in Hongkong, so that there are splendid avenues bordered by large shade trees and many of the English residences

Peak Railway, Hongkong

are set in beautiful gardens of camellias, roses, poinsettias and many other flowering shrubs and plants that combine the charm of the English suburban villa with sub-tropical vegetation, always green-leafed and brilliant flowered. Despite the torrential rains and the sultry climate, it is likely that the island of Hongkong, previous to settlement by the English, was rocky and barren. At the present time, there is little ground space for agriculture, which is confined almost entirely to garden truck raising; but trees seem to cover the hillsides and thrive in the valleys. One colonial governor of Britain was instrumental in having over one million trees planted during his administration. There is a fine botanical garden along the route of the Peak cable tram, which, by the way, was the first to be placed in operation in Asia. It is an inspiring view to look down upon the city and harbor from this height, and then again from still further up at the terminus of the line. One should go in the daytime and then again at night. Beautiful on a clear day, it is all no less so in the evening, when the ships in the harbor have lights and hundreds of sampans, each with a lantern or candle, flit over the water, seeming to be fireflies flashing in the tropical night.

The streets of Hongkong are either shelves on the hillside or long staircases, which make all vehicles, excepting sedan chairs and rikishas, useless. The stranger from the West who has not stopped en route in Japanese ports or the Straits Settlements will thus have his first ride in the little pneumatic tired sulkies of Nipponese origin, which are becoming popular in countries as far distant as South Africa. Excepting when it rains, however, or when it is very hot and one has a long distance to travel, walking about Hongkong is preferable to riding. Many of the principal streets are arcaded as in several European countries, and one may visit the principal shops without going from under cover except at street crossings. Hongkong is not one of the shopping centers of China, however, and the stranger is advised to wait until he reaches other cities before succumbing to the lure of embroideries, ivories, lace, linen and jade that cannot escape his eyes and are likely to drain his purse elsewhere. In these matters of trade, the Hongkong merchants cater chiefly to passengers from incoming steamers who remain but a few hours and go away satisfied with usually inferior materials, for which they pay a price double, treble or quadruple that charged further inland.

Hongkong is the most distant outpost of the British Empire, the Irish soldier remarking that his government could not send him further from home without bringing him nearer. Its shipping has grown to vast proportions. In the year 1861, only slightly over one thousand ships cleared the port;

LI HUNG-CHANG

just before the outbreak of the European war, the number had increased to over twenty thousand. It is difficult to obtain exact figures concerning the value of the exports and imports, owing to the fact that Hongkong is a free port, but the amount is supposed to be over a total valuation of six hundred million of dollars. Hundreds of ships seem continually rocking nervously on the great watery expanse before South China's great waterway, but they are foreign ships assembled at a point which seems to be most blatant example of foreign exploitation on earth.

Almost the first question asked of the returning tourist is regarding the foreign accommodations at Chinese hotels, concerning which ignorance seems to be general in Western countries, and a point on which books of Eastern travel have been ominously silent, excepting where endurance ceased to be a virtue and a tale of suffering, privation or disgust was unfolded. Hotel accommodations at Hongkong are fairly typical of what one finds in other parts of China at the present time. Probably conditions have changed in the past few years, they are not what they were; but there is still a chance for improvement. The principal cities have commodious hotels, where comfortable and hygienic sleeping accommodations, ample service, and a fairly good cuisine need cause no qualms to the prospective tourist. The hotels are not equal to those of Broadway, New York, not even equal to the larger hostelries in Japan, but they are superior to many "leading hotels" in outlying districts in America, and compare very favorably to what was encountered in our own Western cities down to the beginning of the Twentieth Century.

The food is cooked in European style and the service is in kind. One might travel the length and width of China, at least where he is able to penetrate by railroad or steamer, and never so much as taste what is generally known in America as "Chinese Food." In fact, many of the concoctions served at "oriental restaurants" at home are purely American inventions, not procurable in a restaurant or hotel in the vast Chinese republic. What we know as "Chop Suey" in its myriad forms, is one of these and is known only by name in China, "the name given something prepared for the viceroy, Li Hung-chang, when he was in America." In general appearance, even in flavor, there is a similarity between "chop suey" and popular and very common dishes prepared by native cooks for the Chinese coolies, but one would not find them at the tables of a Chinese who made any pretense to "class," and he would not find them at the large native restaurants in the larger cities of China, some of which make a specialty of catering to tourists and other foreigners, who have a desire to have at least one meal in the style of the country in which they are traveling. But the tourist must go out of his way to obtain even this sample of Chinese dishes. No "native" dish is served at European hotels, as is often the case in foreign hotels of Spain or Italy. These dishes cannot be ordered and obtained at the hotels. At all of them, the menu card for each meal is practically the same as it would be in a first-class hotel at home, excepting that there is less variety. Meats may not taste exactly as they do when they come from American kitchens, there is less skill in the preparation of vegetables, and the milk is likely to be absent, or present only in condensed form, but the fowl is good, so are eggs, and the same is true of bread, butter, ordinary pastry, ices and puddings. Strangers do not eat "green" vegetables, owing to the Chinese methods of fertilization. Bottled waters are practically imperative, but they are abundant, and the well-known brands are always obtainable. "Tansan" and "Hirano," familiar to all travelers in Japan, are most popular, but French and German waters and wines are listed on all hotel cards.

Prices are about the same as elsewhere; perhaps a little higher than in Europe, but no more so than in Canada and the United States. All foreign hotels are operated on the "American plan," which includes breakfast, luncheon, dinner and sleeping accommodations with "tea" at five o'clock in the afternoon if desired. The customary charge is from five dollars a day up, although some hotels range their prices a dollar lower than that figure. This includes all service, and fees to servants are usually much lower than at home. In this matter one may suit his purse, however, as most of the larger hotels have suites of rooms to which figures are attached which seem strangely familiar and reminiscent of our own large cities. In China, as elsewhere, one gets approximately what he pays for; and charges in the Orient are not more exorbitant than in the Occident.

CHAPTER II

CANTON THE INCREDIBLE

THE first excursion from Hongkong is likely to be one of the most remarkable the Westerner has undertaken during many wanderings far away from home, because it will bring him to Canton, in many respects the most amazing city on earth. There could be no such city beyond the borders of China, and conditions are such that there will never be another. Among all the large cities of the earth it stands unique; and, built upon a sound foundation, it has not only endured throughout the centuries, but seems likely to endure, unchanged, when later centuries have passed. It is in Canton that many of the great changes are propagated and nursed. There began the revolt in the early days of the Twentieth Century that freed the country of Manchu rule and placed a president at the head of a republic which had been ruled by imperial dynasties dating back further than authentic history. Canton was the revolutionists' stronghold; its people have been noted for their independent thought down through the ages. But Canton itself does not change. New buildings of granite or sandstone may replace tumble-down structures of wood or brick, but they remain the same in architectural essentials and purpose. New generations come and go. Many of Canton's citizens go to the ends of the earth, make their fortunes, return home and, suffering no "taint" from contact with the outside world, take up their life where they left off when they went away. Again they become Cantonese, as if they had never seen anything beyond the walls of their strange city. They quickly lose themselves in the great swarming mass of humanity in Canton's narrow streets. Even the boat-life does not change, and the boat-dwellers form a distinct and numerous class by themselves; it is remarkable that they are born, live and die on tiny craft of probably the same size and shape that were the dwelling-places of their ancestors when Marco Polo visited the city and, being much impressed, wrote so much truth about it that he was suspected of exaggeration and untruth by his own and following generations. Perhaps their status as individuals experiences a slight change with the passing of dynasties. Perhaps they are better housed and fed than they were a few centuries back, and it is probable that there is less human suffering, a slightly greater respect for human life than in the days of Marco Polo. But in a broad and general way, Canton is the same as it was in the dim yesterdays of history; it will be the dim to-morrows of the future.

It is possible to make the trip between Hongkong and Canton by rail, a distance of slightly over one hundred miles, usually consuming about five hours and affording a peep at village and country life that is not to be ignored. But the stranger should preferably go by boat, which leaves the Hongkong docks each night and arrives in Canton early in the morning, when the city's weird activity is just coming to life, after the only quiet hours of the twenty-four, those between two or three and five o'clock.

The boat ride is not without many thrills, first of which is provided by the vigorous precautions against sudden attacks by pirates. White passengers aboard are assigned to a certain portion of the deck space, the whistles and other signals of departure are sounded, heavy iron gates are drawn across companion ways and locked, so that passage beyond them is impossible in either direction. Two guards, armed with loaded rifles, begin to patrol the deck and never discontinue doing so until the steamer is safely tied up at the dock in Canton's principal waterway.

Some of the precautions seem to be unnecessary, but who can be certain pirates have not taken passage in the second class and that at a signal they will swoop down upon the first cabin passengers after the boat is in the silent reaches of the river that flows between hills known to be inhabited by water thieves? They have done that very thing in recent years, as the file of the Hongkong papers will prove. Not long ago they came close to one of the river steamers, set fire to it and there was a great loss of life and property. The government seems to be powerless, so the steamship companies, native and foreign, take the matter in their own hands, and their guards carry rifles to pick off the suspicious characters which they see at a distance; they also carry revolvers and pistols for use at close range.

It is a pleasant cruise among the islands of the harbor, and in about two hours the ship passes beyond the old Bogue fortresses into the muddy waters of the Pearl River. There are extensive plantations on the banks of the river devoted to rice, lichee and banana growing, with occasional groups of houses and other buildings that remind one of the landscape along the lower reaches of the Mississippi, where it flows on to the Gulf below New Orleans. On our first trip over the route, however, we took the night steamer for the purpose of making sure of the wonderful experience of getting our first impression of Canton at dawn.

No Chinese pirates interfered with our progress and we could see the city in the distance as the sun was rising. But this was merely our good fortune and should not be taken as a suggestion that steamship officials are too watchful of their boats and passengers. It is a well-known and proved fact that at least thirty thousand pirates live in Canton and along the watery arms that lead into the country from the metropolis. Sometimes the ships cruise close to the shores where the law-breakers are known to be hiding, but they conceal themselves in the underbrush that grows close to the water's edge and up among the trees on the hillsides. They do not attack every day or every week, but one never knows when the steamer sails from port whether it is to be an uneventful voyage or one of great dangers. When the pirates are captured, as they are when they become too bold, the authorities have little mercy and order them shot immediately. Not long ago fifty were shot in one week in Canton and two hundred in five weeks. Still, it is believed that the number of pirates increases as the years pass.

Canton officials admit their inability to cope with the problem. And this seems strange, perhaps, in a city that recently has pretended to uphold the loftiest modern civilization standards in all China. There are reactionaries who complain that the younger element is too modern. For example, I saw the translation of a report that the city is now quite hygienic, because a law has been passed forbidding the eating of rats, which are plague-carriers, and allowing for rat depositories at the corners of the principal streets, where residents are requested to bring dead rats, which they find in their houses. The edict has gone forth against rats as food, but many are still eaten as "medicine" by the weak people, who desire to become strong. One sees them exposed in the market places for sale; and there is no law that protects cats, dogs, cockroaches or snakes. I saw many old Maltese cats and young dogs, as well as four-foot snakes, being peddled through the thoroughfares in crates, almost as frequently as vegetables or other wares.

As we looked ahead from the deck of the steamer we could see the vast city over which the famous Five-Storied Pagoda was rising fantastically among lower structures, even the substantial structures that are characteristic of all Chinese cities, the pawn-shops for the poor, which are also store-houses for the rich. The poor go to them when sorely in need of a few pennies for

Boat-dwellers, near Canton

clothing which they are able to discard during mild weather, and the rich, who are possessors of vast wardrobes, place their unseasonable garments in the buildings that are supposed to be "fire-proof," although it is likely that no such thing exists in China.

It was no effort to rise that morning on the Pearl River, because the din was terrific long before we reached the city. The people seemed to be shouting to each other as if doomsday had come. Many of them were horrible looking old women who carry on much of the trade of the city in small sampans, which can penetrate to the city's heart by means of the foul, narrow canals. They stand at the bow of the boat and steer it, while it is rowed with one big oar by boys or girls. And they shout in husky voices at each turn of the oar, yelping as loud as the coolies who scream for people to make room for the chairs they are carrying. Their mission down the river may have had a dual purpose. They may have been delivering merchandise to the small villages or the plantations, but they were also dipping nets into the river, and threw long lines overboard for the purpose of catching fish for breakfast. So far as we were able to observe, their energy was not rewarded, which may have accounted for the noise. Certainly they seemed to be particularly angry, and it was not unusual to see one of them pull up a net, observe its emptiness and then abuse the members of her crew in her disappointment and disgust.

At frequent intervals we passed funeral boats, but they were the noisiest of all. Some of them equaled the din of a boiler factory with the additional "music" of a siren screeching and bells ringing. Perhaps the corpse was four or five months old. The priests or fortune-tellers had not found a proper time for burial, so coffins were carried to the decks of these boats where they remained. The sun was rising, so servants of the departed were smashing together great Chinese cymbals, to frighten away the evil spirits.

The name of the big city is derived from the Chinese *Kwang-tung;* but this is only one of the various names it has had during the passing of the centuries. On the opposite bank of the river are the cities of Ho-nam and Wa-ti, which might have some interest for the traveler were it not for the fact that Canton is always more interesting than anything else in the neighborhood, and no matter how often he has plunged into the swarming streets, no matter how often his eyes have been offended by what he saw, his nostrils by the fetid odors, or his ears by the incessant hum of many voices, he will gladly repeat the excursion as often as time will permit. Canton has a tremendous fascination for everyone who enjoys looking upon unbelievable sights.

The steamer from Hongkong comes up to the street that runs along the river front; but passengers discharged from the steamer quickly take sedan chairs and are carried a short distance along what is known as the *Bund,* and, after crossing a bridge, are deposited on the pleasant island of Shameen.

As we approached the landing it seemed certain that the pirates had come at last. There was a spiked, high iron railing to keep back the crowd, but a hundred men and boys scaled those pickets like monkeys going through the branches of trees. They jumped from the decks of river boats to other boats, like Eliza crossing the ice in "Uncle Tom's Cabin," finally landing on the sides of our steamer, howling and gesticulating like the worst piratical crew that ever boarded a ship. They surged around us and yelled at us through the bars that held them back. It seemed difficult to tell whether they or the ship's passengers were held prisoners. But they were comparatively innocent porters and chair coolies, fighting for a job that would give them a few pennies.

Finally, the officers ordered them back, and we reached the shore intact. Having telegraphed the hotel to send chairs and coolies, as well as a courier to meet us upon our arrival, a plan that is to be recommended to all travelers making their first visit to Canton, we were soon lifted over the heads of the mob on the river front. The steel gates on the bridge were opened for our chairs to pass and we were deposited in a garden on the island, where breakfast was awaiting us, and we completed arrangements for our first plunge into the city across the river.

The commercial importance of Canton is such that many Europeans, consular officers and merchants, are obliged to live there. But it was almost an impossibility for them to live within the city, so the French and British governments spent a large amount of money in making Shameen habitable. Supposedly, the people on Shameen are safe, cut off as they are by the guards, gates and bridges. But there is still the river to be reckoned with, so the banks of the island have high barbed wire entanglements, through which it would be very difficult to pass. Chinese are not allowed to step foot upon the island, without permission from the European owners.

One sits in front of the comfortable hotel, beneath big shade trees, and views the great walled city across the river much as a boy would sit outside a big circus tent curious to know what is going on inside. The walls date from about the Sixteenth Century, but they are doubtless built upon older walls. At present they are twenty-five feet high and from fifteen to twenty-five feet wide at the top, with a circumference of about ten miles. There are seventeen gates, and those who go in and come out are searched for firearms, excepting the Europeans, who cross the bridge from Shameen and seem to pass unmolested by the guards, apparently vouched for by their respective governments.

It is impossible to take an authentic census of the city, although several serious attempts have been made to do so in recent years. Down to the beginning of the present century it was usually supposed that about one million persons dwelt within the walls, but recent estimates have placed the number at two million, with a rough estimate of over one hundred thousand boat-dwellers. When I first saw them poling along for space, much as if a hundred gondolas were caught in a narrow Venetian canal, I thought it possible that people who could afford it took to the water after a day in the city. But 'this is not so. Canton also has its class distinctions. People who live in boats have no social standing. In fact, until the republic was established at Peking, they were not allowed to marry with land population. Presumably, they are pirates or the descendants of pirates and political refugees and escaped prisoners. And they look like their ancestors must have looked.

One seats himself in a sedan chair, gives the signal and plunges into the city, as he would descend into a mine or enter a crystal maze. Once beyond the walls no stranger could find his way back to the river front. To walk is practically impossible, for anyone who wears clothing, particularly during the summer season. The jostling of a stripped-to-the-waist population may be disagreeable, if one pause to think of it; but a suit of clothes or gown rubbed against a thousand or ten thousand perspiring Chinese would be a financial extravagance. It is necessary to pay coolies about seventy-five cents a day to undertake the task. So the white people and the better class Chinese ride high in the air, over the heads of the swarming masses, and come through the ordeal with clothing intact—and wiser men in regard to the manner of living of a million brothers and sisters with yellow skin.

Of course everyone knows that Canton is a city of narrow streets. But other cities of the world have narrow streets; at least a few of them will be found in all oriental towns. But nobody can appreciate how narrow streets can be until he sees the principal thoroughfares of Canton! Some of them, with solid structures four or five stories high at their sides, are not more than three yards wide. One street, with great marble and granite fronts, is not more than four yards in width.

Anyone who would attempt to write a description of the city in detail must needs devote a volume or several volumes to it. There are many stereotyped

Pearl River, Canton

sights and sites that will not be overlooked by the chair-bearers or the courier. Incidentally, the guides of Canton are very dependable, intelligent fellows, who speak English fluently and seem to take a personal pride in making certain that the foreigner is enjoying himself. It is not a guide-book "sight," however, that will be of particular interest or amusement to the tourist. The street life viewed en route to the temples, shrines, theaters and stores, is too commonplace and natural to prompt comment from the guide. But the eyes of the stranger will behold sights such as they have never witnessed before, and what is unexpectedly encountered is likely to linger in memory after special buildings have become confused with those of similar architecture elsewhere.

There are seventy-five trade guilds in Canton. Most of them have streets or sections devoted almost exclusively to their particular industry. For instance, one may find the jade dealers and cutters in one section, the shoe dealers in another, silk dealers, embroiderers, hair, wood—and everything else under the sun, all in its own quarters. For example, I saw one large section of several streets devoted to the manufacture and sale of toothbrushes, most of which were said to be destined for America.

In one large shop I saw a large circle of workers spitting into one particular spot, I could not understand this effort, until I glanced over their shoulders and saw that young chickens were eating the spittle.

A disgusting spectacle! Yes, but not a fourth as disgusting as many things that we saw that first morning, when we penetrated Canton from one wall to the other, passing through the heart of the big city.

But perhaps one becomes accustomed to everything. In the afternoon—we were unable to eat lunch on the pretty island of Shameen—things did not seem to be quite so bad. Dinner and a good sleep were refreshing. The sights were as disgusting, the odors as foul as the day before; but we were less nauseated than the day before. We saw that entrails of pigs, chickens and ducks cover the tables of the butchers' stalls, and an endless variety of truck better left to the imagination of the reader than enumerated, is met with in all parts of the city. Cockroaches in honey is one delicacy that I observed was doing a thriving trade. A million people consume much food every day, and although there is much poverty and filth, the Cantonese are quite plump specimens of humanity and rarely show the expected effects of living in the airless vat, which they call home.

One of the amazing sights of Canton is the City of the Dead. It is an odd affair in which there are stalls arranged along an arcade of flowery avenues

AN OLD COOLIE

bright with big porcelain jars, banners and altars, piled with strange objects of tinsel and gilt, representing flowers and animals. In each stall there is a coffin and in each coffin there is a corpse awaiting burial. How long they will be obliged to wait seems to depend upon the wealth of the individual, or the amount that his or her family is willing to pay in rent while the priests and sorcerers are deciding upon an appropriate place for burial, one where the body of the deceased will be "comfortable."

"Who runs this place?" I asked the courier.

"The priests and sorcerers."

"They collect the rent and also decide upon the time for burial?"

Still an affirmative answer, so I was not surprised when we saw two coffins in one stall and learned that they had been there for four years, to find that they enclosed the remains of two brothers, members of one of the rich families of Canton. It is difficult for a rich man to find burial, once he reaches the City of the Dead, as the Bible says it is for him to enter heaven.

After what seemed to be almost a ghoulish visit, we went to the temples, many of them, although one cannot expect to visit the hundred-odd structures answering to the general name of "temple," and with the exception of the colossal and ornate structure known as the Ancestors' temple, owned by the powerful *Chan* family, we found everything in decay and filth. The stone-paved courtyards were overrun with weeds and grass. In what were once temple ponds were heaps of rubbish, broken crockery and greenish water that sent up a vile stench to the nostrils. The interiors were tawdry, shabby and filthy, compared to the similar structures of Japan, and there were few worshipers. Those who came brought food and drink, which they placed on the altars, or they burned punk sticks. They rattled slats in a bamboo vase, took out one that called for a number and the number called for a prayer. This latter was written out on a sheet of red paper, which they purchased from the abominable looking priests, ignited them at the altar tapers and threw them blazing into an old bronze receptacle that was shaped like a base-burner stove. Then they threw down sticks to see from the way in which they fell on the floor whether or not their prayers would be answered.

At the temple of the five hundred Genii, where there are many idols, we spied the gilt image of Marco Polo, and asked the guide why it was that this was included among the Buddhist saints.

"Marco Polo very good man," replied the guide, so we bought punk sticks, lighted them at the altar and left them burning in the big vase in front

WA-TAP PAGODA, CANTON

of the image. Perhaps we were not very devout worshipers; but in this we compared very favorably with the chattering, laughing Chinese crowd that placed punk sticks in front of other images. The temple is not a very solemn place to the Chinese.

Coming back through the narrow streets, our chairs were suddenly halted. When we complained, the coolies explained that all traffic was stopped for the time. The funeral procession of a prominent mandarin's wife was about to pass. First came the bands, playing on absurd instruments, pounding terrible metal drums and creating a horrible din. Then great pieces of fresh flowers, so large that four coolies balanced them with difficulty. There were so many of these pieces that it became tiresome looking at them. But we were rewarded for the monotony of the flowers. On a raised dais, over which hung a beautifully embroidered canopy, was a big roast pig fresh from the oven. He looked quite crisp and tempting. Next were huge trays of food, all neatly prepared in the best Chinese fashion and daintily distributed on plates of fine glass and china. Then came the male relatives of the deceased—seemingly about a hundred of them—dressed in white robes and walking. Then the female relatives in sedan chairs.

A huge canopy, carried by perhaps twenty men, had a top like a long umbrella, with curtains hanging at the sides to the ground. Inside this walked the children of the deceased, but they could not be seen by the crowds in the streets. Then the "official mourners" among the women. I observed several who were so stricken by grief that they carried huge Turkish bath towels to wipe away their tears. Then followed more flowers and more bands. Finally, we were permitted to proceed, while the distinguished lady passed along to the City of the Dead, which we had visited an hour before.

During my visit in Canton I presented a letter of introduction to a prominent merchant, a man who was well-to-do and of considerable reputation in the community because as an officer in the local military, he had distinguished himself on the occasion of riots. Although he had the natural reticence of a Chinese, he made a visible effort to be cordial and not only invited me to accompany him to the theater and to weird midnight restaurants that were the rendezvous for native gamblers, where foreigners are seldom admitted, but also invited me to his house and introduced me to the female members of his family, a somewhat unusual proceeding, even in progressive and revolutionary Canton. One day, when I felt that we were sufficiently well acquainted for me to ask the question without offense, and at the same time obtain a truthful answer, I asked him if he had ever tasted

Interior of Temple of the five hundred Genii, Canton

rat, cat, or dog meat. It seemed incredible that these things should be offered for sale in a great metropolis; and, although they were offered for sale, was it not a mistake that foreigners believed they were eaten?

I recalled an experience of a Welsh regiment stationed in China. The boys had a pet goat, which they considered a mascot and took with them everywhere. It had a fine silver collar and was led ahead of the regiment even when marching to divine service. As the story goes, however, they were prevailed upon to leave the animal behind, when they learned from the missionaries, who had conversed with the people in their own language, that the Chinese believed the regiment to be a group of goat-worshipers! Was it not possible that Europeans and Americans had drawn a similarly absurd conclusion from what they saw and could not understand?

"No, I have never eaten rats," declared the merchant. "Only the poor or ignorant people do. There is the belief that rats are good 'medicine' and will assist the weak in becoming strong. At the present time we have regulations prohibiting the eating of rats, because they are known to spread disease. Anyway, I believe they are not good food, and in the past, as now, were eaten only by people who could not afford more expensive meat. But as to dogs and cats, yes, I have eaten them, but I cannot say that I am partial to them. But neither one is so bad as you seem to think. Old cats and young dogs are most in demand by the Cantonese, who do value them as food. But do not be surprised, for I have a still greater surprise for you, two of them. One is that food eaten by Europeans and Americans is often as offensive to us as cats and dogs are to you. And now the second surprise! What do you suppose is my favorite dish?"

It was a difficult question, after what I had seen in the Canton markets, so I made no attempt at a guess.

"Snake," shouted the merchant of Canton. "Yes, sir, snake! I assure you it is very fine. I cannot tell you that it forms a principal item of diet at my table, but I will say that when I am entertaining my friends—no, we did not have it to-night—I feel that I am giving them something of a treat when I serve snake stew. The particular variety that I like best is a nonpoisonous fellow that costs from six to eight dollars, according to the state of the market. It seems rather extravagant when we dine alone, but when I invite friends—Canton friends—that is our *pièce de résistance*."

Sedan Chairs

CHAPTER III

THE WIDOWS OF AH CUM

ONE of the ancient Chinese customs is that a widow shall wear a skirt, blue, black or white, but a skirt of some kind, thus when a man is said to have married the wearer of a white skirt it is understood to mean that he has married a widow. Of course he loses cast by the ceremony, and so does the bride who has been the bride of another. The widow who marries should go to the home of her prospective husband in an ordinary sedan carried by only two coolies, rather than in the beautiful red chair reserved for brides. There is no such thing as "slipping away quietly and getting married" as in many other countries. In China everyone is supposed to know everything that is commonly considered of a personal nature in Western countries. To close the front door or the front gate of one's home is an indication that something is going on inside, of which one should be ashamed. One is not only responsible to his family for his conduct, but also to the community as well. When he does anything so grave as to marry a widow, the bride has no right to attempt to conceal her widowhood in view of the life she is about to undertake, but if she follows the established customs, which are almost as important as laws, she must flaunt her shame in the face of the throng. Her husband must let it be known that he is marrying a white skirt. It is reported that when Chu Hsi was asked if it was improper for a penniless widow to marry again, he replied: "What you are afraid of for her is cold and starvation; but starvation is comparatively small matter and loss of reputation is a great one." The widow who does *not* marry again is respected, and arches of finely carved wood or stone have been erected in her honor in various parts of the country. She who consents to matrimony the second time is nevermore above suspicion, and the man who marries a "white skirt" never again holds exactly the status that he maintained before marriage.

The Widows of Ah Cum

I was invited to the residence of three "wearers of white skirts" and pleased beyond measure to receive the invitation through their nephew, but surprised to find the trio dressed in black when they received me. But it was a rare privilege to enter a better class Chinese house, be entertained and privileged to chat with its female occupants, and receive at least a hurried impression of the domestic circle in South China, if not actually within the walls of Canton, only a short boat ride on the river in the city of Ho-nam, which seems to be separated from Canton by the narrow river and for political rather than geographical reasons.

The widows were still mourning the death of the arch polygamist, Ah Cum, who guided many foreigners around Canton during his lifetime and received ample "credit" in several books of travels, not only for his excellent knowledge of English, but for wit and humor that impressed itself upon all the Europeans with whom he came in contact. But Ah Cum has been in his tomb these many years. His widows are "faithful to his memory," declared the nephew, but they are not opposed to receiving foreigners in the foreign manner. Their late husband enjoyed the company of foreigners; so why should they not see the people whom he had liked so well? And, in addition, the nephew had not paid them a visit for some time. Would I not like to go with him? He assured me that the youngest of the three was as beautiful as a lotus blossom sprinkled with morning dew, one of the ladies who made the stars of heaven rejoice when they saw her.

So one day, shortly before noon, we set out to visit the widows of Ah Cum at Ho-nam. We left the hotel on Shameen Island in sedan chairs, and, after proceeding for some distance along the crowded river bank, we transferred to a strange old hulk of a boat, propelled by an old woman and two girls, who operated a sort of ferry between the two cities.

The old captainess was very interesting, or at least she tried to be. When she was not trying to talk to us, she was hissing and shouting at the girls, who diligently dipped the big oar in the water, to make the passage as quick as possible. But the old lady was disappointed in her passengers, whom she had taken to be "distinguished men." We were going to call on the widows and she thought better of us. Perhaps we were going to see the "king of the pirates." He also lives on Ho-nam, of which he is sort of a governor.

"Velly much good man alla time," said the woman, as she endeavored to recount the virtues of the man who became rich by piracy. For several years he remained in exile, after his deeds became known, but he reformed and was pardoned. And because of his personal acquaintance with all of the cut-throats of the district, his authority is respected and Ho-nam is said to be one of the safest districts of the vicinity. Of course her white passengers were going to call upon him, and, when the old lady learned differently, she spat in the water to show her disgust. Perhaps she rowed more vigorously than ever on account of her disgust, and she soon brought her boat to a string of log piles leading up to a big house, which resembled the entrance of a Venetian palace. The big pile of masonry had steps running down into the water, and when the old captainess pounded on them with a hollow bamboo pole the door opened and servants from the house rushed out to assist us in the landing. They said that we were expected, and quickly ushered us through several rooms with ceilings about twenty feet from the floor, finally arriving in a big hall, which seemed to be quite empty. Teakwood chairs and tables were shoved back against the walls, and there were a few red banners with big Chinese characters on the walls. Otherwise there were no furnishings, yet this was the principal room of the big mansion; the parlor or reception room.

As soon as we were seated, servants brought us tea, and as soon as this was poured the Mesdames Ah Cum put in an appearance, each hobbling across the floor as if she were on stilts. All three had "lily feet," and the youngest had the smallest feet that I ever saw in China. Her tiny slippers were not quite three inches long and not more than an inch wide.

It seemed a marvel that she was able to walk at all, yet, before I left, she hobbled into the garden with me to show me her azaleas, and kept her balance even when crossing the stepping stones near a pond.

A guess would put the respective ages of the widows at sixty, forty and twenty. The youngest, it was explained to us, had barely left the altar before her husband, who had had thirteen wives before her, left this world, presumably for a better one. Strangely enough, the old man was survived by his first and last wives and by one who was probably about number seven or eight.

"She is very kind to the young wife," explained the nephew of Ah Cum, who pointed to the eldest widow. "My uncle left the greater part of his fortune to the first wife, but she keeps the others here in the house with her and all of Ah Cum's children."

It seemed quite cozy. Three widows of a man living together, being mother to one another's children and to the deceased wives' children by their beloved departed husband! One by one, the children were brought in and introduced. They ranged all the way from two years to twenty-five years. Then came their teacher who spoke English. Altogether, we quite filled the big room, leaving space only for the servants who took their places and violently fanned the company with big feather fans. The widows were great smokers, all puffing excitedly as they chatted with us about such vital things as the weather, how many children we had in America and our ages. I also observed that they frequently spat on the tile floor, scuffed the spot with their tiny feet and had not the slightest idea that this was not strictly in accordance with the European manner. Even with their manifest desire to be "modern" and "foreign," nobody had hinted to them that it is not customary for ladies to spit on the floors of their drawing rooms when they are entertaining guests, or at any other time.

"Of course she will marry again," I said to the nephew, indicating one of the most attractive young widows I have ever seen.

But my question caused him to smile, as if it was too absurd to require an answer. "Certainly not," he replied at length; "my aunt is from a very good family. She could not marry beneath her station, or her family's station in life, and no Chinese gentleman of her caste would think of marrying a widow. It would be disgraceful, you see. So, under the circumstances, she must always remain a widow."

And the cute little girl smiled, because she knew that we were talking about her. She seemed to be quite contented with her lot, and we saw no reason why we should waste sympathy.

"I wish I could go to America," said the nephew. "I would like to go for five years, make much money and then come back to my wife and children."

"Then you would not take your wife with you?"

"Certainly not. I would send her a letter now and then, and that would do just as well. You see, we do not care much for our wives in China, if we have only one; and they do not care much for us. Take my case. My wife was selected for me by my uncle, Ah Cum, because my father and mother were dead. I had never seen her before our marriage but once, and then only a moment—just a glance. So you see that we cannot have the love for one another that American people have. Do you understand? What a Chinese wants is children. I have five of them and I am only thirty-two years of age. Perhaps I shall take no more wives; I have not decided, and then, perhaps, I should not try to afford it."

The little servant girls, who were perhaps ten or twelve years of age, kept up such a violent fanning that our attention was attracted to them.

They were not dressed like the other children of the household, so I inquired who they were.

"The children of family slaves," said the nephew. "They will be taken care of by our family and may always live with us. Perhaps they will marry children of other slaves; we may arrange that."

"Is it possible for them to marry above their class?"

"Possible, yes, if we gave them their freedom; but that is not likely, so they will probably remain here always. They are better off."

"How is America getting on in her war with Mexico?" asked the eldest widow, her question being interpreted by her nephew. For a moment it was impossible to determine if there was a slight tinge of sarcasm in the inquiry, or whether it was the first question which she had thought to be appropriate to a renewal of the conversation that seemed to be drawing to a conclusion. Probably I hesitated for an answer. It is difficult to obtain news in South China, at least it is difficult for the foreigner who has no access to official dispatches from foreign countries.

"My aunt is trying to show you that she keeps well informed in the affairs of the world," explained the nephew, and although I gave an optimistic reply to her question, I doubt if she received a correct interpretation, as she and her nephew engaged in a lively debate upon the "Mexican situation," the elderly woman maintaining that Mexico must be in the wrong. Apparently she did not have a very clear understanding of what had caused the "war," but she knew that Mexico must be wrong and that America must be right. She had often heard her late husband speak of the Americans whom he had piloted around the streets of Canton, and he had admired them so much that she was certain they could do no wrong. The Mexicans she did not know; she did not recall that she had heard her husband speak of them. What kind of people were they? Barbarians? It must be that they did not travel to China. Within memory, none of them had come to see the wonders of Canton; or, if they came, they did not employ her worshiped husband as guide.

The teacups were filled and drained many times, tiny rice-cakes were served, and, at length, small cubes of bananas into which ordinary toothpicks were placed to serve as a convenience in picking them up—in a household where there were no forks, and where hostesses desired to spare their guest the embarrassment of endeavoring to manipulate chopsticks. More tea was served as topics of conversation of mutual interest were taken up and quickly exhausted; and we were about ready to leave when it occurred to the youngest wife that as we had arrived by the canal or back-door route, we might like to go through the house and look at the street. The front door was swung into the narrow thoroughfare at the suggestion, and three widows, the twenty or thirty children, the majority of which were their own, but some of which were the children of the late wives of the late Ah Cum, and the two guests filed through the portal to the pavement, from which the front of the house could be inspected. Once arrived there, the group attracted considerable attention from passersby, many of whom put down the baskets they were carrying, apparently returning from market, and the youngest widow chatted noisily about the architectural wonders of the street, her words being interpreted briefly by her nephew. I saw many window shutters and lattices being thrown back in the neighboring houses, and although most of them had bamboo curtains or slats, I could see dozens of eyes peering at us from darkened interiors. Still, the little widow chatted. Perhaps we would like to walk down the street for a short distance. Would I not like to see some of the front doors of a Ho-nam street, as well as the back doors? I nodded, and immediately we started, the three hobbling widows with the "lily feet," carefully finding their way along the uneven pavement in advance of what soon formed itself into a small procession of men, women and children. Here lived the wealthy Mr. So-and-So. There was the residence of Mr. Somebody Else. Had I never heard of them? The girl widow was surprised; she thought they were known to all the world. Did I not think that Ho-nam was a beautiful place? Would I not rather have a home there than in Canton? Where in all the world would one rather make a home for himself?

Perhaps I do the little lady, one of my kind hostesses, an injustice; nevertheless, I suspected that she was very human that day. I suspected that she was forgetting some of the traditional restrictions that compel women to remain silent within the walls of their own home. It was a girlish prank, no doubt, but it was what in America is called "showing off to the neighbors." It is a rare thing for Chinese women to receive foreign men in their own home. Ah Cum's widows, being very "progressive," were not afraid to do so! and the youngest of the trio seemed to take delight in making sure that no neighbor should doubt the truth of the story that would be repeated from house to house during the next few days. Fearing that someone might be overlooked, the young lady talked in a louder voice than when we were indoors, thus demonstrating her skill at entertaining a white man. Perhaps a gossiping neighbor said that it was all scandalous; perhaps they wished that they enjoyed similar freedom of action. I shall never know; but I do know that the little lady wanted to keep my visit a secret from nobody on the street. I think that she had ideas of her own. She was a widow, she was properly chaperoned by two other widows of the same man; why should she not receive whom she pleased?

A bright little youngster of six or seven years, observing that I was paying more attention to the youngest widow than to the others, came up to me, caught hold of my hand, and said in correct English as proudly as if the lady had been Empress of China: "That lady is my mother!"

"And are the other two ladies your mothers?" I asked, indicating the older widows.

"Certainly not! A boy has only one mother, this lady is mine."

"And all of these little boys and girls, are they your brothers and sisters?"

"No, sir, I have no brothers and sisters. They all belong to the others."

"Yet your father was Ah Cum?"

"Yes, sir."

"And their father was Ah Cum?"

"Yes, sir, that's it."

"Where did you learn to speak English?"

"Our teacher was in Manila and learned English there. He teaches us to speak correctly."

"I speak English, mister," echoed a half-dozen young boys and girls as they gathered around us, the young widow continuing her spirited address on the beauties of Ho-nam, which seemed relative to the stranger in this part of the world.

At length, when it seemed that we had been thoroughly inspected by half of the inhabitants of the street, we went back to the house. The doors were closed again, more tea and more banana cubes were served and Ah Cum's nephew and I made our departure through the back door, where the sampan and the veteran captainess were awaiting us. As the boat was poled away from the stone steps, we looked back and three widows, aged respectively sixty, forty and twenty, stood on the narrow balcony, vigorously puffing their pipes and watching us make a safe start for the island of Shameen!

CHAPTER IV

THE CELESTIAL RIVIERA

THE trip to Macao, and Macao itself, form a pleasant interlude in the early part of the China tour that should not be over-looked by any foreign traveler. The Portuguese city in the Far East is usually called "The Monte Carlo of the Orient," and the appellation is apt for several reasons. Here are some of the notorious gambling establishments of the world, but, in addition, there is a beautiful bay, the city is perched on a hillside and contains many subtropical gardens, splendid drives along the water-front, shady walks in parks, where flowers bloom in profusion, and a row of palatial dwellings, some of which belong to the officials, and some to the men who have prospered elsewhere and for several reasons have selected the beautiful city for a home during certain months of the year—others that may be traced directly to the pernicious traffic of one kind or another that prospers here as in few places on earth. Few geographical comparisons have been so well made. Macao seems to be the Mediterranean paradise transferred to the west banks of the estuary of the Canton River. It is easily reached by daily steamboat service from either Hongkong or Canton, a night's ride from the latter and a pleasant afternoon's cruise from the former, among verdant islands, along rocky shores, and frequently passing the strange ships and smaller fishing craft that make Macao a home port.

Immediately we went ashore, we admitted all of this favorable comparison to the winter resorts of the French or Italian Riviera; but there was much in addition. There was the unmistakable oriental atmosphere about the place that any European city lacks. The streets seemed to swarm with Chinese, who form a large majority of the eighty thousand population that dwells upon this three-mile tongue of land that reaches toward the sea from the island of Heung-Shan, but here we saw more priests, nuns and clergymen than we had observed elsewhere in the Far East. We heard Christian convent and church bells chiming at almost every hour of the day or night. It would have been possible to imagine that it was not China at all, but southern Italy, if the faces of the majority of the population had not been Mongolian.

"At last we have come upon a Christian community in this far-off corner of the world," I commented, but my traveling companions laughed. They had been in Macao before.

After twenty-four hours in the beautiful city I am afraid that I was willing to admit that it was one of the most vicious and most contemptible cities I had ever visited. There was still no doubt that it was making a splendid outward pretention to being a Christian community, Portuguese missionaries and laymen are always zealous in that direction: but it is also as true that Macao is doing more to corrupt the yellow man, encourage his natural and inherited vices and hinder his progress toward the light than any other single force. In many ways it seems a libel on Western civilization. That it has not been more roundly condemned and denounced to the Western world is doubtless accounted for by the fact that it is too far away. Comparatively few people know or care.

For many years the world has recognized opium as the worst enemy of the yellow man. It took the world a long time to recognize this fact and do something for humanity by attempting to forget its worldly greed and diminish the supply to users. Even Christian England was unwilling to give up the profitable trade from India. But, despite these handicaps, opium-smoking has been very well checked throughout China. At least, it is checked compared to former conditions. The habit has not been entirely eliminated, that everyone knows would be an impossibility; but it has received a heavy blow and is staggering for breath. Practically all of the nations of the world, including old China herself, have said that the young men of the East shall not fall under the pernicious influence of the deadly drug. We have heard much of these things. We have had encouraging reports from the missionaries and statesmen. The Chinese may have substituted other vices, but they did not go so far toward the corruption of a nation. Probably most of us believe that there was a comparatively small amount of opium left in the world; from some of the reports that have reached us we might have come to the conclusion that it was only used for medicinal purposes, and then in small quantities.

But Macao is Portuguese territory, lying at the heart of the greatest nation of opium smokers in the world. When I arrived in its beautiful streets that first morning I asked a local guide to take me to the "principal sights."

"First, we will go the opium factory," he said; "it is the largest in the

Waterfront, Macao

world." And, inside of ten minutes, I saw more opium in the process of manufacture than the Western world believes exists in all the world. Here was a great institution, employing hundreds of men, women, boys and girls. It was like entering a great weaving establishment at Osaka, or a steel mill at Moji.

A row of perhaps one hundred great brass caldrons were "cooking" the stuff, each caldron said to contain something like two thousand dollars' worth of the drug. This was a figure that we could easily believe, when we were shown tiny packets that retail at seven dollars each, and boxes that could be slipped into the ordinary vest pocket that fetch thirty-two dollars in the market.

And is there still a market for opium? The fact that the factory pays the Portuguese provincial government the sum of $1,560,000 each year in revenue for the privilege of manufacture, should show something of its enormous output. It is smuggled into China by the wholesale, and it is smuggled around the world in smaller quantities. I had pointed out to me palatial residences with gorgeous gardens, in which dwell the men who have become fabulously rich from the forbidden traffic, and who are still drawing an income from it that reach the figures of Standard Oil magnates' earnings.

It is this great industry of Macao which helps to maintain such a splendid Portuguese colony with its terraced avenues and stately gardens, public and private. There is even a stone embankment and paved thoroughfare along an extensive seafront that would compare favorably with that of any European city. For once, something belonging to Portugal seems to be prosperous! But when one thinks of the frightful havoc caused by the trade that makes it possible, the surpassing beauty seems almost unbeautiful. Some of the devices for getting opium into forbidden territory are quite remarkable. There are said to be men who make a regular business of traveling between Macao and the regular points of distribution. They might be suspected, so they employ agents who carry the stuff with them in their shoes, concealed about their clothing, and in hand-bags, where it escapes the eyes of the authorities. One man in Canton, who rather boasted of the fact that he was a confirmed smoker, told me that his opium always came to him packed in Mennen's Talcum boxes, which looked so innocent to custom authorities that they were regularly passed as "merchandise." He asked me if I did not think that it was a clever idea of the agent, who supplied him regularly.

It seems probable that opium was introduced into China in the Thirteenth Century by the Arabs, who brought it as a commodity of trade from their own country and from Persia. It seems to have gained a quick foothold, and opium-smoking soon became a favorite pastime of all classes. There are scientists who declare that it may be indulged in with no more disastrous results than follow excessive tobacco smoking; but the weight of evidence is against these scientists. Opium, as much as anything else, has retarded the progress of China and has made millions of her people less able to cope with the struggle for existence that seems to be the chief obstacle in the march toward Western standards of living. Even before the so-called Western invasion, however, when China was a hermit nation and cared for little beyond her own boundaries, a Chinese emperor realized the effect of opium-smoking upon his subjects and threatened severe penalties for all who engaged in the practice. The matter came to such extremes in the Eighteenth Century that the smoking of opium was punishable by death. But the trade continued to increase. Means were found by white men to bring the profitable drug into Chinese ports. At one time, over two centuries ago, the traffic was chiefly in the hands of the Portuguese, but in 1773 they brought only two hundred chests containing it to the China coast. When the British East India Company took a hand in the trade, the number of chests increased to four thousand and fifty-four in 1790, and again, in 1820, the figure had risen to over sixteen thousand chests.

England, as usual, maintained the right of her subjects to trade even in such a questionable material as opium. It was one of the chief exports of India. What would become of vast numbers of her colonial subjects if the opium trade with China were cut off? But the Chinese officials were as stubborn and declined to recede from the avowed determination to stamp out the national vice by removing the drug from the country. There were several historical and sensational events as a consequence, as when the Chinese Commissioner Lin superintended the confiscation of British opium valued at ten million dollars. It was thrown into the sea, having been mixed with lime and salt. Commands were given that no Chinese should attempt to obtain the smallest particles of it, and it is recorded that one man who found a small quantity on the shore and attempted to save it for himself, was promptly beheaded. But British sailors continued to smuggle opium into the country and events finally led to a war, which was ended by the Treaty of Nanking in 1842.

In 1906 another imperial edict placed opium smoking under the ban, because the practice increased with the passing of the years; not only men, but also women being addicted. A bride, on her wedding day, was proud to exhibit her opium pipe, as she was carried to her future husband's house in the grand procession that is supposed to be the principal event in a Chinese girl's life. It was considered the proper thing in society to offer opium to one's guests. Under official ban, the habit had persisted until it was sapping the vitality from the nation. A prohibition ban by the President in 1913 made it less public, but nobody who knows China doubts that the curse remains, and that Chinese of all classes are confirmed opium-smokers in private. Smoking apparatus and large quantities of opium have been burned in public places by the authorities, but these spectacular demonstrations have little effect. The average Chinese knows well enough that the officials who preside at the destruction of confiscated pipes are likely as not secret smokers. It is the consensus of opinion that not only the best, but practically the only way to remove the curse from China, is to make it impossible for the Chinese to procure the drug in any quantity whatever; but while "heathen China" attempts the prohibition, the "Christian" nations continue to make the task almost impossible of accomplishment.

And the Portuguese do not stop at opium manufacture and smuggling. Next to smoking the drug, they know that the most popular of all Chinese vices is gambling, so they cater to that too. The unwieldy government at Peking has made it rather difficult for the people to engage in the pastime on Chinese soil, but Portugal comes to the rescue. Macao is known as "The Monte Carlo of the Orient." This is the proud boast of its citizens, but the criticism of the world leveled at Monte Carlo and its operators is more deserved by Macao.

Some of the principal streets of the city seem to be practically given over to gambling halls of various kinds, in which the games continue for twenty-four hours a day, seven days a week. Some of them are luxuriously appointed, where the wealthy folk fritter away their time and money. But one feels little sympathy for them. Usually, they know perfectly well what they are doing and they can afford to play. In a country that is so old that it has outgrown a desire to indulge in almost all of the pleasures of life, gambling comes as a real recreation. One feels little sympathy for them, for many Chinese are extremely rich. They want to be entertained, and as they sit at the fan-tan tables, tossing thousands of dollars into the basket, one feels almost that it is putting money into circulation that might otherwise be in banks, or accumulating dust, rust and ten per cent, interest from the pockets of the poor. Around the tables one sees the staring eyes of men and women, as at Monte Carlo. They sit and watch the men poke little brass coins with a stick,

Opium Smoking

as if Judgment Day had dawned and they were about to receive the final verdict. All there is to the game: a man throws a heap of the coins into the center of the table and covers them with a cylinder, so that they may not be counted by on-lookers. People bet on one, two, three, or four, the four sides of a square in the center of the table. Amounts sometimes go staggeringly high. Then the cylinder is removed, the coins are counted out in fours. One, two, three, or four remain at the final count, and the lucky number wins, while the "house" takes a percentage of all bets. It seems simple enough, but I have never seen men more excited at the roulette wheel, at faro, or at any other gambling device. And the women, too! Chinese women patronize Macao establishments in large numbers. I saw a little lady enter a saloon alone, remove her outer wraps, give them to an attendant and take her place at the table, apparently for all day. In a short time she had been lucky enough to accumulate a good pile of coins. Probably she was in luck that day; the next, she might lose it all again.

Servants flutter around these gaming halls and bring choice fruit, cigars and cigarettes to all comers. One may go into the game for ten cents, and while sitting at the table, within three minutes, two dollars' worth of food and smoking materials, as well as beverages, will be placed before him. It is not in the way of the proprietors of these places to let anyone feel slighted, at least no opportunity will be given for one to escape while he still has a dollar remaining in his pockets.

I remarked to the guide that I wanted some bird nest soup, shark fins and other Chinese delicacies to eat. He said: "Let's go to a fine gambling house. You take your place at the table. Do you happen to have plenty of bills in your purse? If so, make a show of them, while pretending to make change. Bet ten or twenty cents and then watch the game. The men in charge will have observed your fat purse. I'll tell them what you want to eat, when they ask me; and in that way you can get the best food in China for nothing, if you want to do it. It's a rather clever scheme for getting even, don't you think so?"

But the real evil of the gambling of Macao is the opportunity it offers to the man of limited means to go to the tables and spend his earnings. It is in the Chinese blood to desire to gamble on everything. The average Chinaman, like Lloyd's, will place a bet on everything and anything. You think it will be a pleasant day to-morrow; the Chinaman thinks otherwise for the sake of putting up whatever money he has in his purse. He usually works very hard for a little money, but as soon as he has it, he wants to gamble.

The tables at Macao invite him. I saw several of these men, not of the coolie class, but apparently shop-keepers or clerks, rush to the tables, throw down the profits of the last sale, and attempt to win. Usually they lose, but I saw one young fellow, who rushed into the place excitedly, winning time after time. When I left, he was still there and perhaps he had a hundred dollars, made from a pittance at the beginning. It is this that lures them on. They know the chance and they see the others winning. They risk everything, and, of course, there are many tragedies. The difference, however, is that a Chinaman goes out with the same expressionless face that he wore when he came in, excepting for the staring eyes. One is unable to tell from a celestial gambler's face, whether he has won or lost.

Some of the means for gambling devised for the Chinese are too oriental to have originated with the Portuguese and must have come from the Chinese themselves. For example, the butcher will hang a fine piece of meat in front of his stall throughout the day, drawing customers to his shop by announcing that for a penny one may guess the weight of the meat which will go to the winner at the end of the day. Other merchants lure the crowd by receiving guesses on what the weather will be to-morrow, the next harvest, the depth of water in the canal on a certain day, the first appearance of the fruit tree blossoms, the color of a flower from an exhibited bulb. A few *cash* are deposited for the privilege of gambling, and, of course, toward building up the bank account of the merchant; but the Chinese does not think of that. His concern is the prize that goes to the winner. A popular game is known as the *Thirty-Six Beasts.* The names of that number of animals are placed on counters and shuffled. In the morning one counter is removed from the pack and placed in a paper sack, which is drawn to the top of a pole. All day long the gamblers wager on the name of the animal enclosed in the bag, and sometimes large amounts of money have changed hands and excitement has run high over the "animal's name." The banker retains the bets placed on six animals as his share of the proceeds, and the winner's stake is multiplied by thirty, as a grand prize. Abbé Huc relates that he saw Chinese gamble until they were obliged to stake the clothing they were wearing. He saw men who were obliged to keep in motion to keep warm, because necessary covering had gone to pay gambling debts. He even saw men staking their own fingers and chopping them off to pay the winners.

The Portuguese have been in Macao so long that there is mixture with the Chinese race as perhaps nowhere else in the world, and the stranger has great difficulty in distinguishing the half-castes who are numerous.

My guide, for example, seemed as Chinese as any laundry-man who ever wielded a flat iron, but his name was Francesco Xavier. He spoke English and Chinese fluently, and when I asked him if he also spoke Portuguese, he replied, "Certainly, that is my native language."

Chinese have the reputation of being "good husbands" and they are married to many foreign women who reside here. Vice versa, there are many foreign men married to "native" women. Many of the older families of the city have been here so long that they call themselves "Macaoese" instead of Portuguese; because if they retain the pure occidental blood, it is likely that some of their children will not do so. I was told, when I asked the question, that not more than ten or twelve pure blood Portuguese families reside in the colony, in addition to the officials, some of whom remain only a short time and then go to other colonies or return to the mother country.

Before there was serious thought of occupying the territory, Portuguese sailors knew Macao as a haven of refuge for themselves, their ships and cargo. In fact, it was first known as an excellent place for the drying of wet cargo, but in 1557 they were permitted to build factories on the strip of land, after the payment of twenty thousand Taels. Until the cession of Hongkong to Great Britain, Macao was the only open port in China, but it soon began to decline after the rise of Hongkong, similar to the shifting of trade from Amalfi to Venice in Italy, and, like Venice in her day of grandeur, Hongkong is now of far greater importance than the older colony. In 1887 the Chinese government consented to recognize Macao as a Portuguese possession in return for the aid of Portuguese officials in suppressing the trade in opium smuggling. As far back as the Sixteenth Century the Jesuit missionaries were active in the district, and in 1560 Gregory XIII constituted the Bishopric of Macao. The large church of St. Paul was destroyed by fire early in the last century, but its ruins, surmounting a hill approached by wide stone steps, are still one of the routine "sights," and modern Macao delights in the belief that the church is to be rebuilt.

After a pleasant ride along the sea front boulevard, shaded by ancient banyan trees, one comes to an attractive garden in which is what is known as "Camoëns' Grotto." Great granite boulders have been left in their natural state, but there are pretty flower-bordered walks, ornamental shrubs and many shady nooks in which rustic benches beckon to the pedestrian unused to rather vigorous hill climbing. In one of these retreats is a bronze bust of the celebrated Portuguese poet, Luiz de Camoëns, and beneath it are carved in the rocks selections from his immortal epic, the "*Lusiad,*" which relates the valorous deeds in arms of the Portuguese in Asia and Europe. Lopa de Vega, the world's most prolific playwright, has written of Camoëns: "Strange fortune that to so much wit and learning gave a life of poverty and a rich sepulcher."

It seems likely that seven cantos of the great Portuguese national epic were composed while the poet was in Macao, other portions belonging to the period of his lengthy exile in Centa, Mozambique, Goa and other places. Tradition says that he sat among the rocks of this garden, overlooking the roofs of Macao, and that much of the "*Lusiad*" was written on the exact spot that now supports his effigy. At any rate, it was in the vicinity that the luckless poet of an ungrateful country glorified his nation's accomplishments, and Macao is not behind the mother country in paying him honors today.

I was invited to spend my last hour in Macao in the garden of one of the wealthy men of China, who finds it convenient to live in foreign territory. His house is one that would be a show place at Newport. His garden covers perhaps ten acres, and is given over to ponds, bridges, lotus beds, a rare collection of azaleas so trained as to resemble mandarins, and grottoes of rocks over which piped water trickles as in a natural woodland. Nothing was more characteristic of the place, perhaps, than the remarks of the guide as we were strolling around the mosaic walks.

"This man very rich. He has mines, and I imagine that he has interests in some of the gambling halls. He is very, very rich, as you see. The stones in this garden cost one hundred thousand dollars to bring them here, for this was all a barren hillside before he came. Think of it, so rich and he has only four wives. That big house and only four wives!"

Francesco made a gesture of contempt. It seemed to be more Latin than Oriental. It was Macao.

CHAPTER V

"PARIS OF THE FAR EAST"

A WEALTHY Chinese gentleman told a foreigner that he thought it would be advisable for his son to learn the English language, because he believed it would be much more necessary in the years to come than it is now, so he engaged an English tutor for him. "I could have sent him to Shanghai," he explained, "but I did not want his future life ruined. Shanghai may be what the foreigners want it to be; but it is not the place for a young Chinese."

But this would not be the Occidental opinion. To the average Westerner, Shanghai is more attractive than Paris. The principal reason seems to be that Paris has the reputation, although it always seems a libel to call the French capital gay, for it is one of the most sedate and proper of all European capitals; while it would be just as much of a libel to call Shanghai anything else than gay. It is gay with a determined vengeance, and as cosmopolitan as Cairo. Throw Russians, French, Americans and English together, with a good sprinkling of Spain, Italy and Portugal, cast them in a city anywhere from three to five thousand miles from home, give them plenty of leisure and money, and it is quite safe to suspect that they will find means of amusing themselves.

They do! Never waste sympathy on the foreigner who is "obliged to live in Shanghai for business reasons." It is a certain guess that he is enjoying himself about ten times as much as he would at home. It is a hardship to be separated from old friends and relatives, but even this has its compensations. First of all, the man who comes to Shanghai to live finds what a distinction there is in being a white man. Others of his race have been here before him for a long time and they have paved the way. Here is the great cosmopolitan gateway to China. The nations of the Western world have been prowling around that gate like vultures for many years. Their various representatives of state and commerce saw to it that Shanghai should not be a dull place in which to spend their years of "exile." The young generation is clinging tenaciously to the traditions. Shanghai is really one of the great cities of the Chinese republic, but Chinese Shanghai is a shabby, narrow-streeted section of city, smelly, and a most unhealthful place in which to live. European Shanghai along the river front in many ways compares favorably to the banks of the Seine or Thames in Paris or London. View any prosperous American city from the water front and the buildings are of much the same sort as those which border the harbor along what is known as the Bund, which is ornamented with gardens, walks, drives and parks. Several of the consuls of the foreign governments have offices and residences that would compare favorably with American bank buildings. And this is China! One would barely suspect it but for the predominating element in the streets.

But a dozen Chinamen will scoot when an American, Russian, Frenchman or Englishman yells at them. And that seems to be the fashion. The Caucasian comes along the street where a group of Chinese are talking and blocking his path. It is China and these men are in their own country, but what does the white man do? Turn aside to pass them? Instead, he yells: "Get out of my way, you loafers," or stronger words, and the Chinese scatter. Perhaps they do not understand the words, but they know the tone of the speaker and what it means, so they do not need a second invitation. Verily, it is better to be white than yellow in Shanghai!

An American resident took me for an automobile ride. Automobiles seem out of place in China; the streets are too crowded with people. They were scampering to right and left as we smashed along through the crowded streets. The chauffeur was a young Chinese, who highly valued the honor of driving a white man's car. He did not seem to be a respecter of human life at any time, but we came to a street where there were so many people that they blocked the pavement from curb to curb, and a traffic policeman, standing in the center of the crowd, held up his arms and shouted for us to stop.

"Get out of our way, you old yellow fool, or we'll run you down," shouted the host. The Chink dropped his arms and stepped aside with the others. He understood English and was afraid that the American would do literally as he had threatened.

Chinese are aggravating to the person driving a motor car, and they seem to be tempting fate as they stand still when they see a car approaching, dodging out of the way as few seconds as possible before the rubber tires actually brush them aside or run them down. I asked the editor of the Shanghai *China Press* about it and he explained: "Like many other things Chinese, this may he traced to superstition. The average Chinese thinks he is pursued by many devils. He thinks the auto is the most powerful devil of all, so he likes to stand until the last minute, hop out of the way, and he believes the auto smashes the devils that are after him."

"White folks," as they like to be known in Shanghai, run things as they please. Whether they do it well or ill depends upon the point of view. At any rate, they do it entertainingly. Practically all the large countries of the world have warships floating in the harbor with guns eternally turned menacingly toward shore. They are to "protect foreign interests." This is diplomatic language perhaps, because they seem to say: "Do as we want you to do, or we'll blow you to atoms. Perhaps we quarrel among ourselves, but we are all agreed upon one thing, you must behave exactly as we tell you."

The tourist may come direct to Shanghai from Hongkong, a two-days' trip by sea on the splendid *Empress* steamers bound for Vancouver, after stopping at Japanese ports, or he may desire to know more of the native life in the early days of his tour and avail himself of the opportunity to visit such cities as Foo-chow, Swatow, or Amoy, in each of which there are temples and other sights of interest, modern hotel accommodations, and where one feels plunged into the filthy, opium and incensed air of China that has not changed so much in recent years as the coast centers more frequented by foreigners. The trip may be made by steamer, and at the landing stage one may step to a waiting rikisha or sedan chair and visit the principal points of interest with barely so much as touching his foot to the ground—which may appear to the new arrival to be desirable. Unless one has considerable leisure, however, and an overwhelming desire to see "everything" in China, the side trips to the cities mentioned are not to be strongly recommended.

Arrival at Shanghai seems doubly interesting by reason of the fact that after leaving the fine ocean liner, he is still thirteen miles from his destination. The steamer runs into the great yellow flood that sweeps down to the sea from Thibet, dividing China into halves, but it proceeds only as far as the bar that is near the junction of the Whangpoo-Kiang and Yangtze-Kiang, drops anchor and swings around in the muddy current awaiting the tenders, upon which passengers and baggage are carried to Shanghai. It is a fine ride up the river, the bosom of which seems dotted with the world's shipping. After many twists and turns, the city begins to loom in the distance, boats seem to be more numerous and before long one distinguishes the flags of many nations from the ships at anchor and from consulates and foreign concession buildings. Here is Shanghai, on the same parallel as Cairo and New Orleans, but a nice cool breeze is blowing and it seems a relief after Hongkong.

Street Scene, Shanghai

Shanghai seems so hidden away that one might anticipate trouble in finding it; but there is no such trouble. Apparently, every one finds it. Most of the fashionable trippers from America and England "do China" from a hotel veranda at Shanghai. It is more expensive and gives one very little idea of what real China is like; but as I heard one American debutante remark: "It seems to be the most fashionable place in the Far East."

There is no doubt about it, Shanghai is fashionable. There are several fashionable hotels where it would be unpardonable to attempt to dine before eight or nine o'clock in full evening regalia. There are large foreign orchestras in some of them. One restaurant that boasts of being the gayest in the city, has a choir of the "best Hawaiian singers who ever left the islands," and a cabaret entertainment that would be gay in Paris or New York. Here Mr. Foreign Consul or Mr. Foreign Representative of a Commercial House, or Mr. Officer of a Warship promenades with a flashily gowned and bejeweled lady. Of course everyone else sits along the rows of tables and gossips. But gossip means less in Shanghai than elsewhere. Nobody wants anybody else to become homesick or lonesome, so when any one is not actively engaged in gossip he tries to give everyone else something to gossip about. So goes the world in Shanghai! It is likely to be the biggest surprise of the whole China tour. It is not a place of Chinese sights, although it claims a population of a million Chinese, but rather it is gay Cosmopolis with a foreign population estimated at twenty thousand, about fifteen hundred of whom are Americans. There are several clubhouses on the Bund and in the suburbs that would not be out of place in American cities. Society drives out past the Bubbling Well in the afternoon, as society drives in the Bois at the same hour in Paris. I saw a fine string of expensive automobiles going along a fashionable drive about four o'clock in the afternoon. I stepped into a rikisha to go and see them pass. The white women were gowned as smartly as the women of Fifth Avenue, New York. They had Chinese chauffeurs, footmen, and sometimes servants on the steps of the cars, all in natty oriental uniforms. I thought that perhaps the ladies of the diplomatic corps might be down from Peking for some celebration. Crowds of people were watching them pass, and I am sure that they attracted as much attention as if they had been ambassadors' wives. I enquired and found that from four to six o'clock is the fashionable hour for the foreign demimonde to take its airing.

Verily, Shanghai is gay, and even the local guides feel certain that it is the gaiety that all Westerners enjoy. One of the craft smiled when I told him that I wanted to see the principal "sights" of the city. It was in the forenoon and he assured me that there were few "sights" until the lights were turned on at night. "Are there no temples, pagodas or monuments?" I asked.

"Oh, yes, there is the old Mandarin's Tea House, supposed to have been the original for the willow ware pattern which ornaments chinaware. There is the statue of old Li Hung-chang, and I believe that American school teachers go to the old city and see the bird market when they are in Shanghai. Of course, most people gave up looking at such things many years ago. Say, are you fooling me, or are you a missionary?"

He was hopeless, but he was more polite about it than guide Number two. When I told this worthy gentleman that I would like to see the Mandarin's tea garden, he seemed to enjoy the best laugh of his life and said: "Quit your kidding," after which he explained, "Americans don't give a whoop for the old tea house."

Yes, I repeat that Shanghai is gay, and a part of this gaiety consists of turning night into day. "Everything worthwhile" is running at top speed and full blaze at two or three o'clock in the morning. Clerks must have heavy eyelids when they come to their desks at ten, for, if the truth must be told, there is much "society" here that is clerical. But there is a good rest at noon, business being practically suspended until two o'clock, and every one must be at his club, golf links or tennis court shortly after four. Business hours are short in Shanghai, and nights are long. The whole city seems to be afraid that somebody will become homesick or lonesome—or spend one hour of the twenty-four quietly. That would not be according to the proud boast of the "Paris of the Orient."

One may not have noticed it until he reached Shanghai, but the rather amusing spectacle of men walking along the public highway, bird-cage at arm's length, will no longer escape the eye of the foreigner. Perhaps the first instance goes unnoticed; the man may have purchased a bird and he may be taking it home as a pretty present for his wife. The second, third or fifth bird-carrier may not cause a remark, but the twentieth or fiftieth is likely to do so, and the real truth of the matter is too odd to occur to the tourist's mind. Sentimental people, these Chinese; they are much attached to birds and flowers! They squander huge sums of money on a dwarfed pine tree, the shape of which strikes their fancy. Rich men often count azaleas among their prized possessions, particularly when the branches have been trained into grotesque or fantastic shapes, held in place by wire frames or sticks, giving them the appearance of men, birds and animals. One takes it for granted that the little Chinese housewives also love birds and flowers!

But the Chinese who are carrying birds in the street have not purchased them for their women folks! The smartly dressed young men of the cities, who promenade the streets bird-cage in hand, are not thoughtful of their wives, who have been selected for them by their parents. They would "lose face" by carrying anything for such an insufficient reason as to bring light or sunshine into the lives of their companions at home. They carry birds because they are bird fanciers—or pretend to be. The more literal truth might be that it is fashionable as similar whims are "smart" in America, but because it was fashionable when their grand-father's father was a boy—and before. In an older day, however, one's favorite bird went for his airing perched on the forefinger of his master, still a favorite recreation for the older men of China. But the wooden and bamboo cages were attractive to the youth of China, and, in addition, the cages gave them the opportunity to promenade with birds that were not wholly domesticated, feathered creatures that were more beautiful than hawks, even brilliantly plumaged warblers that previously had been confined to the house, garden, or store. Nearly every Chinese shop or home, however small it may be, has room for at least one bird and sometimes for several of them. Every garden has them suspended from the trees or bushes in bright cages or tied by a string or chain.

In reality, the Chinese are great bird fanciers. The variety seems to be of little consequence; pigeons, hawks, pheasants, parrots, or canaries seem to be equally popular. The bird market is usually one of the interesting corners of every city of China, because one not only sees the great variety of feathered creatures, some of which are perched on ropes, hoops or bamboo hung from roof to roof across the narrow streets, but also comes into close contact with the vari-colored Chinese of all social classes, and observes them bargaining for birds that have struck their fancy. Here one hears a strange medley of voices, the bird language being as easily understood by the foreigner as the "bally-hoo" of the merchants who chant the merits of the creatures that are offered for sale at prices that seem to be ridiculously low to the American. While many Chinese youths may promenade the city streets, bird-cage in hand, making their choice of companion seem to be an affectation; one who goes far from the cities to the distant tombs, shrines and the surrounding parks with ponds and pretty gardens will come upon many pedestrians or holiday-makers who have brought their birds with them to enjoy the fresh air and the beauties of nature.

The bird-market of Shanghai is in the filthy but interesting native city called *Hu-tsen* or *Sen-tsen,* surrounded by a wall about three miles in

The "Mandarin's Tea House"

circumference, and in the narrow streets of the neighborhood one may spend several enjoyable hours. The "Mandarin's Tea House" is close by, and so are many narrow lanes, in the shops of which splendid collections of Chinese jewelry, ivory, porcelain, carved chop sticks, idols, brocades and rare antiques of various kinds are offered for sale. Both the native and foreign parts of the city are fascinating places in which to shop. Jade, Chinese coats, linen and silk may be found in greater abundance elsewhere, but the quality of the merchandise in the Shanghai shops is not excelled in the other cities.

The late dinners and drawing-rooms of the hotels, the foreign restaurants or ballrooms patronized exclusively by the foreign residents and visitors, may make a strong appeal to the Western tourist and cause him to believe that Shanghai copies much of its manners and customs from cosmopolitan Cairo or Port Said, but there is a much more interesting native night life, which, of course, one will not mention to foreign residents, because they are not supposed to look with favor upon an excursion that brings one elbowing the Chinese crowd that fills the streets and surges into theaters, tea-houses, and baths, some of which are luxuriously furnished. And in addition to these older re-creative institutions, around which there is always the bedlam caused by masses of chattering men, sing-song girls, musicians who vie with boiler-makers in the matter of tone production, dozens of cinema theaters have lately come into existence, and are so rapidly gaining in popularity that they seem likely to become the most popular institution that ever came out of the West.

The Chinese are becoming infatuated with the motion picture exhibition to such an extent that they will gladly attend a performance, the program of which extends through four, five, or even six hours, which is quite in keeping with the time limit of native theatrical representations. I saw a crowd quite overcome with joy at the vicissitudes that befell the heroine in the American-made film, "The Hazards of Helen." The thrilling scenes were greeted by outbursts of applause, many of the spectators rising to their feet and shouting lustily when the hero saved Helen and her baby by venturing onto the railroad bridge and jumping into the river with the two in his arms as the express train whizzed across the screen.

Such a demonstration meant much more in China than it would mean in a Western country. It is not "good form," not even "proper," for a Chinese to betray his emotions; at least, he must not let them rise to the surface. He may applaud at the theater, but even while making this demonstration, which is not in accordance with ancient custom, he must not smile or laugh. The comedian may grimace; gentlemen in the audience are not supposed to do so. The scene may be very thrilling and tense, but Chinese gentlemen should have better control of themselves than to show by any facial movement that they are excited.

But Helen, assuredly very modern, as seen in the motion pictures, caused them to forget some of the things that they had been taught by their fathers. They not only betrayed the fact that they received the thrill, but they seemed to be delighted to do so and seemed to desire to let the hero know that they appreciated what they had done. When "close-up" portraits of the characters were shown, smirking and "looking pleasant," which is so contrary to all the canons of Chinese theatric art, they stood up and waved their hands. When the express train was flashed on the screen, whizzing along at a mile a minute—in a country where trains seem likelier to move a mile in ten minutes—they applauded as we in America applaud when a favorite star makes her "big speech" in the third act. Certainly they enjoyed "The Hazards of Helen." It was the first time that I saw a Chinese audience witnessing a film that was "Made in America." If I had never seen another Chinese audience beholding a "Made in America" film, I would have had the impression that the motion picture was more popular in China than in America. But I saw many of them. I saw audiences only mildly interested, and I saw some that were quite visibly bored, because they did not know what it was all about, and, not knowing, they could not feel an interest any more than the popular American audience would feel for Greek tragedy or the sacred dances of Siam. At Chinese motion picture houses a lecturer frequently stands on the stage and explains the action, even in such stories of primitive situations as "The Hazards of Helen."

"Now you see the little child going out on the railroad bridge," he says. "She is a thoughtless infant, who does not know that death is lurking in her path. She is as happy as any innocent little child can be. She skips over the railway ties, having found a new amusement. But what will happen when the fast train comes thundering along the track? What will become of the child?"

Oh, he is an eloquent extemporaneous speaker, this Chorus who explains the play! He weaves much into his "explanation" that is prompted by the picture itself, much that never entered the mind of the scenario writer.

"Helen sees the little girl," he continues; "What can she do? How can she save her?" (Helen is flashed on the screen gazing bridge-ward, with a sort of hunted-deer expression.) "Will she stand there and see the child run over by the train, or thrown into the river below? No, she does not think twice, but rushes out onto the bridge and snatches the child into her arms. But the cruel train is coming; see, it is coming around the mountain. It will plunge into the tunnel and then out onto the bridge." (Business of express train plunging into a tunnel.) "The hero sees Helen and he, too, rushes out onto the bridge. Will he reach her and the child before the train comes? That is the great question. See! He has reached them, but it is too late! In ten seconds the train will be upon them. There is no time to escape, so the hero takes both Helen and the child in his arms and jumps off the bridge into the river. Will he be strong enough to swim and reach the shore in safety with his precious load?"

And so forth, the "lecturer" creates action, when he thinks the interest is flagging. During the scenes that make merely an "exposition" of the characters and plots he is obliged to keep up his story, or at least he does so. He invents enough plots and counterplots to provide another installment of the serial. I was unable to learn the origin of these gentlemen, who seem so important to the movie in China, but they must have had much theatrical experience in their native country. They must have as ready knowledge of all the old plots as the average dramatist in America. Perhaps some of them have acted in Chinese plays, the plots of most of which are the same as the stereotyped plots in American drama. They remember, but the audience does not, apparently, because, as in America, it appears to enjoy the unraveling of the same old stories. It is the "lecturer" who makes the American motion picture intelligible to the oriental audience, at least the Chinese audience, which insists upon knowing something about what is transpiring. Chinese actors carry "suggestion" so much further than the Americans would attempt to do their speeches are so absolutely inaudible, on account of the strumming and squawking of the various instruments of the orchestra, that people do not expect to hear too much and have learned to trust to their eyes. Or perhaps they do not care to understand. In the course of a six-to-ten hour entertainment, which is not an uncommon length of time for a Chinese play to run, they will hear enough to satisfy them and reward them for going to the theater. It is useless to permit one's self to become overwrought and excited about mere play acting. Life itself is much more comic, much more tragic; and they do not become excited about life, seeming to value it very lightly, and not worrying about death.

Their attitude toward the theater in China is very well expressed by a question asked of some Shanghai Chinese after they had witnessed the first

CHINAMAN WITH BIRD-CAGE

game of tennis in that country, as played by Englishmen. "Yes, it is all very well as a game," they said, "but why run around, hitting the little rubber balls when you can hire coolies to do it for you?"

Charlie Chaplin has "invaded" the Orient and he is winning friends for the "American drama," where acting and singing companies have failed to do so. They told me of an American comic opera company that visited Shanghai some time ago. My informant declared that the troupe gave creditable performances, but the Chinese ears were tortured by the singing. At first the audience calmly endured it, thinking that the agony would soon be over. Then they looked at one another absent-mindedly, and, finally, before the evening was over, most of the men had folded their coat sleeves over their mouths, so their laughter would not be audible. But they all have heard about the popularity of Chaplin in America, and for once in their lives Orient agrees with Occident. Chaplin is a great entertainer! The Chinese enjoy him, because his antics coincide exactly with their ideas of what comedy should be; and think he is the funniest man who ever lived. It is amusing to attend a theater in China where a Chaplin exhibition is in progress. When I first saw him in the country it was in a rather imposing theater and "Our Best People" were said to be in attendance. The first glance at them, however, was rather shocking. Here was "full dress" with a vengeance; "full dress" that quite put into the shade any similar effort at undress in the Metropolitan horseshow in New York. Many Chinese were stripped to the waist and wore either a pair of bathing trunks—the idea was borrowed from America—or the long, baggy Chinese trousers that are tied around the ankles with ribbons. As I looked out over the audience from the back of the house, the bathing trunks, trousers and ribbons were invisible. What I saw was an ocean of bare backs and shoulders. I took a seat among this strangely costumed multitude, and finally recovered sufficiently to note that a Charlie Chaplin comedy was being shown. Bang! Something came down and hit him on the head. Zipp! He tripped his toe and fell headlong. The audience laughed as I had never seen Chinese laugh. There were few ladies present, because it is not yet considered quite the "proper" thing for a Chinese matron or her daughters to attend a cinema exhibition, but I carefully observed the perspiring gentlemen close to me. They seemed to be having the time of their lives, sometimes laughing so violently that it seemed to pain them, doubtless because it pained them to realize that they were so far forgetting themselves. Whenever "Our Charlie" took a particularly heavy fall, or whenever something fell on his head, apparently causing him great suffering, the Chinese closed their eyes, sat back on their benches and laughed facially and inwardly. It was a typical July night and it was very warm. The perspiration flowed down their backs in streams as they literally undulated with glee.

But no better exhibition could be devised for the entertainment of the Chinese audience. He is supposed to have a "heart," but the Chinaman derives much satisfaction when he sees another man suffering, particularly if there is a remote possibility that he deserves it. Let a villain strut upon the speaking stage, with those artificial strides so affected by native actors, and the Chinaman will literally shout with joy when he comes to his downfall. "What is, is right," he argues, and if a man on the stage, or off the stage, comes to misfortune, it was destined so to be. Let a mason drop a heavy stone on his foot in the street, and almost instantly he will be surrounded by a giggling multitude that seems to gloat over his suffering. There is nothing funnier to the Chinese than to see someone in great difficulty endeavoring to extricate himself. For example, it is very funny when in the native drama a flirtatious mandarin is walking with a "sing-song" girl favorite and comes face to face with his wife. Or he may be chatting with the sweetheart of another man when approached by her lover. This is very funny; but, after some time, the fun passes and then there is a "scene" which the Chinaman likes almost as well as the first grim joke. He likes the quarrel, the duel, the escape, the fight or the killing. It is action.

In a country where everyone dotes on a "sight," the drama must the lurid. Executions in real life are "well attended." Head-choppings were among the popular amusements of the week in that older day when sometimes twenty or thirty victims fell to the headman's knife in a single city. This was counted a gala event and the crowds remained until the heads were exposed on fence posts or poles at bridges and street corners, where they served as an "example" to passers-by. Missionaries have reported that they have seen small boys at these spectacles, tossing heads about in a game of "catch," as if they had been rubber or wooden balls. Head-choppings are rare nowadays and occur only in the far interior of the country. But men are still put in the stocks, and they are obliged to wear heavy wooden or metal collars that speak their guilt to all passers. They are hung up by the hands in iron cages placed on the street, and men so punished are always certain to "draw good houses."

One day my Chinese "boy," age forty-six, one of his kind readily attaching himself to every traveler in the Celestial republic, serving as valet, interpreter and "guide," came to me and excitedly told me that a famous dramatic company would give several performances of centuries-old plays in a native theater of Shanghai.

"May be you no like, because plays very old," he said, while attempting to whet my appetite for the native drama, but he had so much to offset any misgivings that I accompanied him, permitting him to believe that as he had arranged everything he would "lose face" if I did not share his enthusiasm. When the curtain was raised—or parted, for the sliding curtain is an ancient Chinese device, although I had been led to believe in America that it was of comparatively recent origin—we were seated in an orchestra box, Hong Mai-fong delighted with the music, while I attempted to be deaf to the orchestra and give my attention to the stage. And, almost immediately I had the theatrical surprise of my life. Misunderstanding my enthusiasm, Hong continued to repeat: "Play very old," which seemed to be his formula of apology for enticing me to this exhibition palace.

"That man belong great emperor," he explained; "beautiful lady no belong his wife but belong wife other man. Other man come pity soon now."

I made no reply, from which Hong took it that I was not interested. In reality, I was looking at a set of folding screens that formed the scenic background for the drama. Here was "Gordon Craig's scenery!" And I found later that its speedy shifting schemes of presenting various ocular impressions to an audience and even its "suggestion" rather than fully developed decoration oration was much as the son of Ellen Terry has been urging Western nations to adopt! But Gordon Craig's meanderings are vague, tinged with precious theories, apparently not intended to be too well understood by *hoi-polloi*. With minor exceptions, however, usually in such technical matters as the employment of calciums and other electrical contrivances, it seemed apparent to anyone who had followed Mr. Craig's writings on the subject of stage decoration and scenic manipulation that he has received credit for being an originator whereas he was but an adapter.

"You no like?" asked Hong, eager to converse, as all individuals of the Chinese audience seem to be during the enactment of a play.

"Yes," I replied, "Hike."

"This belong very old play," he continued, quite unable to appreciate the irony of his words in the light of my thoughts about the "new" stage and scenery of which we have heard so much in recent years. But my thoughts quickly turned from Craig. To encourage my "boy" to be quiet, I assured him that I had never enjoyed a theatrical representation so much in my life, and I had no sooner done so than the "Emperor" on the stage summoned all

MARKET-PLACE, SHANGHAI

his retainers, vassals and slaves. That particular moment of the play called for some sort of conclave, preparatory to the inevitable combat. Somebody of high degree had "sinned," he was to be put to the test in the presence of his emperor. Hong did not make the plot exactly clear to me, and I have my doubts if it was wholly clear to him. He caught some of the dialogue, as did the rest of the audience, but there was much that was drowned by the continued din caused by the orchestra, and the idea of "suggestion" was carried so much further than our most prominent suggesters would think of going that one not thoroughly acquainted with the subtle technique of Chinese pantomime could not hope to fathom it. For instance, as the clans arrived in the palace courtyard (represented by a wooden gate that may have cost ten cents) before they were ushered into the presence of His Majesty, the actors gave a jump, and after landing on their feet, at a point a yard from the gate, they stood still for some seconds while a young lady undulated a small stick on the floor. I could not understand, but Hong explained:

"When these men come up to the courtyard of the palace there is much water, because the palace is on an island, and they are unable to reach it without a boat. See that young girl! She is rowing a boat, a ferry. The men they jump into the boat and she takes them across to the palace gate."

But I had another surprise before the crowds reached the palace. Some of them came from the right of the stage, some from the left—but the larger number came from the front of the house! "What I have known as a Max Reinhardt novelty," I whispered to myself, because the actors were streaming along a run-way, level with the heads of the audience. It was exactly as the famous German stage manager floods his stage with people at a moment's notice. That certainly was an innovation, because all the articles that have been written about Reinhardt have told us so.

"Very old," harped Hong, when I mentioned the matter to him. "That is called '*The Flowery Way*' in the Chinese theater." And on later investigation I found that this run-way was in existence in China several centuries ago. It is a feature of the usual equipment of the Chinese theater, as much so as seats for the audience, or the orchestra, and will be found even in the most provincial theaters.

Although the particular spectacle that I was viewing made use of shifting screens for scenic background, I attended a smaller theater sometime later, and at the close of the first act I was astonished to see the small stage begin to turn on a central pivot. The second act setting came suddenly into view—after a few seconds of boisterous music by the orchestra—and the play proceeded without intermission! I had no opportunity for inquiring further into the matter while in China, but a few weeks later in Japan, having seen the same device there, I sought out an American who has been making a special study of the native theater in the Orient and said: "Certainly this convention has been borrowed from the West. We have all been told that these stages are unique in England and in America."

"That may be," he laughed, "unique in America and England, but there are hundreds of them in operation over here. Probably the Japanese first took the idea from the Chinese; but it is certain that the revolving stage, permitting the settings of the next act to be put into place while its predecessor is in view of the audience, has been used in Japan for centuries—just how many I am unable to learn. The device may have existed in China at least a thousand years ago."

Finally there was an intermission, and Hong, still doubtful of my opinion concerning the ancient Chinese spectacle that was being enacted, advised me to stay and see the next act. "It will be more better," he said, "more better than the other part. Man belong emperor now hold court because he marry beautiful lady. Mandarin come from many province to bow before him. Beautiful costume!"

And Hong was a good prophet. It was a "more better" spectacle than was offered in the earlier scenes; in fact, it was a "more better" spectacle than I have ever seen on a stage in any other country. The costumes were "more better" than any ever worn upon the operatic stages of London, Paris, Berlin, Munich, Bayreuth or New York, because here were realities, whereas those in the theaters and opera houses of the Western world are tawdry imitations made to glow and glitter by the clever manipulation of calcium lights and colored globes. It is a well-known fact that the finest mandarin robes and head gear in China now belong to the actors and theaters. They have owned gorgeous costumes for many years, but after the establishment of the republic the impoverished Manchu nobility suddenly was obliged to open its chests of fine raiment that reposed within palace walls and was obliged to sell for whatever could be obtained in a hurry. Ready cash was a necessity and they had no other means of procuring it. They had little in addition to their wardrobes and jewelry.

Europeans and Americans, long resident in the Orient, affect to despise everything "Chinese." An American who had lived in China for fourteen years told me that he would not have so much as a Chinese plaque or vase in his home. Instead of availing himself of the opportunity to stock his domicile with beautiful teakwood furniture, inlaid with mother-of-pearl, each piece an almost priceless gem, he preferred the Grand Rapids article. So beyond a few buyers for antique dealers in the West, there was no active demand for these things among Europeans or Americans. But the Manchus required money. The husband of the Princess Der Ling told me that after the fall of the Manchus he visited palaces of the nobility at Mukden in which rooms were literally stacked with chests in which the gorgeous costumes of mandarins and courtiers had been placed, sometimes after garments had been worn but once, although many of these things were gorgeously embroidered satin or silk robes which must have occupied their makers for months—even years. They were offered for the proverbial "song," but, often enough, there were no buyers. "Money, money, money," was the despairing cry of the owners. At length, the second-hand dealers of China took them, and many of them are being scattered around the marts of the world. But the best of them were bought by the actors and the theaters of the country. In design they were exactly in accordance with the requirements of the native stage, because there is practically no such thing as modern drama in China. The nearest approach to it is a slightly varying method of producing the old stories culled from the legendary lore of bygone centuries. The stores themselves do not change, and the "periods" do not change; consequently, there is no change in the costumes as to style. They are always of that grand period when emperors sat on their thrones and when feudal lords ruled from behind moated castle walls. And although Chinese theaters seem to eliminate accessories and scenic investiture, even to the point of negligence, sometimes setting a pole that resembles a broom-handle in the middle of the stage to "represent" a magnificent banyan tree in the palace courtyard, while the palatial pavilion itself is often represented by another pole set atop two sticks placed in an upright position, they are never lax in the matter of facial makeup and adornment or in costumes, The masks of an older day—the idea for which doubtless came from the ancient Greeks by way of India—are not so commonly used as formerly, but I have seen Chinese actors made up to represent black demons, with gilt or vermillion designs from Persian patterns on their faces that at a distance were scarcely discernable from papier mache masks, unless the scenes required a movement of the face in singing or speaking lines.

  As one of these demons came on the stage at Shanghai I recalled that Nubian slave in the American production of "Kismet" in which Otis Skinner was the featured performer. This ebony-hued gentleman attracted

CHA PIH-YUNG

nation-wide comment for his artistry at makeup, as did the gilded figures in Granville Barker's production of Shakespearian dramas. But they were as a child's water color painting beside a Rembrandt when compared to the makeup of the actors in even a provincial Chinese theater. A glance at these actors showed plainly enough the "source" of many of the "pet theories" of modern stage operators in the West. Many of our "new" ideas seemed to be about contemporary with the building of the Ming tombs when viewed on the Chinese stage, "which has not changed in essentials in a thousand years."

But the greatest surprise and discovery of all came later, as the wonderful pageant approached the stage along the *Flowery Way*, as I caught glimpses of Chinese lords coming to pay their tribute to the mighty emperor costumed in magnificent robes of silk, heavily embroidered from the collar to the tip of the train, often so long that it required the service of four pages, as I observed the odd head-gear, ranging from pointed caps resembling bishops' miters to grotesque diadems which spread out over their shoulders in curves and twists that resembled the roofs of temples and shrines, and my mind quickly turned to the costumes designed by the very modern Leon Bakst, of Paris, which have lately caused much comment in the Western world.

The stage was flooded with people, and at the height of what seemed to be a barbaric oriental orgy a young lord recognized his favorite as the lady in whose honor the festivities were given by the Emperor. He had no means of redress, so with posturings and posings he approached the base of the throne and committed suicide. The lady rushed to him, thus betraying their "secret," so the Emperor ordered her to be killed. Confusion, terror—everything but artificial thunder and lightning! The music crashed and piped in unearthly noises!

"Serge de Diaghileff and his Russian ballet!" I said aloud, but Hong did not understand and asked me to repeat the words. "The Russians have accentuated the action of the scenes," I continued; "the Chinese do not care for rapid action, because they consider it to be vulgar and common."

"Play very, very old," parroted Hong, now assured that I must be displeased.

"You must get permission for me to go back on the stage," I said to him.

"That is not possible," he regretted.

"It must be possible. Tell them that I am an American actor, a Russian manager, or the Prince of Wales; I don't care what you tell them and I will take the consequences, but go and procure permission for me to go on the stage." And, after considerable difficulty, the "boy" returned, bearing a slip of paper that gave me the coveted permission. During my first visit, there was the expected oriental reticence. "White people" do not go on the stage of a Chinese theater, and neither the stage manager nor the actors could understand my interest. They treated me politely and courteously offered me tea that had been poured on jasmine flowers, the petals of which floated on each cup—a potion constantly imbibed by the actors. And they gave me an invitation to "come again," so, a night later, I not only saw the show from "behind the scenes," but sat by actors' tables as they put on their remarkable makeup. On a later occasion they not only let me examine the wardrobe that was being worn, but brought out rare robes and head-dress that was put on for other plays. Stage hands spread out marvels of color, design and workmanship.

Yes, the plays were very old, the costumes and manner of presenting them were very old, the *Flowery Way* through the audience was very old, and even the makeup of the actors, because it was all in imitation of ancient masks. But Hong was a Chinese peasant, before he became an interpreter and valet. He may be excused for not knowing. There is not such a good excuse for Americans and Europeans who have accepted the "new" stage and the "moderns" and never thought to look to that decadent "father of all things," old China, for stage "novelties" as well as for the origin of printing and fire-crackers.

One night the stage manager introduced me to a young actor named Cha Pih-yung and told me that his salary was $2,000 a month. In a country where there are almost daily reports that this or that movie actress has placed her name to a contract calling for that amount of money for about forty-eight hours' work the amount may not seem to be so large. It may not mean to the casual reader that it is an amount almost unheard-of for a public entertainer. Nevertheless, this is the case in China. Where coolies work for eight or ten cents a day, where artistic embroiderers receive twenty cents for working from dawn until sunset, and where porcelain artists and wood-carvers sometimes receive the munificent salary of seventy-five cents a day, it will be observed that by comparison Cha Pih-yung is well paid. Also, there is the fact that actors of all grades are looked upon with unpitying contempt in China. The "Brethren of the Pear Orchard," as they are called by polite Chinese, are on a social scale with barbers. People who understand the Chinese language will realize better than the rest of us just what it means to be called by numbers, rather than by names. It gives the actors the general class distinction of animals, quite similar to the German *fressen* used in connection with eating.

It is not the popular opinion that actors deserve to be well paid. Perhaps there is no country on earth where theatrical performances of all kinds are more enjoyed than in China; but the status of the actor does not improve with the passing of the years. At best, the clan is about at the level of the strolling actor of the Middle Ages in Europe, and there are many other points of similarity between the stage of the Middle Ages in Europe and the present day in China. The services of professionals may be requisitioned at any time by a powerful mandarin, who commands them to put up their stages and act in his front court-yard fittingly to celebrate his birthday, or who desires to celebrate the festival or birthday of a provincial idol, and commands them to go to the most inconvenient places, where they must act under the most distressing circumstances. Male and female parts are played by men, as in the days of Shakespeare in England.

In such a country, and under these circumstances, Cha Pih-yung receives two thousand dollars a month! I could not find any actor in China who receives anything like a similar amount, anyone who had risen to a point anywhere near his importance in stageland in the Flowery Republic, and it seemed strange that he should be an impersonator of female characters. At least I expected that he would be cast for the extravagantly costumed and much over-played parts of the triumphing hero which are so common in Chinese drama. I thought that he would be one of those gentlemen who strut around the stage and prance down the *Flowery Way* to the back of the auditorium with pompous strides that are supposed to indicate wealth, authority and dignity, according to the celestial stage technique.

The stage manager explained that Cha plays the "fair princess," who is a figure of importance in the old style drama. In the offering of the evening, he was playing the lady who had been commanded to commit suicide. A Western critic would believe that "the lady protesteth too much," in these Chinese spectacles, but the native audience would not agree. "She" had scenes alone with the Emperor, and the latter seemed almost on the point of relenting, while in almost the exaggerated emotional manner of the out-of-date Western stage, "she" begged for her life. Then at length, "she" put on ceremonial robes, and after visiting numerous idols, with a specially constructed appeal to each of them, took her own life. The reader will appreciate that here was an opportunity to act, and it seemed that for fully

A Manchu Woman

two hours Cha occupied the center of the stage, reading a part that seemed to be as long as Hamlet's.

Judged from any critical viewpoint, oriental or occidental, it was a remarkable performance; and, in addition to whatever technical points of excellence I was able to observe, there were countless details that passed my eyes which would have been detected quickly enough in their neglect or elimination by the audience. There are a thousand little conventions relating to women's "inferiority" that must be observed to the letter in such a play, or the feelings of the audience would have been outraged. There are details in regard to the arrangement, draping, and hanging of costumes that would never occur to the Western actress or audience. And, in addition, there is a technique for every gesture of the arm or hand, every step or posture, and for every tone of the voice. This technique must stand as law in the Chinese theater. The actor who attempts to deviate from any of the traditional conventions would soon find himself in bad odor with his audience.

Most difficult of all, however, seemed to be the strange, mincing gait of the "lady with the golden lily feet," for no princess of the period would have had large or natural feet. Those of Cha Pih-yung were in plain view of the audience, bound with golden bands and incased in golden slippers. I had the opportunity to examine them closely on the stage, after the performance, and they appeared to be about two and one-half or three inches long. He actually walked on the tips of three toes for a period extending over four hours, excepting for the intermissions, when he sat on a chair back-stage. Yet he did not indicate that he was enduring pain, and he has acquired the "grace" of "lily feet women" still admired by the Chinese, who will not admit that binding of the feet is a barbarous practice.

Cha Pih-yung, who may be taken as a representative of the best in Chinese theatrical art, chants his lines in an amazing falsetto voice that is laughable to a Western auditor, but quite in accordance with the traditions. All the other men who enact women's roles attempt to do likewise. It would not be "in the picture" for them to wear female costumes, take the parts of princess-heroines and recite their lines in a sepulchral basso. Cha becomes funnier still when he sings. He literally squeals with a ridiculously nasal tone that is terrifying when heard for the first time.

"I would like to interview this famous actor," I said to the manager of the theater, as he was appearing in the closing scenes of the play.

"I will present you to him," replied the manager, "but I doubt the 'interview.' Chinese actors never heard about interviews. If you ask him questions, he will think you are an English police investigator of some kind. He will not want to let you have a photograph because that is 'bad luck.' They get this idea because a photograph of the deceased is carried in funeral processions."

As Cha came hobbling from the stage he made a dash for a tea-pot from which a servant poured copious draughts. The manager attempted to explain to him what an "interview" was like, and he was not much taken with the idea. He said, however, that he would think about it, while changing his costume, and disappeared. When he came back, I would not have recognized him but for the prompting of the manager. The rouge and paint had disappeared from his yellow face, he was dressed in street attire and stood on two man-size feet.

"I have been on the stage fourteen years," he said in masculine, almost brassy, tones. "I am twenty-seven years old. I have acted in Peking theaters for ten years. I have five hundred costumes, and sometimes I change my clothes four or five times during one act, never wearing the same costume twice in one evening."

"How much longer do you expect to play female parts?"

"I do not know."

"When you stop playing them will you leave the stage?"

"No, then I shall play the parts of old men."

We were standing near the doorway and a uniformed Chinese came up behind us. He took Cha's big topcoat and stood at attention.

"Pardon me," said the actor, bowing profoundly, "it is very late and I am very tired. I desire to rest."

Outside the door was a waiting brougham, a most unusual conveyance in a city where everyone rides either in an automobile or a rikisha. On the box were coachman and footman, uniformed like the valet who had entered the theater to meet his master. After the carriage started, this boy ran ahead and shouted at the top of his voice for people to get out of the way of Cha Pih-yung's carriage. Here was "importance" such as actors have never acquired in an occidental country.

"Just as I expected," said the manager, who had acted as interpreter. "Only he was more communicative than I had expected. I never actor. But, as I said before, nobody knows nor cares about these things in China. There are always more actors for the parts than can get employment. Never any difficulty in getting all places filled. There are so many people in China—actors, singers, musicians and everything else!"

In a country where actors are despised, Cha Pih-yung receives two thousand dollars a month, a salary by comparison to other Chinese artists that would equal a thousand dollars a day in America. And he has a slave to run before his carriage and shout his name. Perhaps here is "recognition." And celebrity is this that comes to few thespians in lands where they are heroes!

CHAPTER VI

CITY OF HEAVEN BY HOUSEBOAT

EVERY one from the West who goes to China and has the leisure should spend at least a week upon a houseboat. At first thought this may seem to be rather expensive and uninteresting experience, but it is neither, and one will gain an actual knowledge of interior China by sitting on the deck of a little boat that pokes its nose into the great network of China's canal system that can be gained in no other way. And, in addition, it is possible to find comforts, and what Westerners are likely to consider the necessities of life that are little dreamed of by the foreigners who tarry a while at the big city hotels and then take the train for Peking, and gain only the slightest knowledge of the country. Perhaps Shanghai is the best city from which to embark upon the houseboat excursion, because the river there abounds in luxuriously appointed little craft that may be leased for short periods. Even the tourist agencies have some of these boats for rent, and gladly undertake to provision and equip them in Western style, similar to the arrangements that are made for trips up the Nile. But likely as not, it will be unnecessary to make the request of an agency. One is certain to meet someone who knows of a boat that may be leased for a small sum of money. Guides are glad to undertake a commission to procure the boat and provide its necessary equipment and crew.

Perhaps I know of the great number of houseboats owned at Shanghai because I had seen what appeared to be hundreds of them moored to the river bank, and I may have had some previous knowledge of the many pleasant excursions into the surrounding country that are available to one who controls the movements of a boat; but I paid no attention to the matter until I recalled what my "boy," Hong, had said the day that we visited the *Wa-lam-tsz*, or the Temple of the Five Hundred Immediate Disciples of Buddha at Canton. Hong was very religious, on occasion, particularly when we were in the vicinity of a temple or a shrine. He was somewhat non-denominational and felt inspired to burn incense or recite a prayer whether he stood before an altar dedicated to Buddha, or one to Confucius, or to somebody's ancestors. And so it happened that when we were in the Cantonese temple Hong lighted a punk-stick and placed it upright in the ashes that almost filled a big jardinière in front of the god who loves little children—amply proved by the fact that they are sprawling over his lap and shoulders.

"This is Marc' Pol'," said Hong, pointing to the figure of a man who looked to be less oriental than the others.

"Marc' Pol' ver' good man," he explained, so to give him the respect due him, I lighted a punk-stick and placed it upright in the jardinière before the statue.

"Marc' Pol' he like China ver' much and stay here ver' long time," continued Hong. "He have see all the world, yet he say in China is best and grandest city on earth."

"Which city?"

"Hangchow, City of Heaven, at the end of the Grand Canal. Marc' Pol' was right; it is beautiful place. Mister would like to go there by houseboat?"

At this time I gained the first knowledge of this interesting excursion, having previously anticipated going to the ancient capital of China by railway. "By houseboat to the City of Heaven!" The words were haunting, and although I made slight reference to the matter during the days that intervened, we went to the riverbanks to see the craft of which I had received such flattering accounts from the boy. A hasty inspection proved that he had not over-praised them. "But these cannot be rented for the amount you say," I insisted. "Yes, mister; boat, servants, food and all will not cost more than ten dollars a day." There was but one discouragement: all the boats seemed to be occupied, or were soon to be. A few days later, however, Hong came to my room as nearly smiling as would be possible. "I can get one ver' nice boat from rich Mr. Cho. I have seen today. Seven servants and boat." Two rikishas speedily took us for an inspection, and, as so often afterwards, I found that the servant had not exaggerated, even in his enthusiasm. There were two cabins, a kitchen and ample quarters for Chinese servants. There was a good size deck over-spread with an awning; with wicker chairs and table.

At Shanghai I succumbed to the lure of the water. Since I arrived in China I have seen thousands of people living on houseboats, running the gamut from miserably poor sampans to palatial affairs with gardens of potted plants, ornamental balconies and other luxuries that would do credit to a houseboat on the Thames. And some of these boats are vastly more interesting. For example, they have a big eye painted on one side of the bow. The Chinaman says: "Boat have no eye, can no see, have no see, can no walk." And as even the enlightened owners of some of the boats find it to their advantage to cater to the whims and superstitions of the serving folk, who do so much to make life agreeable or very disagreeable, it is always the safer way to give them much latitude.

The average Chinese knows how to enjoy himself. He dotes on pretty things and he knows how to surround himself with them if he has the money.

There were some strange Chinese characters gilded on the bow of the boat. I asked Hong what they were and he said: "That belong name of boat." He pronounced them and they sounded surprisingly like "Chilblain," which seemed to be a strange enough name in English for such a beautiful little boat. Probably in Chinese it means something like "Morning Pearl" or "Sunset Dew" or "Misty Landscape." That would be more in the Chinese manner. But I preferred to call the boat "Chilblain." It was not much to look at from the outside, with the exception of the comfortable observation deck just outside the cabin door. But once inside, I saw literally a vision of beauty. The furniture was gilt and carved teakwood. The wall panels were of white embroidered silk, with roses, butterflies and storks in that splendid manner known only to Chinese artists of the needle. Couches and chairs had snow-white cushions, as clean as if they had just come from the laundry. At the doors and windows hung bright coral-pink cretonne curtains. There was a dining-room with teakwood table, sideboard and chairs. The panels of the walls were mirrors. An ornate chandelier of glass beads was suspended from the center of the ceiling. There were quarters for servants, a kitchen, and, most surprising of all, a bathroom.

"Seven servants and one captain belong to this boat when you rent him," explained Hong.

I held my breath before receiving the blow. I wanted to know what it would all cost, but hesitated before asking. It seemed sure to be too luxurious for my purse, but I realized that cost was an important part of the whole enterprise, so I asked.

"Houseboat, seven servants and captain cost four dollars a day," said Hong, naming Chinese currency equal to the amount. He knew that I was paying five dollars for a rather disagreeable room at the hotel. "I know very proper Chinese cook," he continued. "He get fifty cents a day, but very proper cook, and make better chow than Astor Hotel, Shanghai."

"The world is mine—for about five dollars a day," I shouted, slightly paraphrasing Alexandre Dumas; and the bargain was struck immediately.

Only a word to Hong was necessary and in a few hours the "Chilblain" was mine, and I floated along toward the interior of China in lordly state, literally in taste becoming a mandarin. Lordly state comes cheap in China. I saw young Englishmen at Shanghai who were little better than clerks, yet they maintained bachelor apartments that would cost three hundred dollars a month in America. One young American who had apartments on the top floor—consequently the coolest—of a seven-story apartment house with an elevator, a fine new building equipped with all modern conveniences—which are still rare in China—told me that his rent was fifteen dollars a month. He was waited upon by a troupe of servants and maintained the social position of a New York clubman, yet the total outlay was only about one hundred dollars a month.

There are thousands of Chinese boys sitting around waiting for someone to engage them. In the cities, most of them have some experience and make splendid waiters and household servants. About half the time they seem to anticipate the wishes of their employers, and it is unnecessary to tell them more than once what is wanted, when or how. For example, one morning Hong saw me eating watermelon for breakfast, and not much else. So he put down in his oriental mind that I wanted watermelon for every morning, and because I ate little that first day it was difficult for him to understand why I wanted anything more on other mornings. But once they learn, they never forget. You explain anything once and there is an end of it.

"I go buy chow for one week," said Hong, after I had acquired a lease of the "Chilblain." That also seemed to be something of a task, but he did not think so. "Tell me what you like for drink and I buy chow myself."

"I think I will go with you when you buy."

"All right, but, when you go, the store charge more, because you are rich foreign master. I go better alone, for I am China boy and they charge me not much."

My appreciation of Hong had increased when I saw his success with finding a houseboat, so in this rather important matter of food I decided to leave everything to him. If worse came to worse, we could doubtless purchase chickens and eggs in the country. I thought I could trust him well enough not to turn me into a Chinese canal and let me starve, so I gave him his way and paid no attention to the "chow" order. He was away two hours and came back with a smile of satisfaction over his bronze features. He presented a bill for sixteen dollars' worth of "chow," but said that he could return all unused goods at full price. The articles in the bill looked as if he had been equipping a hotel kitchen, even if the price did not. I knew that he could not have done wholesale buying of provisions for sixteen dollars, so I decided to say nothing and await developments. It is always the better way to say nothing to the orientals. They seem to understand without words and rather resent the intrusion of questioning. But I had not been a day away from Shanghai before I was obliged to call a halt. I was living too high. A six-course dinner, four of them having side-dishes, may be all right once a day, but when it is repeated three times a day, in addition to "tea," the occidental stomach rebels.

It was at dinner. After soup and fish and three meat courses, Hong placed more meat before me and I saw that the time had come for a lecture. I merely declined the dish, but he was inclined to argue. It was excellent, he said, "more better" than any of the others which I had eaten. If I did not eat it, I did not like the "chow" that he was providing. Would I not try it? And he placed the dish on the table a second time. No, I would not, and I gave him instructions that he must never again serve me more than two kinds of meat at one meal. He looked crestfallen and went back to the kitchen, after which, to make amends, he brought me not only a portion, but a large steaming cabinet pudding and placed it all before me. It was delicious, and the sauce might have been prepared by a French chef. I ate and ate, but much more than half of the pudding remained, not counting a large piece which I threw out of the window when Hong was not looking. It was monotonous to explain to him that I could not eat everything, and he seemed to fear that I must be ill unless I could do so. Orientals must have observed Westerners with enormous appetites when they were forming their opinions of a white man's capacity for food. The pudding prompted a question. Where did he capture such a cook for fifty cents a day? Hong grinned. The cook was an old Chink from a ship, and the boy found him somewhere around the riverfront looking for work.

"He long before cook in London," explained Hong.

"I thought so," I replied, although I had not thought so when trying to account for the miracles that came from the kitchen.

That cook was a wonder, and he will live in memory as long as I live. He had a full knowledge of Western culinary arts, but this was mixed with an oriental desire to make everything look appetizing. Eggs in the morning were set in cups on plates garnished with mulberry leaves, which the cook had snatched from overhanging trees as we passed along the canals. Baskets of fruit were arranged as one expects to see them arranged in the windows of an expensive fruiterer. Fresh flowers were placed in the saucers of teacups, with perhaps one jasmine petal dropped into the cup—a favorite delicacy with the Chinese. And all this work, knowledge and almost loving care with food for fifty cents a day! It seemed too good to be true.

A few hours after we had left the city we were floating along an old canal and I spied a boy rowing his shell-like craft frantically in an endeavor to reach us and attract our attention. His boat was loaded with two hampers, one of peaches and the other of loquats. He asked us to buy.

"How much for the peaches?" I inquired. Hong named an amount equal to twelve cents in United States currency.

"How much for the loquats?"

"Eight cents."

"And how much for the two baskets that hold them?" They were beautiful things, hand woven of bamboo and rattan, and I wanted them for a week, even if they were too cumbersome to take home.

"Two and one-half cents."

Needless to add, perhaps, that the boy discharged his full cargo on our deck. The twenty-three cents were willingly placed in the boy's palm, he was much pleased, and thus everyone was happy at the bargain.

An hour before our departure from Shanghai Hong rushed into my room at the hotel, saying that the train would leave in an hour and that we must be on board in forty-five minutes.

"Idiot, we are not going on a train; we are going on a boat!"

Visions of the worthy Mr. Cho's floating palace came before me and I wondered if there had been some hitch in the arrangements after all. But, as usual, I did not understand, so Hong explained that it was the boat train to which he had referred. A steam tug, in place of a locomotive, was scheduled to come along at four o'clock. All boats bound for Hangchow would throw it a line. Then, as they went along, all the craft would be lashed together, forming a long train that would go in and out of the circuitous windings of rivers and canals, under arched stone bridges, through cities, towns, villages and farms.

"What clothing do I want to take along for the trip?" I inquired.

A Chinese Canal

"That belong my business," replied the squint-eyed one, meaning more correctly, "I will look after that for you," because no slang was intended, Immediately my trunk was in the hands of Hong. I was in the hands and at the tender mercies of Hong, or at least I felt that I was; and a well-known and often quoted epitaph would apply to him: "He seen his duty and done it noble."

I was in possession of the "Chilblain" fully twenty minutes before the train came along, and it gave me the opportunity to look over the crew. They seemed to be decked out in holiday attire to welcome the new master, for although they usually scampered around the decks stripped to the waist later in the trip, looking more like apes than men, that first afternoon they wore shirts, or what corresponds to shirts in China. They had fixed up for the occasion. Although most Chinamen have taken advantage of the opportunity to cut off their queues, the river and canal men, most of whom come from the country districts, have retained their pigtails. There was one "missie" aboard, the wife of the captain, but she wore trousers like the rest, and her hair was dressed in pigtail fashion, so it was difficult to tell her from the others, and she handled a pole with as much skill as any of the men when quick action was needed.

Hong has no queue. His hair is clipped and looks strangely bald among the others of the crew. But there is considerable class distinction among them. Hong speaks of them as "coolies" and pokes out inch-long fingernails to prove that he is not a "working man." I asked him about his queue and he said that he clipped it off four years ago at the time of the revolution. "Too much catches on something," he explained, adding that one of his class could not think of being seen with his queue wound around his head. It must fly at full length, the longer the better, so he braided cords into it to make it longer. When the wind blew, it blew to one side, caught hold of things in passing and gave him much pain. And, besides, he believed that queues are foolish. He thought he was very much enlightened and rather looked with disdain upon most Chinamen, whom he described as "velly bad men." But he is a Chink. He said that his last master took him to Singapore on a business trip. The food on the voyage didn't agree with him. He had pains in his stomach, so he took the next steamer back to Shanghai.

"Why didn't you go to a doctor?" I asked him.

"Master wanted me go English doctor," he said. "Doctor was good friend of he and master say all right, but I no think right. I want Chinese doctor, so I come back to him and he make me well again."

"Why did you not want an English doctor?"

"No, master, maybe I go English doctor and he cut out my stomach with a knife and I die. No, I go English doctor no time. I go Chinese doctor and he make me well again."

And when one recalls that the stock in trade of Chinese physicians are such things as plasters made of snakes and spiders, pills made of rat blood, tiger hair and a dozen such delicacies, he is inclined to believe that there is much in having faith in one's physician.

"I took off my queue to be like Englishman," continued Hong. "My wife say to me that I am much like Englishman she had seen, because I think that all good man go up when they die, and that all bad man go down. I cannot tell much about that, but I can tell that I am not. Like Englishman when I am sick. I want China doctor."

The pigtail was imposed upon the Chinese in 1644, when they were conquered by the Manchus, who remained in power until the death of the late dowager empress and the rise of the late Yuan Shi Kai as president. It was considered a sign of subjection, but the wily Chinks soon turned it into a badge of honor and respectability by enacting a law that nobody in prison or guilty of crime should wear it. During the long period in which the queue was worn it was an insult to call a man "tailless." As an added punishment a man's queue was sometimes cut off before he was executed, if his crime was great and there was a desire to "humiliate" him before taking off his head.

Murder has not been the only crime for which a man could be executed in China. In the older day his head came off if he was in the way of a political rival. Men are still executed for robbery in such centers of European enlightenment as Shanghai. And not far away from Shanghai they are shot, but their heads are cut off afterwards, in deference to ancient custom. It isn't so much just to kill a man. There are so many of them in China that one does not count for much, even in the eyes of the Chinese themselves. They value human life lightly. The other day a man told me that he had been obliged to give a fellow man over to the bamboo-beaters, when I asked if the system still was in vogue in the interior districts. "This man took money from me and would not confess it," said the white man. "I told him that if he would confess I would take him out of the hands of the police, but he would not, so I felt obliged to give him over to the magistrate. Still he would not confess. So he gets fifty lashes of bamboo today, and you know that will ruin him for life."

The practice of head chopping is still allowed, because with his head on his body it is the popular belief that a man may meet his ancestors in the next world without being ashamed of his earthly life. They clip off the head, and no man would dare approach his ancestors with his head missing. This is the awful blow that every Chinaman fears. A queue was put to many uses in the older days. It was used to chastise children. It was used as a noose for the suicide. Now that they are tailless, Chinamen have been obliged to find a new way to fight. The good old style has become obsolete. One day, however, I saw a fight between two men, both of whom wore pigtails. They stood stock still, hurled abuse at one another and squealed like pigs. Each had hold of the other's queue and jerked it violently to emphasize his words. In the older day, the policeman nabbed his man by the pigtail and held him securely. The swinging of the queue had its "technique" in the art of the public story-teller, just as there is a technique in speaking or walking on the theater stage. The queue was always doubled back and served to hold taut the necks of men who were about to be beheaded.

In the days of queues every Chinaman wanted his to be as long as possible, and it speaks volumes for the vanity of oriental men when it is known that they used false hair or braid to make it appear to be longer than it really was. When the Chink was in mourning, he put white braid in his queue, for white is the mourning color, and it looks strange to the oriental to see foreigners eating their meals from white table cloths. Boys put red braid in their hair because red is the lucky color. In fact, so much time was spent by Chinese gentlemen in dressing their hair that the reformers said it was a serious drain on the resources of the country.

All these things—and many more—Hong told me as we sat on deck and moved in the train of boats that pushed the thousands of sampans and junks out of the way and passed along up into the Grand Canal, which runs all the way to Peking. I saw life that I had not been led to suspect existed in China. For instance, whole villages were built of grass and placed on the tops of poles set in the water. There were huge duck farms penetrated by little canals in which the fowls were so thick that they were fighting for swimming room. One day I saw a Chinese "dandy" out for a walk with his pet pig. He stepped along as blithely as did ever American Johnny with his bulldog.

Wonderful sights I saw by day, and in the evening heard remarkable music. The men and women in the surrounding boats stopped their work after

Watching the Canal Boats Pass

sundown and sat on deck, piping weird strains from flute-like instruments, accompanied by brass chimes or gongs. On the banks people walked along toward the villages, carrying torches instead of lanterns.

Days were spent like this, days followed by peaceful nights; and then, one morning, I saw a city in the distance, but its greatness has been diminishing for thousands of years, and today it is but sorry remains of former glory. I was arriving at "Hangchow, the City of Heaven." This was the oriental Venice so glowingly described by Marco Polo, and thousands of oriental and occidental writers since his day. Hang-chow, the ancient capital of China, the cradle of learning and the arts in this vast empire. Ancient emperors of China loved Hangchow so well that their advisers told them they spent too much time there for the good of the country. We tied up to a funny old five-arch stone bridge, and my attention was attracted to a big coolie who was carrying a well-dressed maiden astride his shoulders and was cantering along at a lively gait. Inquiry proved that she was a "sing-song girl," a public entertainer, who was going home after a night in the city. Sing-song girls are too "wicked" to live in Hangchow but they reside just outside. And at sundown there is a big procession of coolies carrying them into the town for the evening's festivities. The one I saw was late in getting home. That was all, said Hong, and he could not see anything unusual in having a coolie for a "vehicle." All sing-song girls do.

But as I looked out over the vast distances in which there were groups of buildings and large open spaces, there was little that was different from the endless canal banks, staring populace and the sounds and odors characteristic of a Chinese city which have become so familiar to my eyes, ears and nose in recent days.

I thought of the words of Marco Polo, who wrote: "It is doubtless the best and grandest city in the world," and his references to the hundreds of merchant ships that filled the port. Also Friar Odoric's "It is the finest and noblest city, and the finest for merchandise that the world containeth." He compared it to Venice, which he had seen, saying that it was built upon lagoons, connected by twelve thousand bridges. And one who has seen them knows that Chinese bridges are not things to be passed over lightly. They are still marvels of construction, lending beauty to almost any landscape. My enthusiasm had been aroused for the feast that would meet my eyes. I recalled that even the Chinese emperors, after the capital had been moved from Hangchow, spent so much time here that it called forth protests from the people. One emperor dissipated so much wealth on his state journeys to Hangchow that his prime minister reminded him that each inch of his journey cost his people one inch of silver.

But as I stood on the deck of the houseboat that first morning I could not see the great merchant ships of the world. They seemed to have all departed for other ports less "heavenly." The bridges had also departed, at least eleven thousand of them, as not more than three hundred and fifty remain. Great palaces and libraries—for Hangchow was the literary repository of the empire—had crumbled into decay and were toppling over into the channels, and filled many of the waterways. The "Queen City of the Orient" has changed mightily, but it still remains a city of pretentions and vast proportions. It vies in antiquity with Damascus and Baalbek for interrupted existence of centuries.

Hangchow is, today, a city of nine square miles, within the ancient walls, and it has about one million inhabitants. Its silk is counted among the best that comes out of China, just as it was in ancient times, when the quality was so superior that the imperial court ordered vast quantities for its own use, even when residing at other capitals, and the various products of its artisans compete fairly with all others in the marts of the world. And yet Hangchow is in decay. Its principal asset is its beauty.

It is still the "city of heaven" to the Chinese, but this city is not visible from the canal bank. A large per cent, of the population lives in junks and sampans on the water, although there is still wealth in the city and some fine ancient residences. The boats were crowded around us, and I watched them that first morning as they pushed aside the sheltering straw mats and the people made their toilet for the day.

Gone are the three thousand public baths of which Marco Polo wrote. "The water is supplied by springs," he said. "They are hot baths, and the people take great delight in them, frequenting them several times a month, for they are very cleanly in their persons."

But the baths that I saw were of muddy canal water. Sometimes there were eight or ten people on a sampan no larger than an American row-boat. One by one they appeared for the morning "spray." They had a long-handled mop of rags, which they dipped down into the muddy water, and, standing erect, they splashed it over their bodies by strange manipulations of the handle. When the bath was over, the principal benefit derived must have been that it had been cooler than the air. Certainly it had not cleansed them, and from the staring crowd that assembled to look at the "foreign devil"—I could not say with Marco Polo that they were very cleanly in their persons.

I watched a little housewife on a neighboring boat as she prepared rice for the morning meal. Milady had "lily feet" and hobbled about the square-yard deck of her "kitchen" as if she had been on stilts. She had a big earthen jar, in which rice had been soaking over night, or longer. But apparently she did not consider it a clean jar, because she dipped several handfuls of rice into a fine-mesh basket and threw it over into the muddy canal, where she "washed" it by spinning the basket round and round. Then she put it into a copper pot and placed it over an earthenware stove the size of the pot, in which she fanned a fire made of twigs and charcoal. In what seemed an incredibly short time the rice pot was steaming, and when I went inside the cabin for my own breakfast the whole sampan family were squatting around the pot, each scooping a bowl of rice and shoving it into his mouth with chopsticks with a speed that indicated great hunger.

Groups of coolies with sedan chairs, the principal vehicle of Hangchow, had gathered on the bank during breakfast, so when I came out there was lively competition to see who should carry me into the city. Poor, half-starved men—the natives give them but a few coppers for their work, and they thought, when they saw me, that they possibly detected an extra coin. They ventured as close to the railing of the boat as they could come, without actually touching it. They immediately set up, not only a plea, but almost a demand that they be engaged, all of them, and there were enough to carry ten persons instead of two. They made almost threatening gestures, and when I was about to retire to the cabin with anything but "heavenly" thoughts regarding these people of Hangchow, Hong came to the rescue. And he was a good match for them when it came to screeching at the top of his voice, gesturing and threatening. Four men offered to carry me all day for one dollar, but Hong shook a stick at them and told them they were no good. Another set had a chair that was dirty, so they were waved aside. Finally, he picked a quartet that looked as if it were made up of Tartar pirates. He liked their chair and they seemed to be strong enough, so he promised them one dollar for the day, and I walked the gang-plank and seated myself in the ancient "vehicle," for a closer inspection of the city of Chien Liu, commonly known in Chinese history as the "Great Prince Chien," the salt peddler who became a powerful ruler, and who, to this day, is considered Hangchow's most illustrious personage.

An Ancient Bridge, Hangchow

First of all, we came to the walls, which are still in a fair state of preservation. They are the best reminders that Hangchow claims to be a city with almost four thousand years of known history. But the principal interest in the present wall, which is ornamented with ornate turrets, is that the whole thing was constructed in the short space of three months.

For thousands of years every invader in the district has focused his attentions upon the city, which has been talked about as much as any city of the antique world. Always someone has been trying to demolish it, and soon afterwards someone always arose who wanted to rebuild it. This process of total demolition and piece-meal reconstruction has gone on for centuries. In 1360, however, a man named Chang Shih-cheng, a feudal lord, took things in his own hands and said he would work quickly. The wall is thirteen miles long, thirty feet high and forty feet wide at the base; even today it is a masterwork, although the constructive genius took no longer to build it than the ordinary man would take for the construction of a summer cottage. Here was one who must have inspired much enthusiasm, for when he announced his intentions to rebuild Hangchow he had the services of five hundred forty thousand stone-masons, fifty thousand carpenters, three hundred sixty thousand plasterers, six thousand six hundred seventy-five metal workers, and four million five hundred thousand coolies, according to the city's history, which is believed to be fairly authentic.

As I stood gazing at this marvel, a crowd of the people of Hangchow congregated, and when they showed signs of hostility, spitting and shouting at me, I was obliged to move along, and the chair coolies were forced to set up a terrific howl as they shoved the people of the City of Heaven aside and passed into the great street that goes from one side of the city to the other. Marco Polo said: "This street is wide enough for nine carts to travel abreast, and as level as a ballroom floor." Either things have changed much, or Marco was mistaken. In some places it is no more than eight or ten feet wide today. The highway is paved with big flagstones and they are in sadly ruined condition, after centuries of travel over them. It had rained the night before, and in the middle of the streets there were pools of filth into which the coolies stumbled almost up to their knees, causing the chair to rock and pitch like a ship at sea.

Nothing daunted, the merchants piled their wares far in front of their stores and stalls, sheer to the edge of the filthy pools—vegetables, meats, silk and other articles of wearing apparel. They squatted among their heaps of stock and seemed to care nothing about the vile stench that came steaming up from the pavements in the morning sun.

I saw a strange, cobwebbed stall, in which a woman sat sewing, surrounded by a fine collection of carved soapstone vases of beautiful colors and designs. I shouted to the coolies to stop, and commenced to bargain, but the crowd became so dense that I was obliged to leave the chair, go inside her stall and close the front door, which left the place in semi-darkness. Clinging to a particularly fine specimen, I asked her the price. She shouted something and seemed to indicate that she did not want me in her store at any price.

"She say that vase cost sixteen dollars," interpreted Hong. "It is too much; offer her very little and see."

"One dollar," I said.

The woman shouted like a demon and let out a torrent of abuse. I had insulted her, and she declared that she would be disgraced before all of her ancestors if she gave me the vase at such a price.

"She say give her five dollars for it," said Hong.

"One dollar," I repeated.

The old woman spat on the dirt floor, to show her disgust for me and my kind. Still yelling at the top of her voice, she went back to her sewing and indicated that she was through, so I said that we would go, and started for the door. The merchantess seemed to pay no attention and I passed along and climbed into the chair again. The coolies raised it to their shoulders and we would have disappeared into the crowd in a moment if she had not run to me, vase in hand, shouting something that I could not understand.

"She say take it for one dollar," shouted Hong.

"Never," I replied indignantly. "I offer one dollar in shop and she no take. Now I give fifty cents"—attempting the "baby English" which Hong understood better than he did "plain American."

He interpreted what I said and the old lady spat on the ground again and shouted something to the crowd, probably that the white devil was trying to rob her. One would have thought that I had some of her property concealed in the chair. She saw that she must act quickly, so she handed the vase to me.

"She say take it for fifty cents," said Hong, with a chuckle, and the coveted carving changed hands. A sixteen dollar vase for fifty cents! I congratulated myself that I had become a good oriental bargainer.

The coolies carried me along over countless bridges, through filthy narrow streets, halting now and then in front of a shop or a stall that displayed something that was unusual and might attract my eye. They perspired like racehorses. They were stripped to the waist and streams of water coursed down their backs, rippling over ribs that caused the skin to bulge. I felt guilty. To be sure, I saw four coolies trotting along merrily, carrying a stone that weighed three or four times as much as I did, and huge bales hanging from bamboo poles across their shoulders. But I asked Hong about it and told him that I didn't want to overwork them, in reality, not knowing that I was giving them a holiday, because, no doubt, they would have had a much heavier load of merchandise, if I had not employed them.

"That not because you are heavy that they perspire," he explained, "that because they shout so much to get people out of road. Much people get in road because you are foreign master."

At noon we came to the hotel. In many ways it seemed to be the most remarkable hotel in the world. It was a big brick structure, doubtless erected at great expense by the railway. A determined effort is being made to induce tourists who come to China to include Hangchow in their itineraries, so the hotel was put up to accommodate them. The hotel is there, but there is little accommodation. The coolies took my chair into the "lobby" and dropped it on the floor. I stepped out in mud and water ankle deep, and quickly made my way to a staircase, up which I mounted to the second floor, where a waiter said something about the difficulty of keeping the main floor of the hotel clean in such rainy weather as they had been experiencing lately. He might have said "impossible" instead of difficult, because eight muddy feet of coolies for every chair that enters the place soon cover tiles with spattering clay.

As I sat down on a sofa the waiter handed me a sheet of paper, on which were Chinese characters translated into English on the other side. In many ways it was a document as remarkable as the hotel itself. It told of the conveniences and comforts of the structure, and just why it was handed to me, a guest, or at least a prospective guest, when I was there and could see for myself that there was no convenience, comfort, cleanliness or decency, I was unable to ascertain. But at least the paper gave me a smile. Herewith a few quotations, picked at random from the large printed sheet.

"Now since the Shanghai-Hangchow railway has been connected, the commerce is gradually prospered. The masters of the hotel having spent much money begin to build the great building the Railway Hotel. On its

West Lake, Hangchow

upper part there is a roof garden and by using the electric passing the people can go up and down without any on foot trouble while on the lower part the merchant shops supplied with different kinds of things are arranged so that the things may be conveniently brought up. It is built in the foreign up-to-dag style. The hotel in middle consists altogether of about more than one hundred rooms. It is full of bright rays and fresh air. Large and beautiful are the hall and dining-room, which may be let for marriage, feast giving, meeting and so forth. The foreign furnitures, the large iron beds and those fine and useful things are furnished. The hotel also provides with beautiful spreadings, the silk bedquilts, the mosquito nets and the electric lamps and may be used by the passengers without paying any money. The water is filtered and very clean indeed. The diligent and trustful boys and maidens are hired and the passengers may call them at pleasure. The committee who specially has the duty of adhering will do the passengers order at any time. If they want to see some friends, or visit the famous places, the boat, the jinrikisha, the chair and the horse may be hired in a moderate price."

The "committee" which seemed to consist of a group of howling bellboys, who acted much as the coolies acted in the streets, fairly fighting with one another for the privilege of waiting on guests, stood near me as I read the paper.

"Take me to this celebrated roof garden," I said to one of them.

"You must buy ticket," he said, "please come after me."

We climbed another flight of circular steps and arrived in front of a somber-looking individual, who squatted behind a low desk on which papers and books were littered. He was writing Chinese characters in a book, doubtless balancing his accounts. He slapped down a piece of cardboard, when the waiter told him that I wanted to ascend, and named an amount of Chinese currency equal to five cents.

"That is for riding in lift," explained the boy. We went into the elevator and a man looked over my ticket and handed it back to me, whereupon he turned a lever and we shot upward—one story, into the open air. It had cost me five cents to make the ascension, but it was worth it. At least up here there were no odors and no mud. A few potted plants were scattered around and groups of Chinamen sat under straw awnings, enjoying their noonday meal. They were scooping great bowls of rice and chopped meat and vegetables into their mouths.

"Have Chinese chow or foreign chow?" asked a sleepy individual, who seemed to be a sort of head-waiter. His costume consisted of a pair of white drawers and a sleeveless undershirt. I was glad that there was nothing which compelled me to see the cook. There was nothing about the whole place that prompted a desire for food, but I was too far away from the boat to think of returning, so I said "foreign" and we decided that chicken was the best thing offered on the day's menu. I spied a good basket of fruit on the table and thought with this to fill out, everything would be all right. But it was not. The chicken was burned and dried to the bone, seemingly having been cooked before—perhaps many times. The fruit must have been better a week before than it was on that particular day. A man who said that he was not the manager of the hotel, but was acting manager in his chief's absence from the city, apologized for the food when I told him that it was miserable, even to the butter which smelled like axle-grease, and he volunteered to send down town for some sing-song girls to come up and entertain me, apparently in lieu of no food fit to be eaten.

The other day a young white man who was born in China and who has spent his entire life here, with the exception of four years in an American college, was telling me of his hardships during one of the ever-present Chinese revolutions. He was caught at Hangchow, when the trains were not running from the city. He was told to leave and to leave in a hurry. The larger boats were all engaged or already had sought a haven of safety, so he was obliged to engage a sampan. He had only one hundred miles to go to his relatives and to safety, but his boat was rowed by one man with one oar, and it took him eleven days to make the trip through the canals.

"I was obliged to lie in the sampan most of the time because the straw top was so low that I couldn't sit up," he related. "I could stand all this, even the terrible canal mosquitoes at night and such things, but the test came when it was a case of eating Chinese food, prepared on the boats that we passed en route. Chinese food for eleven days! It does not seem possible that a white man who knew about it could endure it and then live to tell the story. But here I am, although I confess that it was the most trying ordeal of my life. I travel into the interior of China every six months—he was a cigarette salesman—but I always take my cook, who prepares and buys my food. Otherwise I would have been dead long ago."

After lunch we started out again. This time I had told Hong that I wanted to go to West Lake, a body of water that has as much classical poetry written about it as any body of water in the world. Ancient poets vied with one another to make their compositions about it better than their predecessors', with the result that a library of volumes is extant with West Lake as the topic of inspiration.

In reality, it is the lake that gives Hangchow its reputation for visual splendor. It was the scene around the lake that drew mighty emperors, princes and scholars to the surrounding hills. Many of them spent their entire lives here, and many who tried to go away felt drawn back to the beauties of the place and came back to die. Some of the rulers who were obliged to go away from Hangchow endeavored to imitate its beauties in the construction of their gardens. Many ancient books were written descriptive of its "eight beautiful places." Later the eight were expanded into "seventy beautiful places" and found their way to Japan, like everything else Chinese, where they became the principal inspiration for the gardens of Nippon that have excited the admiration of the world with their bridges, pagodas and ponds—all in imitation of, or an adaptation of West Lake and the surrounding shores at Hangchow.

Soon we plunged into the narrow thoroughfare again. Starting out to go to any given point in a Chinese city is as much of a mystery as going into one of those mirror mazes that we have at American Luna parks. Five chairs or rikishas may start from a given point and make for the same place, but unless there is one great central road they will soon scatter into different alleys and streets, keeping only to the general direction indicated. But we emerged from the tangle. There was a wide street paved with big flagstones that went down to the water edge. My attention was attracted to perhaps a hundred houseboats, each with screaming polemen who shouted for my patronage. Beyond them, across the lake, I saw the wonderful view that had charmed the world. At last here was Hangchow, City of Heaven, with bridges, palaces, pagodas and a dozen things that contributed to the beautiful scene.

My impression was that of passing from purgatory into paradise. The coolies spattered along through the filthy and vile streets of Hangchow. At the hotel I had told them to take me to West Lake. My earlier experiences of the day had not been the sort that make me think that I was visiting the "City of Heaven." I began to think that the Chinese poets, and even old Marco Polo, himself, must have had lively imaginations. Either that or things had changed in a thousand years. Of course things do change in a thousand years, even in old China; and as the foul odors of the streets met my nostrils, as I looked into the faces of the weird crowds and saw almost savage life, I was about ready to give up my quest for beauty and go back to the houseboat and breathe the comparatively pure air of a Chinese canal.

I merely took one more chance and told Hong that if West Lake did not come nearer to living up to the classical reputation of Hangchow, we would go elsewhere and take the word of historians about the grandeur of the place which was no longer grand, or did not seem to be. But once we emerge from the tangle of streets the coolies put down my chair on flagstones that went down to the waters of a five-mile lake. Immediately I realized that my wily Chink boy had reserved this view for the great climax of our houseboat meanderings. Here, at last, was one of the great objects of all travel in China. From the depths of a squalid, filthy, miserable China I had emerged into the real Hangchow, City of Heaven. Before me lay the original of the great landscape gardens of the world.

Here I saw that Hangchow is still a city of great wealth and oriental indolence. Reconstructed palatial dwellings and pavilions of ancient courts still face the lake, and are tenanted by a dreamy class of Chinese who live in the China of one or two thousand years ago and do not care for the onward march of events. They much prefer that luxurious life of the past. The outside world does not exist for them and they think only of intellectual and sensual pleasures. What else is life for? At least that was my impression when I passed from Hangchow's purgatory into its paradise.

The waters of the lake seemed to be of silver. A great arched stone bridge stretched itself away into the distance to the base of hills capped with pagodas, monasteries and temples. Even from this distance I could see bushes and vines in festoons of green over the balconies of pagodas. And when such vegetation thrives on the mortar with which hewn stone has been put together, one knows that centuries of summer suns have caused the great heaps of stone to disintegrate. A mildewy and musty languor hung over the place, discernible in everything, even the people. They seemed to be people who had lost ambition. Most of them looked like the stone relics of the City of Heaven, the degenerate results of an over-ripe civilization.

It was well along in the afternoon when I arrived on the shores of the lake, and everything was quiet until the houseboat polemen saw a possible foreign customer. They set up an awful howl, but this was quieted when I rented one of the boats. There are no small crafts, for the humbler folk of the city do not come here. Here seemed to be the original idea for something that is now practised throughout the world. Many sacred and imperial edicts have been issued in regard to encroaching upon the waters. Emperors said that it must be preserved as a place of beauty, and now there is no emperor the ruling classes see to it that the same laws hold good.

It seemed all strangely like taxing the people of a Western city to build and maintain macadamized park roads and boulevards so that the poor may enjoy sitting on the grass and watching machines speed past, knowing that the owners of automobiles are suffering no discomforts. But the poor do not go and sit by the shores of West Lake. They know that they will always be poor. There are visiting mandarins and the aristocrats from other cities, visiting Hangchow swells and voluptuaries, enough of them to fill the houseboats every evening. Squalid poverty must have no place in the picture of beauty. Here, at last, was China of which the Western world knows little. Perhaps I am wrong in a measure, but I suspect that here is the untainted China of a long ago.

The boats are splendidly fitted up like a house, with sofas, chairs, tables and other articles of furniture. Some of them have splendidly equipped kitchens that produce food that is considered "classical" because the chefs prepare strange concoctions that date back to the remote days of Yao and Shun, and serve them to the delighted guests. A man who knows told me that for ten to twelve dollars gold a man may take a party of friends for a "tour of the lake" on these boats, feast them royally, entertain them with a group of sing-song girls and a "mystic" juggling performance, of which the Chinese is so fond, and make a night of it. This entertainment has its etiquette similar to that of the chano yu tea ceremony of Japan. Much of it is complicated and would not be considered particularly hilarious by an American "swell," but it is highly appreciated by the people who understand, and there are features of the boat ride that would appeal to the average Yankee, even if the odor of incense and punk sticks did not, and if he were not interested in the scenery, which the host is supposed to point to while he declaims verses from the classics.

After we were poled back to the shore we were just in time to see many of the parties starting out for the evening's revelry. It was all very quaint, and was accompanied by almost a ritualistic ceremony. Every one arrived in a sedan chair carried by coolies, and most of the hosts and guests brought their own personal servants with them.

Poor Mrs. Hangchow! I did not see much of her, and suppose that etiquette requires her staying at home when her husband is enjoying the lake ride. Hosts and guests were ah male. Later in the evening, after the feasting and drinking, the barges would be poled to the shore and the sing-song girls taken aboard. No doubt they had been ordered for a certain hour and would be there on the minute. Coolies would bring them astride their shoulders,

A Garden in Hangchow

as I saw them carried about the streets the night before. They would be dressed in tight trousers, usually white, with dark coats, and sometimes with decorations in their hair.

"Are these men bachelors?" I asked Hong.

"Nobody," he laughed. "Everybody he marry in Hangchow, and the men you see have many wife, because they have much money. Sometimes a man of Hangchow who not rich have two or three wife; the rich sometimes have six or seven."

"But none of them brought their wives to the entertainment on the lake."

"Perhaps have many wife, but do not love any of his wife because they have been picked for him by his family and not by himself," was his rather laconic explanation.

Soon after coming ashore I saw many soldiers standing around the landing piers, which reminded me of something that I heard about the military of the district of Hangchow. There had been a revival of the age-old fighting between the people of Hangchow and the neighboring district or province. Finally, the case came not long ago for a test of arms and strength. The day of the battle was agreed upon, but when it dawned it was raining, so the Hangchow commander sent a communication to the commander of the opposition's army asking that hostilities be postponed until more pleasant weather, which proved to be quite agreeable to both sides. The military of Hangchow were being put through drills the other day and the men were being initiated into the mysteries of modern trench warfare. The commander ordered his men, but they said it was too muddy and dirty, and, to a man, refused to go in, so the drill was abandoned until more favorable conditions obtained.

These stories are fairly typical of Chinese soldiers in the country districts, where they are removed from the "foreign" influence. They hate trouble and will do anything to avoid it. And another fact that is important: the military is thoroughly detested by the masses of people, being quite without any social standing at all, which is a sorry condition in China. Chinese say that when a boy has displeased or disobeyed his parents, and when they have cast him off without money, he joins the army. So, in addition to being considered a family outcast, a miserable condition in China, he is a social outcast. As a result, the typical soldier of the rural districts is a slouchy, slovenly creature, who usually appears to be very sleepy. Notoriously, he is a coward and would be badly startled if someone shouted to him.

But even this is in keeping with Hangchow. Everything has passed, or is passing, to decay. The old city seems to have lived too long, and it may be time for the purging fire to come. Its people have tried all the pleasures, and they have known all the sorrows of life. They have passed through almost every earthly experience, and many of these when civilization was comparatively young upon the earth. They seem to be suffering from world weariness, and merely consult their desires of the moment.

It is claimed that Hangchow was the first city in China to receive Christian missionaries. At least it is known that before the brilliant Sung period, Nestorian fathers had visited the city and established missions. This fact is pointed to by the historians, along with the fact that stone crosses in the interior of China prove that Christianity was practised in this country as early as the Sixth Century. But Christianity has made comparatively little headway with the masses of Hangchow, despite the centuries of labor of the missionaries. It was a difficult field to conquer. In the Emperor's lodge at West Lake there is said to be a library containing ten thousand volumes. There is a private library belonging to the family named Ting which is said to be the largest in China, with one exception, as it contains eight thousand works of about twenty thousand volumes. The superstition is that these libraries are likely to be destroyed by fire from heaven at any moment. Heaven will not permit too many mysteries of heaven and earth to be known by men, and these mysteries are supposed to be explained in books. The libraries are usually a point of attack by revolutionists.

It was after sunset when I finally told the coolies to lift my chair to their shoulders. I never had seen such a place as Hangchow and never expect to see another. It was difficult to leave it, not expecting to see it again. It seemed like smelling some rare perfume only once in a lifetime, tasting a forbidden nectar, or having the veil lifted for a moment on one of the rare things visible to human eyes. It seemed amazing and untrue.

As I stood there and gazed on the original of earth's formal landscape gardens, Hong enumerated to me the "Beautiful Views" of the antique oriental world as we stood where we could see them. They are still more beautiful than the imitations with which the people of the world are familiar. Only centuries of a poetically minded people could have given such places appropriate names. The Chinese did it, and they remain today the points of interest which the Hangchow gentleman recites to his guests as their barge is making an evening "Tour of the Lake." They were as follows:

(1) The Broken Off Bridge of Late Snow.
(2) Pavilion of the Peaceful Lake and Harvest Moon.
(3) Three Pools and the Printed Moons.
(4) Su's Dawning Spring Road.
(5) The Lagoon of Fish and Flowers.
(6) The Winding Hall of Fragrant Breezes.
(7) South Mountain's Evening Bell.
(8) The Evening Illumination of Thunder Peak.
(9) Willow Bay Where Eagles Are Heard.
(10) Two Cloud Piercing Peaks.

I felt a thrill, but was overfilled with musty luxury and decadent beauty and started back to the houseboat to begin the trip back to Shanghai over Chinese canals.

CHAPTER VII

"SON OF THE OCEAN"

I WENT back to Shanghai and quickly transshipped, or at least I considered that I had done so until I used the word in conversation with Captain Carnaghan, the jolly skipper of the big Yangtze steamer, *Poyang*, which plies between Shanghai and Hankow, probably the furthest inland of all important ports of the world. He said it would be much more appropriate to say that I left a tub for a palace, and perhaps that would be a better way to express it, because, in reality, I left a houseboat on the canals and walked the gangplank of a steamer that would compare very favorably with the fleet which runs in any coastwise or inland lake service in America. I was making for the very heart of China, according to the map, one of the most backward nations on the face of the earth, and yet I was traveling in as much luxury and comfort as if I had been going from New York to Newport by sea. And the *Poyang* is but one of the many excellent steamers that run up and down the Yangtze, the second largest river in the world, and very much more important to the world's people than the Amazon, which the geographers usually give a few additional miles.

The exact length of the Yangtze has never been determined, owing to the unreliable information in regard to its headwaters, which rush down from the mountains of Thibet, following the melting of the snows. Some geographers place it at three thousand miles; others give it an additional five hundred. None doubts, however, that it ranks in importance far above the Amazon, having a direct influence upon the lives of a vast population, usually reckoned at about two hundred millions. The magnificent "Son of the Ocean," "Child of the Sea," or "River of Fragrant Tea Fields," to give it only three of its native appellations, is the great dividing line between North and South China. It drains a fertile basin of six hundred thousand square miles, touches nine rich provinces, and finally finds its way to the sea, where its muddy waters are visible for a distance of thirty to forty miles.

The ocean's tide is felt up the river for three hundred miles. It is navigable for nearly two thousand miles and never closed by ice. The scientists place its watery deposit into the Yellow Sea at some incomprehensibly large figure every second, and the silk deposits near its mouth are constantly building up fertile islands, one of which, Tsung-ming, opposite Wu-sung, contains sixty-five square miles and supports a population estimated at two hundred thousand.

On both banks of the Yangtze are the richest tracts of agricultural land on the surface of the globe. It is freely predicted that whatever nation controls this valley in future will have the "balance of power" in the Far East, and it has been said that whoever gains control of it might rule the world, if its resources were fully developed. Certainly it will be one of the most vital spots in the world's activities in the future. Whether old China will hold her own seems to depend much upon China. It belongs to the country, but the other nations of the world have been casting envious eyes upon it for many years. Now they are firmly entrenched and it may be a difficult matter to dislodge them. At least the Yangtze valley is likely to be the arena for one of the greatest world contests of history. The gunboats of the nations are anchored everywhere along the twistings and turnings of the turbulent yellow flood. There are also a few Chinese gunboats, but they seem impotent in the face of the great frowning engines of war that are ostensibly to guard the "interests" of the other nations.

The great day is coming. China is like a tremendous creature with a renewed heart action, but paralysis at her extremities. Notoriously her people are not religious. I asked Chinese repeatedly in various parts of the country why it is that all of the temples are in ruin and that nobody seems to take any particular interest in them as they do in Japan; and the answer always was: "China is no longer religious." But I am firmly of the opinion that deep-seated religious prejudices are responsible for the present condition of the country round about the Yangtze. Observe almost any neglected opportunity and you can trace it to religion or to the prejudices and superstitions that spring from religious teachings and practices. It is generally admitted that the teachings of Confucius have had a splendid moral effect on the Chinese people in ages passed; and it is generally recognized that Buddhism is responsible for the glorious days of Chinese art and learning, but the people seem to have outgrown both of them and together they are passing into a miserable decline. China seems ready for a great religious awakening, as was Arabia when Mahomet came.

See the millions of peasants along the Yangtze poking the earth with sticks and other primitive impleme.nts that were used in Egypt during the days of Moses, according to the monuments, ask why they do not employ modern implements and reap a bigger harvest for their labors and one finds that the priests have warned the people against letting the devil enter China by means of new-fangled machinery, so they struggle and work for a handful of rice, miserable in their ignorance, but content that they are not tempting the furies.

The casual visitor never knew that there was so much garden in all the world. For five days and nights on the rapid steamer, from Shanghai to Hankow, one passes through a continuous garden spot, fertile, well-watered, and, in many localities, capable of bringing forth three crops a year. And then it is possible to change steamers and go on by the same waterway for another five days by steamer. Here might be raised the foodstuffs for the people of the earth. Instead, the millions of people who cultivate the soil are ill-fed, dissatisfied, eternally led to revolution, and always enduring an existence that would be tolerated only by a down-trodden race almost returned to a state of semi-barbarity. And religious prejudice is largely at fault. Back in the distance, during this long cruise, there are chains of hills and mountains, which the prospectors have found to be veritable treasure heaps of minerals.

"Do not let the foreign devils dig into the hills, for they will disturb the spirits of your ancestors and the gods that watch over China," say the priests.

One would think that the people would soon realize that these gods are sleeping and not attending to their "watching," but when some nation or company gains a concession by "squeeze," which is practically the only way that anything is obtained in China, every handicap is placed in the way to prevent or hinder development. In the particular case of one big mine the property and concession was bought back by the Chinese, who closed it. The spirits were being disturbed. Of course, some of the big interests are successful. Great institutions like the Standard Oil Company have ways of doings things where individual effort fails, but along this Yangtze it seemed to a thoughtful observer, at least until he reached Hankow, where all the nations are taking everything they can get their hands upon, that the Japanese are likelier to enforce their demands than any other people. They are less inclined to tolerate any "nonsense." When Japan makes an agreement or enters into any sort of a contract with China she means business. If anything "happens," she makes China pay. It is well known that Japanese agents are working all the time with the revolutionists and malcontents of southern China. Japan asks something of the government at Peking, and when she asks, she lets it be known that she is in a position to make "trouble" in the South. Consequently, she seems to get about what she wants and there is no limit to her desires in this territory. Japan wants iron ore—much of it. So her ships merely sail up the river a little over five hundred miles to Hwang-shih-kang. Here is the famous Tayeh mine, almost at the water's edge. In reality, it is not a mine, nor a series of mines, but a quarry. The iron ore, which is considered of better quality than that of America, Sweden or Germany, crops out of the hillside in vast quantities. I saw the big Japanese ships anchored side by side at this mine, loading ore for the blast furnaces of Nippon. It is said to be sixty-seven per cent, pure, and Japan is said to receive it for three and one-half yen, or less than two dollars a ton, by an agreement with the Chinese government. Not long ago trouble broke out. The ancestral spirits were being disturbed, said the priests, whereupon Japan merely sent a few of her warships up the river and gravely threatened to blow things to atoms if there was any more "foolishness;" and with the threat came a demand that the mines be kept working full blast. Any other action would have made it necessary for Japan to land her troops, "to preserve the peace of the Far East." Japan believes that Europe will be busy with its own affairs for some time to come, and she smiles when she says that America is likely to be busy also; considering it a heaven-sent opportunity in China, and she is making the best of it, her citizens making themselves cordially disliked by the Chinese and by the other nations which have been trying to throttle China by the same means, when there were better facilities at home for backing up demands.

Japan is encroaching more and more upon Chinese territory. Her people are conspicuous in all of the Yangtze cities and villages, where they may be trusted to look after their "Master's" business. One Japanese frankly talked to me about "Der Tag," just as Germans and English did in ante-bellum days. They do not doubt that the great test of strength is coming, and there is no reason to believe that they do not think Japan will one day control China in reality, just as many onlookers believe that she does today, although by underhand means, usually known as diplomacy.

"It is popularly supposed that China has over one hundred million men," I remarked to a well-informed Japanese. "What would happen if your government should harness this energy into a great fighting machine along modern lines. You could rule the world."

"Japan knows better than to attempt that," he replied. "If China realized her strength, she would whip Japan in short order. Japan will not teach her to

A Typical Chinese Village

realize this strength, for Japan must remain uppermost in the Far East! China must be kept in ignorance of the realities."

Although the trip up the Yangtze is started at Shanghai, this great cosmopolitan city is situated on the Whangpoo River, fully thirteen miles from where the rivers unite near Wu-sung, and it is necessary to sail towards the sea before the ship's bow is turned inland for the voyage upstream. Owing to the great sandbars constantly forming in the Yangtze near Tsung-ming Island, passenger steamers usually leave Shanghai at midnight or after, for the purpose of arriving in the shallow districts at daylight. Here, however, the river is thirty to forty miles in width, and one realizes the truth of Marco Polo's assertion that it is more like a sea than a river. For a considerable length of time, land is not visible, but finally a pagoda on a distant island comes to view, the banks of the river are narrowing, and at a distance of one hundred sixty-seven miles from Shanghai, the boat stops at the city of Chin-kiang, which is at the junction of the Grand Canal and the Yangtze. It is an important treaty port, one of the first opened after the British besieged the lower ports of the river during the Opium War.

As a result of this war China consented to open five ports to foreign trade: Canton, Amoy, Foochow, Ningpo and Shanghai, beside ceding Hongkong to England, so the date of 1842 is usually looked upon as the beginning of China's trading with the nations of the world, because over seventy ports have been opened since that time, but it is not correct, because English and French traders had obtained a foothold in China early in the Eighteenth Century, and there was intercourse with Europe through the Portuguese, Spanish and Dutch navigators as early as the Sixteenth Century. The Chinese are born merchants, and there is reason to believe that they have been traders with other nations for many centuries, despite imperial edicts which prohibited intercourse with foreigners. It is on record that the Chinese carried on somewhat extensive commercial operations with western Asia as early as the Third Century B.C. The southern ports of China were trading with Arabia and India in the early years of the Christian era.

Chin-kiang, with its population of two hundred thousand, is the first of the important ports in the voyage upstream and it is typical of dozens of them, where the steamers tie up to floating hulks, anchored in the deep water, by means of which passengers and cargo are taken on or discharged. Looking ahead, one sees a cluster of white buildings with red-tiled roofs, almost like a Spanish city in appearance, excepting for the pagoda, which frequently towers over other structures and seems to brood over the community as the best preserved relic of that day when China considered herself mistress of the world. Hereabouts begins the vast plain that is one of the beautiful garden spots of the world. Here also comes to view the results of what is known as the Taiping Rebellion, one of the monstrous uprisings of all history, which struck a staggering blow to the whole Yangtze Valley, from which it has never recovered. Off the bank of the river from Chin-kiang are what were sacred islands, richly endowed by imperial favor, with temples, shrines and carved gateways. Here were amassed collections of books, equal in importance to the imperial libraries at Peking or Hangchow. In the days of Marco Polo there were two hundred priests officiating in the sacred structures, but the Taipings came and the islands have been the scene of later warfare, so that today they seem to be anything but sacred, although it is said that a few priests still dwell among the ruins of burned libraries and fallen altars.

The Taiping Rebellion which devastated whole provinces, razed great cities, which have never been rebuilt, and caused the ruthless and unpitying slaughter of countless peaceful men, women and children, the reign of a barbarous band of brigands, which extended over fifteen years, had its inception in the teaching of a Christian Protestant missionary, who with some of his co-workers believed in the beginning that it marked the religious upheaval of China and the dawn of the conversion of the vast population to Christianity. After the Opium War there was famine in the land, and the people, in great masses, seemed to be expecting some great deliverer who could promise them relief. They believed very willingly that this Savior had arisen in the person of Hung Hsin-chuan, a native of Kwang-si, South China. Hung had received Christian instruction, and although he never professed conversion, he wrote and circulated various tracts in which he made liberal use of Scriptural references, signing them the "Heavenly Prince" and in them declaring that he was the "Elder Brother of Jesus Christ." In a few months a large following had flocked to his banners, which are said to have displayed the Cross as a symbol of the "Kingdom of Great Peace," *Tai-sing Tien-kuo*, which he was to establish. In a comparatively short time, he had surrounded himself with a large organized band of brigands and peasants. They swept over the surrounding country, burning cities and murdering the inhabitants who did not join them. Hung issued edicts that his followers should not shave their heads in the Manchu fashion, for he claimed a divine mission in overthrowing the Manchu dynasty and his band came to be known as the "Hair Rebels." He enfranchised slaves, prohibited concubinage, prostitution and the binding of feet. In some of these things the missionaries recognized the results of Christian teaching; and hopes arose that even from the appalling disaster good might come. The missionary who had been his instructor visited him at length, but was soon made aware of the real character of the man. He found Hung surrounded by a numerous harem, and found that he was basking in debauchery as the results of his frightful conquests.

The rebellion spread like wildfire and the government seemed to be unable to check it in any way. Finally, it had reached sixteen provinces, and Hung had established himself at the ancient capital city, Nanking, where he ruled with almost imperial authority for many years. He elevated his peasant followers to princely positions and rewarded the most desperate brigands with commands of generals. He did not go out at the head of his troops during a period of nine years, but trusted to his subordinates, who were assured of honors and authority, in keeping with the devastation for which they were directly responsible. For fifteen years Hung maintained his sway, most of the time behind the great walls of Nanking, until Chinese forces, under the command of several officers, famous at home, but the best known of whom was Li Hung-chang and General Gordon with his "Ever Victorious Army," defeated him. He came by his death as a result of drinking poison rather than to submit to the humiliation of capture. Throughout the entire Yangtze Valley one is constantly reminded of this frightful Reign of Terror. Fields now lie idle, or are under cultivation, where once stood large cities; and within city walls there are vast tracts of land, either littered with the remains of burned buildings or structures that have gone to ruin as the result of Taiping raids upon former inhabitants.

Chin-kiang was destroyed by the "hairy rebels," but the citizens who escaped massacre and large numbers who rushed here from the small towns and villages in the neighborhood, after the overthrow of the fanatics at Nanking, quickly endeavored to make this commercial port profit by the downfall of cities further up the river. Large sections of the city were rebuilt and an era of prosperity seemed likely; but immediately there was a serious check to progress caused by anti-foreign demonstrations. Few river passengers leave the boat at Chin-kiang, reserving shore excursions for other towns and cities where there is more of old China remaining to claim attention.

As the boat steams along the yellow current beyond this treaty port, it passes the city of Yangchow, but the celebrated seat of the Emporer Yang-ti is not visible as it lies too far inland. It is a city of at least one hundred thousand inhabitants, and native poetry and history celebrates it as one of the gay resorts of the olden times, whence came men of wealth and official position to enjoy its pleasures. The Chinese declare that Yangchow was so fascinating that the stranger who entered its gates was unable to leave until he had squandered his last coin.

Over by the Grand Canal, and beyond human vision from the deck of a river steamer, lies Hwai-yin, which became immortal because it was the birthplace of General Han Hsin, a hero whose life is held up to Chinese boys as a worthy example to follow, one whose name is not overlooked in the musty and over-crowded Chinese Pantheon. Han was the poor boy who made it possible for his master to ascend the imperial throne. It is recorded that although he was the son of peasants and was very poor, he felt that he had a superior "mission" to perform even when he was a mere lad. Thus, when he was almost famished, he sat on the bank of a stream and fished to relieve his hunger. But no fish came to his net and he was obliged to beg for food from an old woman returning from her day's work in the fields. She gave him food, but he did not thank her for it in the customary manner. Instead, he ate her food and then made an eloquent speech in which he promised her that she would be liberally rewarded for her charity when he became rich and powerful. Such oratory was not likely to make Han popular in his native village, and it is recorded that he was the butt of the jests of the other boys, but seems not to have cared and continued to have absolute confidence in himself and his future. He obtained a sword, which he carried at his side as if he were a military officer, and this prompted frequent challenges from the boys, armed with sticks and clubs. One day, as if he had been a conquering hero, he went to a petty ruler, Han-wang and offered his services, but he met with prompt rejection, which might have discouraged the ordinary youth, but it only aroused Han to renewed activity. Spurned by Han-wang he went to the ruler's most active rival, who became Emperor Kao-tsu (206-195 B.C.) and made a similar proposal. Kao-tsu gave him a commission immediately and soon made him chief general of his forces. Han proved himself to be an unusual strategist and soon subdued so many kingdoms that he was in the main responsible for his master's elevation to the imperial throne. Kao-tsu made him a "King," but the emperor soon died, and listening to a court intrigue that accused Han of high treason, the widow-empress condemned him to death. It was almost with his last breath that Han gave utterance to the words that have been famous in China for two thousand years: "As a good hound is killed and eaten when there are no more hares to catch, or as the bow and arrows are laid away, when there are no more birds to shoot, so I am removed, there being no more need of me, as empire is at peace."

The *Poyang* reached Nanking in the early morning, and the city seemed to rise like a vision of antiquity from the gray mists that hung over the landscape. Junk and sampan folk were astir, and, as usual, were making a loud clatter at their rowing and cooking. Many people were visible on the bank, either dipping up water, or silently watching the large steamer plowing through the current towards the hulks that are anchored in deep water, as a pontoon pathway for disembarking passengers. But the splendid old capital city lay over behind its walls, which are thirty-two miles in circumference and thirty to fifty feet in height. It was impossible to gain the slightest idea of the magnificent stronghold, "the city of magnificent distances," which from outward appearances had been such a fitting capital for a colossal hermit empire. A Chinese city is not one of towers and minarets, which, as for example, Jerusalem, pierces the skyline with tiled or gilded domes and is a thing of unforgettable beauty when seen from afar; but as one approaches great walls, like those of Nanking, there is the fascination of mystery. What lies beyond those seemingly forbidding barriers? What landmarks of the ancient tragedies and comedies there enacted still remain? What manner of people are there today in the stupendous enclosure, which from a Western point of view seems almost like being within the walls of a glorified penitentiary?

Nanking is slightly over two hundred miles from Shanghai and may be reached by rail, but no tourist who has a couple of days' leisure should deny himself the pleasure of approaching the ancient stronghold from the muddy current that almost washes its walls. It has been a treaty port since 1897, and is supposed to have about three hundred thousand inhabitants at the present time. It was the seat of the imperial government of six dynasties between the Fourth and Sixth Centuries of the Christian era, and later became the capital of the Mings in 1368. It has had several names during the passing of the centuries, the present one having been conferred by the Ming emperor, Yung-lo (1403-1424) to designate it as the Southern Capital, when he moved the imperial seat to Peking. It was captured by the Taipings in 1853 and remained in their hands for eleven years, suffering almost as much as the other cities, which were not the temporary residence of the "Heavenly Prince." Laid in ruins, excepting the walls and a few districts occupied by the

Taipings themselves, it has staggered under the blow, despite the courageous efforts of its people to regain lost prestige. Following the fall of the Manchu dynasty and the birth of the present republic, large portions of the country were in favor of returning the capital to Nanking, and it is a popular belief that this would have been done had it not been for the opinion prevailing in diplomatic circles that Peking, being familiar to the world as the Chinese capital, should remain the capital because Nanking was not familiar to the people of foreign countries. This would have brought to Nanking another period of prosperity and fame, but there is likelihood that the future of the city will depend upon its commerce, rather than from again becoming the residence of the ruling classes.

Boats usually remain at the hulks near the city wall about two hours, affording even the hurried Yangtze tripper the opportunity to take a rikisha ride within the walls, which are pierced by thirteen gates, about four of which are usually kept closed. Such a procedure, however, is not to be recommended. One may spend two or three days here en joyably and comfortably. There is a first-class hotel managed by an Englishman, who will offer much valuable advice in regard to itineraries, provide guides who speak English, and assure his guests a well-cooked dinner, and spacious and clean room at the close of the day's journey.

And it is a day's journey, or several days' journey, to and from the various points of interest within and beyond the walls. Perhaps there are more sites than sights, but all of them will be of great interest to the casual visitor or the student of China's history. There are several palaces and temples, numerous shrines and monuments, some of which are familiar to Westerners by some date or personage of historical significance; but even more fascinating are those quaint corners and spaces concerning which the guides spin their fanciful versions of ancient myth and legend. For example, we halt beside the pond into which the great scholar, Yen-lu-kung, liberated the tortoise and fish, instead of having them killed and cooked for his table. Yen was murdered on account of a court intrigue that implicated him in a treason to his country, but, as is commonly the case in China, he received posthumous honors, when his name was changed to "Prince of Culture and Loyalty," and a shrine has been set up near the pond in recognition of his achievements. One hears a hundred of these folk tales, some of which have a slight foundation in history, but whether they have, or merely spring to the mind of the narrator as he recites them, they provide an unmistakable sidelight on Chinese character, and always are more interesting than the exact information of guidebooks. Gone is the wonderful Porcelain Tower, *Lin-li-ta*, which rose to nine stories, a height of two hundred sixty feet, and was accounted one of the beautiful structures of China. The Taipings destroyed it, but there remains the lake, *Mo-tsou-hu*, two miles in circumference, where the first Ming emperor once played a game for a wager and, according to report, won it. Here also resided the beautiful lady, *Mo-tsou* (No Sorrow) whose portraits are still offered for sale, and whose biography, along with the history of the lake, has been written in two large volumes.

It is a long drive to the Tombs of the Ming Emperors, much of which is uncomfortable, owing to the bad condition of the paved roads, and visitors going to Peking will do better to eliminate this journey to the avenue of stone animals that line the way and the Tombs themselves and go to Nankou, beyond which more marvelous carvings and constructions for a similar purpose provide one of the notable side-trips of the whole Chinese tour. But a drive into the country around Nanking will bring its rewards to one who by the time he reaches this part of the country is likely to feel himself drawn by the oriental spell and is anxious to see as much as possible of the Chinese who has not come into contact with Westerners as in the cities of the coast. Of much interest hereabouts are the large duck farms, penetrated by small canals, where the large broods are tended by picturesque "duckherds," whose charges are frequently quick to detect "strangers" in the persons of occidentals and give their masters as much trouble as a herd of cattle gives a cowboy on a Texan prairie. The region around Nanking is noted for its *pi-tan*. Do not know what *pi-tan* is? In plain, or vulgar, English, *pi-tan* is rotten eggs, or eggs that are the superlative degree of rotten. They may have been simply rotten early in the days of the process of evolution, through which they have passed, but they were packed in a mixture of lime, clay, rice hulls and salt. The white of the egg solidifies and becomes a greenish-black color. They are highly prized by the epicures in all parts of China; duck eggs are largely used, and, presumably, are stronger than hen's eggs. The Chinese likes "strength" in his food. Sometimes this strength becomes terrifying to occidental nostrils; but perhaps occidentals do not know what is good to eat. I am firmly of the opinion that this is the oriental belief, and more, I surmise that more than half of the Chinese are convinced that occidentals are raving mad. It depends so much upon the point of view.

After leaving Nanking one comes shortly to Wu-hu, connected by an eighty-mile canal with Tai-ping-hsien. Vast quantities of rice and other agricultural products arrive here from the surrounding country for

A Chinese Junk

distribution to other cities. The Chinese have looked upon agriculture as the basis of society from the earliest times, and in these fertile plains of the Yangtze find ample proof that the theory is correct. "Have you had your rice today?" is a common form of greeting in place of the usual occidental comment about the weather. Methods of cultivation, however, should be improved everywhere, and as the Chinese farmers are unwilling to follow the advice of Western teachers they are being reached by agricultural schools and associations at the heads of which are natives who have received foreign instruction or experience.

The next city is Ta-tung, with not more than sixty thousand inhabitants, but a point for distributing the products of several large cities a few miles inland, which are reached by a famous highway. Soon An-king comes into sight, a city with a half-million inhabitants and commercially important, although containing nothing likely to be of interest to the tourist. Just beyond the city, however, the steamer comes close to Hsiau-ku-shan (Little Orphan Island) which appears to be a great detached rock, rising perhaps three hundred feet above the surface of the river. The Yangtze flood swirls around its base, and approached from downstream it seemed to be uninhabited. Like other islands, however, it was sacred to the people of the early days, and is said to have basked in imperial favor, having been richly endowed by the mother of an emperor, much as the mother of a Roman emperor expended vast sums of money upon the holy places of Judea. Facing upstream, are large temples and monasteries, whose red-tile roofs stand out prominently against the grayish-black shelf of rock on which they are perched. The buildings are occupied by a few monks, who cling to ancient beliefs, but the visitors are few in these modern times and the inmates are said to be very poor. Probably there are steps and staircases carved in the cliff under the shelf supporting the buildings, but we could not see them and wondered how the friars reach their perch, or how they are enabled to communicate with the "mainland." Captain Carnaghan said he had planned a surprise for his passengers; as we approached the side of the islet he tooted the steamer whistle sharply and looked to see the "thousands of birds" fly out from the island at the unexpected noise. Perhaps a dozen of them left their roosting places, but the great number had heard the whistle too often to be frightened and declined to fly for exhibition purposes.

There are many legends connected with the sacred island, one of which has to do with the cormorants, which find the region good fishing grounds, particularly where the waters splash at the base. It is related that a beautiful woman was caught in the Yangtze current and carried downstream to the island. It was in the early days, before there were boats on the river, or inhabitants on its banks. She did not starve, however, as the cormorants brought her food, as the ravens brought manna to Elijah; and although the legend is silent in regard to the manner of her death, it seems likely that she died of homesickness, probably at a ripe old age, which is the only time for a legendary character to die.

After Hu-kow, a little city which has considerable trade with ports of Lake Po-yang, on the sloping banks of which some of the most highly prized tea of China is grown, the steamer arrives at Kiu-kiang, a name fairly familiar to Westerners, because the famous pottery of the entire district is usually known by that name. Local history records that the city possessed eight hundred eight temples at one time; but many of them, like Marco Polo's bridges at Hangchow, have completely disappeared. There remain several that repay a visit, but the commercial life of Kiu-kiang seems to be more important than the ancient fanes. Notably at King-teh-chen, only a short distance away, pottery has been made from the earliest times, beautiful pieces that are today the most prized specimens of Chinese art in foreign museums. Here was made the ancient pottery for the Chinese court that inspired the earliest Jesuit visitors to write lengthy descriptions of the manufacture, which gave an impetus to the art in Europe, where attempts, most of them unsuccessful, were made to duplicate the colors and designs. Small value is placed upon the modern product of many ovens, but the process of manufacture is jealously guarded and foreigners are not welcome in the region, although many of them go armed with official letters that open all doors, much to the disgust of the workers, who have the reputation for being a riotous crew, easily led to outbreaks, which hold local officials in the constant position of apologists to someone who has been "insulted."

Captain Carnaghan had two beautiful vases, which he had purchased from an itinerant dealer at Kiu-kiang, who spread his wares on the landing-stage and begged for purchasers. Certainly they were of modern manufacture, but in imitation of ancient pottery, and exactly the article that brings a large sum in the American market. It is likely the pieces would have been held for about sixty dollars each in this country. "They cost me thirty cents each at Kiu-kiang," laughed the skipper. "But this is not so remarkable. Over there is the district where these came from, the tea-growers are said to receive about two cents a pound for the leaves they sell to natives. Money seems to have a great purchasing value at this point." This seemed to be encouraging and we watched the deck of the hulk closely, but no pottery salesman appeared while we were in port. A boy who had brought fruit or other provisions to the steamer, held in his hand a beautiful tray inlaid with mother-of-pearl, and gazed with envious eyes upon the flashy colors of a fifteen cent American magazine which I had been reading and which remained in my hands. I offered to buy his tray, but he was adamant, and although he was probably in sore need of money he would not sell it. When I offered to exchange the magazine for the tray, however, he seemed to think that he had struck a great bargain with the "foreign devil" and quickly ran away with the magazine, leaving the tray in my possession, fearful that I would change my mind and repent of the bargain.

The steamer plowed into the water of Lake Po-yang, the second largest lake in China, just as night was falling. We could see thousands of twinkling lights from the cities on its banks, but did not visit and could not see any of them, with their swarming population. Po-yang is eighty miles long at one point, and in summer it is deep as it is filled by the Yangtze, swollen by the spring floods; but in winter it sometimes falls so that a water depth of three to five feet makes navigation impossible. The Yangtze flows through the lake as the Jordan flows through the Sea of Galilee, and Po-yang has been held in great reverence from the earliest times. Its spirits have received worship and sacrifice for many centuries, while an epistle from the emperor was read at the temple and burned each year, a ceremony not unlike that at the sacred lakes of Thibet.

Wu-sueh, the first port reached in the Yangtze trip after the steamer has again entered the river, is known principally as one of the markets for salt, which is a government monopoly in China, and in some districts said to be held at such a high price that it is considered a luxury. The government appoints a number of salt merchants in a district, and none other may sell it. The country is divided into ten districts and the price is regulated in each by the provincial governor. The price is not uniform, but is supposed to fluctuate in response to demand and supply, but is likelier to be dictated by the governor, who may be depended upon to extract as much "squeeze" as possible.

The Tayeh mines, mentioned early in this chapter as being chiefly in the hands of the Japanese, are connected by a nineteen mile railway with the port of Hwang-shih-kang, which is five hundred and twenty-eight miles above Shanghai. Japanese steamers are always lying in the river at this point, loading the precious ores for the furnaces of Nippon. While mining is still conducted in most primitive manner, when in the hands of the Chinese, who are not in favor of penetrating far into the earth, because, as before mentioned, the excavations are likely to disturb the peace of ancestors, it is certain that mines have been worked for thousands of years in this country so rich in precious ores. It has been proved that the Chinese knew the use of copper as early as the time of Huang-Ti (2698 B.C.) and mining laws were in force as early as 1122 B.C. In mining, as in practically everything else, the Chinese claim originality. For example, they are now pointing to the fact that a celebrated Taoist teacher recorded that he spoke his message into a box and ordered it delivered to a disciple, who resided at a great distance from him. What was this, they ask, but the Western phonograph?

Hwang-chow, a city of thirty thousand people, is unimportant, save for the fact that it was the home of Su-Tung-po, an essayist who lived a thousand years ago. After passing Kiu-kiang the scenery changes and hills sometimes suggest those magnificent gorges that lie many miles upstream and are reached only by trans-shipping at the port of Hankow. Time permitting, one should go nearer the headwaters of the magnificent river to Ichang, a trip of three days, only to find it possible to transship again to a ship of lighter draught for further progress on the bosom of the same "Son of the Ocean." The trip abounds in sensational delights, even perhaps a quarrel with the unruly natives who are constantly encouraged in their anti-foreign sentiment by pamphlets from the literati, and who despise everyone and everything foreign. The ports are being opened to international trade, however, and the fertile lands of the Upper Yangtze, with their teeming millions of population, are slowly but certainly coming to a realization that China's days of sleep and isolation are over; a great fact that seems to penetrate inland in a leisurely manner and against tremendous obstacles. If one leaves the steamer at Hankow, however, rapidly becoming the "Chicago of China," and glances at the map, he will see that he has reached the heart of the wonderful country, and in reaching Hankow he has had most of the experiences of the Yangtze voyage, with the exception of the grandeur of the gorges. The cities further upstream seem to be repetitions of those encountered on the banks of the yellow serpent that brings life to so many millions of the sons and daughters of earth. The average visitor will not care to go beyond Hankow, although the way has been paved for him to do so with comfort, convenience and no danger; and the opportunity should not be passed lightly, if one has the time and inclination.

CHAPTER VIII

CHINA'S TRIPLE HEART

WHERE the Han-shui river joins the Yangtze, about six hundred miles above Shanghai, there is an amazing population, which the amiable Abbé Huc estimated at eight millions in 1845. Later estimates have reduced the figure considerably, but there seems to be no better reason for accepting one as authentic more than another. The Westerner's first thought as he beholds the miles of junks in the water and the swarming humanity on the shores, is that he had never before believed there were so many people in any given spot on earth's surface. For the territory covered by the three great cities of Hankow, Han-yang and Wu-chang is not great; but one's impression is that every square yard of this territory is the "home" of a numerous family. Every boat in the river seems overcrowded and the land population pushes down to the water's edge, so that many families actually live on mats or boards spread over the tops of sticks which are poked into the soft mud. Yet the district has suffered disasters that have cost countless lives within the last few years. In modern times the Taipings were here, and it is recorded that miles of junks were in flames at one time and the swords and fire-brands were at work on land. Even so late as 1911, there were desperate struggles here between the revolutionists and imperial forces. The native city of Hankow seemed to be almost totally destroyed, but it is being rapidly rebuilt. Loss of property and countless lives seem to retard and check the growth of the place for a brief time; but soon again the streets are filled with a population as vast as before. The Chinese call the three cities "The Collecting Place For Nine Provinces," and, whatever befalls them, they seem to be eternal.

Population and prosperity seem to drift first to one and then to the others. Thus when Hankow was only a fishing village, Wu-chang, which seems of minor importance today, was a celebrated city. In fact, Wu-chang had attained considerable prominence as early as the Third Century of the Christian era. But just now the tide has turned to Hankow and it has assumed proportions that are comparable to Yokohama in Japan in much the same length of time and for the same reason. And, in many ways, Hankow is one of the delightful cities of the vast republic. It is one of the cosmopolitan cities of the globe. Large concessions are given over to the British, Russian, French and Japanese. A foreign census shows that nearly two hundred Americans make it their home. Verily, it is a vast rendezvous for East and West. The peoples of the world do not assemble for social reasons as at Cairo, or for religious purposes as at Jerusalem, but for the transaction of business. It is supposed that produce passing through Hankow each season amounts to fully Taels 60,000,000. In the streets one meets the people of practically every part of earth; and they all seem to be occupied with business, most of which, directly or indirectly, has to do with the vast quantity of tea that is assembled here for shipment in every direction. London held a monopoly over this vast product at one time and it was not uncommon for twenty or thirty steamers to be in port for the purpose of taking on the cargo; but Chinese tea is out of favor in England, where the leaves of Ceylon and India are preferred. The market has drifted to America, Siberia and Russia, and in season the experts from those countries come to Hankow to purchase every quality from the first young leaves of May to the final pickings, which are pulverized and become an important staple in the Northern countries, where the dust is not only consumed with hot water as a beverage, but mixed with dough to give a flavor to bread. At times the newcomer feels that Hankow is an outpost of Russia. One hears Russian in the crowded streets, sees Russian signs over shops and is often recommended to a Russian bank when concerned over the inevitable tangles caused by the coin in circulation.

It was in this neighborhood that General Li Yuan-hung, the president of China at the present time, distinguished himself as a strategist. Li was proclaimed vice-president at the fall of the Manchu dynasty, but he remained at Wu-chang at the head of the army, when he was induced to take up his residence in Peking, and succeeded to the executive chair on the death of President Yuan Shi-Kai in 1916.

There is a first-class foreign hotel at Hankow and although the city is not one of guide-book "sights," it is worth a few days' visit, in the course of which one may ramble at leisure around the native quarters, take a ferry to Wu-chang, at the present time notable for its cotton mills, to Han-yang, where are the arsenal and colossal iron works, or chartering a small boat, drift around the waterline of the three cities and behold sights which no tourist is likely to have encountered elsewhere in his travels.

One feels that he is beginning to arrive in Hankow long before the steamer ties up to its terminal hulk along the Bund, where there is a wide boulevard, shaded by large trees, and along which the foreign concessions are located, with the characteristic architecture of Berlin, Petrograd, Paris and London. Here seems to be the central pivot of the nations' grapple for the possession of China's resources and trade. The river banks display huge signs in English, French, Russian and German, marking the plants of tremendous concession-grabbers. It is as if one passed along a wide avenue in which rival showmen announced the superiority of their attractions over all competitors. It is confidently believed by careful observers that here will occur one of the great scenes of the almost inevitable international tangle arising from a desire of each nation to "protect its interests" and attempt to see to it that no other nation receives a larger share of what all Western governments seem to consider spoils, which must be apportioned among them.

There are only two or three streets of consequence in Hankow where one may drive an automobile or carriage. The motive power is the coolie. He swarms the streets day and night, either pulling rikishas, or carrying the great bundles and bales of commerce. Some of the tea depots have a constant line of coolies passing between their doors and ships on the river, which may be five or six blocks away. These lines are crossed by others carrying the imports, or the local trade. As one sees these heavily laden, perspiring and plodding slaves, he recalls those figures estimated by modern scientists as the number of workers enlisted by Egyptian kings when they built their pyramids. Hankow is in about the same latitude as New Orleans or Alexandria, Egypt. The summers are hot and the days of the tea harvest almost warm enough it seems to "fire" the tea, which is cured by other means in the great receiving plants. Here a Chinese compradore, in charge of perhaps a thousand coolies, told me of the origin of tea. It is a well-known fact that it was used at a very early date by the Buddhist monks whose eyes would become weary at night, and who might have missed their nocturnal devotional exercises but for deep draughts of the hot beverage; but I had never heard of the miraculous beginnings of the fragrant shrub, which it seems had to do with Daruma, an Indian saint. He endeavored to devote his life to endless prayer; but one night he became exhausted, fell asleep and did not awaken until morning. When he realized what had happened, he was so angry that he took a sharp knife and cut off his offending eyelids and threw them on the ground. And lo! they had no sooner struck the earth than they

Hankow

were transformed into tea-shrubs, the leaves of which should minister to the vigils of holy men.

When I made inquiry about the time of departure of trains over the railroad that runs between Hankow and Peking I did not receive what seemed to be a definite answer, and the station, being only a few blocks away, I stopped at the iron grating in the principal station of the great railway and asked the question: "What time does a train go to Peking?"

"One starts in two hours," grunted the agent.

"But how is anyone to know that this is the case? It is not posted on the schedule at the hotel," I complained.

"Oh, plenty people know," he smiled. "Every train is full. If train go before people come today, they go to-morrow. That makes alla same. Train go every day, once a day to Peking now."

Ordinarily, this would have been plenty of time, but it happened that I had left a part of my luggage aboard the *Poyang*. This was anchored some distance away, so I sent word to the hotel to send the hand luggage to the station, while I would take care of that which remained aboard the steamer. And immediately the trouble started; "trouble" that seems to be serious at the time, but which becomes laughable when recalled in later days. I made the mistake of indicating that I was in a hurry. Haste is detested by the Chinese coolie or gentleman; to the former it is merely ridiculous and unnecessary, while to the latter it is vulgar. Hankow is practically horseless and likewise cartless. Around the landing-stage there seemed to be ten thousand coolies, but all of them seemed to be engaged. Not one indicated the taxi sign "For Hire" and none paid any attention to me when I endeavored to indicate to them that they could earn extra money by helping me in what seemed to be an aggravating situation. Finally the chief steward of the ship shouted something from the deck, probably that a rich prize awaited the man who would carry my trunk on a bamboo pole a few blocks to the railway station. Ordinarily, they would have been carrying heavy bales of tea for a few cents an hour: the trunk was no heavier, but the trunk belonged to a white man, and he indicated "hurry," the most objectionable word in a coolie's vocabulary.

Four stalwart coolies presented themselves, however, doubtless having agreed upon their demands. Also, I was charitably inclined. They were helping me out of a difficulty and I thought that instead of giving them a few cents, their rightful wages, I would reward them for appreciated services with a nice silver dollar. After all, why not be liberal with these poor slaves and give them the opportunity to think of a white man's generosity? My thoughts quickly changed, however, as the four took up their places on the deck and declined to touch the trunk until I had paid them in advance. I smilingly offered them the dollar, expecting a reciprocal smile of gratitude. But they sneered and made a move to leave the ship and return to the carrying of tea bales. Two! I doubled my generosity, while cursing them mentally. Still they refused, however, and to make a recital of the conversation as brief as possible it may be truthfully recorded that I paid six dollars to have a trunk transferred on a bamboo pole from the river bank to the railway station! It was doubtless the highest wages ever obtained by coolies in China since the birth of the first Ming emperor or before. But even the ignorant coolie is no fool. He saw my necessity and he capitalized himself.

Arrived at the station, I visited the ticket window, only to learn again that "very much people go to Peking today," so it was necessary to place me in a sleeping compartment already partially occupied by two Chinese. Nothing is more likely to terrorize a "Westerner than to be quartered in this fashion, and nobody is likelier to know it than the seller of tickets. But I took my pasteboard and started for the baggage-room. The coolies had already deposited the trunk near the scales. "Baggage very, very heavy," mourned the baggage agent. I protested that it was the identical baggage that had been checked free elsewhere. "Very heavy" he repeated, paying no attention to what I said and telling the coolies to put it on the scales. He threw up his arms and chuckled when he saw the weights rise into the air. "That cost you eight dollars to Peking," he said. The guide books say that each passenger is entitled to two hundred pounds of free baggage. But the court of last resort, under the circumstances, ruled against me and the guidebooks, knowing that I was playing against time, a fact which he had doubtless learned from the coolies. The train was due to leave in ten minutes. Did I desire to have the baggage put aboard the train? If so, I could hand him eight dollars and the coolies would take it to the baggage van. Yes, I paid it, eight dollars excess, on slightly over two hundred pounds.

Arrived at the car, the conductor inspected my tickets. Could he not give me a compartment that would be "all white"? He could make no answer, until the train started; at least he said so, but two dollars smuggled to his palm quickly opened a compartment that had not been sold, and the ticket agent knew that it had not been sold. Presumably, the conductor and ticket-seller are obliged to divide "earnings" at the end of each round trip.

In many ways this railroad is a mighty achievement; in others, it is to laugh. It was a feat to put down the rails and keep them down in the interior of China. The Chinese do not like railroads as a general proposition, or they say they do not, although they patronize them liberally enough, once they are in operation; but they have a way of ripping up the rails after the builders are gone, if they are sufficiently aroused. Either the government is powerless, or it is indifferent in such matters. There is one case on record in which the people objected to the railway too strenuously, and the government, fearing complications, purchased the line, ripped up the rails and sent them with equipment to an island possession. The natives would have sent them to a less attractive place, if there had not been quick action.

Nevertheless, the Hankow-Peking Line is remarkable. It pierces the interior of China, going through the fertile agricultural land of three provinces, and sends its trains among people who only a few years ago were as primitive as the natives of interior Thibet. It has had a civilizing influence that has had some sociological advantage, no doubt, because it brings the outside world into contact with the hermit-like people of densely populated cities and towns. They still congregate around the stations, however, and stare in open-mouthed surprise at the steam marvel. They peer into the windows of the compartments like blank-faced sheep. Shout "shoo fly" at them and they run like a herd of frightened cattle.

The train stopped near a farm where many peasants were at work in a corn field. There was something the matter with the engine, and they all came running to get a closer view. Eight or ten of them poked their heads into the windows of my compartment. I was reading, and suddenly looking up from my book, I confess that they startled me, for they were a weird looking lot. But I gave them a military salute and said simply: "Good morning." This terrorized them and they immediately ran away, their long pigtails flying in the wind, for these interior people have not "followed the fashions." Their fathers and their grandfathers wore queues and they do not care for the new-fangled notions of "looking like a criminal." They crossed a big field before they ventured to look back. Perhaps they had heard stories about "foreign devils," but they probably had seen few of them and they were not taking any chances. But the railroad has been a blessing to these people, whether they appreciate it or not. It has given them a better market for their produce. They are too dense to realize this advantage at the present time, however, and look upon arriving and departing trains much as we would look upon airships at home in America.

It seems that the trains run regularly several times a week, but nobody takes any pains to let anybody else know about it. The line was built by a Belgian syndicate, and an amusing feature of this "contact" is that the trainmen speak tolerably good French, but do not understand English. A Chinese porter or conductor, speaking the dialect of Brussels, is amusing in itself; but these men are otherwise amusing. They are slouchily dressed in shirts that gap and expose several inches of bare stomach, because they must be "uniformed," and once-white trousers. And they wear wrist-watches! Probably the superintendent of construction who came out from Brussels was so adorned, so no self-respecting Hankow trainman would think himself dressed, unless his "dollar watch" was strapped to his arm.

The Chinese government purchased the line some years ago, so the railroad is now run like everything else in China. It almost runs itself, until it strikes a snag, and then it merely suspends trains until matters are adjusted or adjust themselves. When there is a revolution on—and there is usually some political trouble brewing in these districts—the government does not take any chances, and merely sends a telegram that stops railroad communication so far as the populace is concerned. People who want to travel can wait until things are settled.

On the car there was a porter who made up the beds, and there was another porter who served tea. There was a porter who took charge of hand luggage and there was a porter who adjusted the electric fans and rubbed the dust off the passengers' shoes, and brought towels dipped in hot water, every half-hour or so, for passengers to wipe their perspiring brows—a luxury much indulged in by all traveling Chinamen. We had a merry party of them aboard. I never saw so many porters in my life and could not see why the railroad gave so many of them free rides. But this was understood before the end of the journey. The railroad gives them next to nothing and they are glad of the jobs, to get as much as possible from passengers. They were all on hand at the end of the journey, looking for "tips." These first-class attendants have comparatively few passengers and they make hay while the sun shines and the wheels move, if pestiferous attention can be considered "service."

But just as everything else was expensive, the meals were ridiculously cheap, considering their quality and quantity. Almost all the passengers ate Chinese "chow," but the line boasts that it also provides European food, and it does. Nine course meals were the rule. They ranged from soup to delicious peaches, apricots and pears and included one fish and three meat courses, each with vegetables. And the charge for this banquet was sixty cents in American money. They were meals that would cost four or five dollars on a Pullman car in this country where we are told that diners are run at a loss. Most of the passengers at the tables were European, however, the natives preferring to patronize the swarms of "hucksters," who shouted their wares at each station, selling unusual food, ranging from whole roast chickens—which were offered for twenty cents—to gourds and radishes about a yard long. Most of these things were eaten as "relishes," however, and boiled rice from the dining-car was ordered in quantities astounding to the Westerner. Here the Chinaman is again the opposite of his Japanese brother, who prefers to dine in private in a hotel or inn, sending for his food to be served in his room, and eating his rice and fish in a closed compartment on the train. The Chinese like to eat in "public," just as they like to appear "publicly" at most times when other people consider it preferable to remain behind closed doors.

All sleeping cars in China have a "lounge" in the center of the car as long as several compartments. It provides a chair for travelers who become "cramped" in sleeping dens, and the open space is usually filled with natives, either smoking vigorously or holding bowls of rice to their mouths, while poking great lumps of food between their lips, with noises that are not considered "polite" at western tables, although eminently proper at Chinese boards.

After dinner, when the sun had set and electric lights were turned on, the Chinese passengers seemed to take it as a signal to commence a slow preparation for retiring. Many of them seemed to feel that they were cramped for space in their compartments, so they stood in the corridors or the "lounge" as they removed various articles of clothing. Most of them seemed to take a "night cap" smoke, after being fully prepared for bed, prancing up and down the corridors as they did so! And be it understood that the Chinaman who wears little more than a long coat in the daytime does not put on additional clothing when he retires.

Woe to the passenger who hurriedly boards a train on this line without having purchased a ticket! Unless such passenger can prove to the satisfaction of the conductor that he boarded the train at Tschoue-tcheon, Lion-li-ho, Wang-ton-sien or Pao-ting-fou—the difficulty of which will be apparent to any one—the company, which is the government, gives the conductor full authority to collect fare from the starting point of the train. In addition to "teaching folks to come early to avoid the rush," the paternal government thus gives the train crew another opportunity to turn a dishonest penny, a privilege which in large measure takes the place of salary. The Chinese government was never generous in salaries, but it "gives every man a chance" to prepare for a comfortable old age, from the president to the railway conductor.

But railways are comparatively new in China, so that their operators may not have been connected with them long enough to have mastered the "tricks of the trade." The mileage is being rapidly increased, however, and it is certain that the railway has come to stay. The great obstacle still difficult to overcome is that a railroad track cannot avoid the numerous graves of ancestors that dot the entire Chinese country landscape. The first line was built from "Wu-sung to Shanghai, a distance of about twelve miles. There were several accidents and so much disturbance in the district that the government purchased the line, tore up the rails and shipped them with the rolling stock to Formosa, at that time a Chinese possession. The line was not rebuilt until 1898, when several Chinese bought shares, and it soon became popular with the natives who had opposed it in the beginning. The real start of railways in China, however, is usually dated from 1881, when a line was built between the Kaiping coal mine to a canal seven miles distant. At first it was merely a tram and the change was brought about by deceit and strategy, the owners trusting to diplomacy to keep it open. It is related that a British engineer built the first locomotive by stealth, and almost before the officials of the province were aware of it, there was a fifty-mile narrow gage line in full operation. But there were many difficulties to be overcome. The Chinese of the district were careless, and the number of deaths resulting from the operation of trains threatened to destroy the profits of the mine, which had prompted its construction, for the company, fearing mobs or other violence, paid indemnities to the families of victims without the customary investigation of accidents. It was soon learned, however, that in China, where life is held to be of so much less importance than death, there was what amounted to a suicidal mania among the people. The head of the house, who could not provide food for his family, willingly placed himself in front of trains, assured that survivors would profit by his sacrifice. The company stopped paying indemnity and the suicidal mania was quickly suppressed.

Following the Sino-Japanese war, however, Chinese officials realized that railroads must be encouraged and an era of railway construction began in various parts of the country. The opponents argued that there were over seventeen thousand miles of waterway in China which had served all purposes of transportation for centuries, augmented by a system of national highways that had been in operation from ancient days. But the progressive won and are still winning. By 1911, there were four thousand miles of railway open to traffic in China and the mileage is supposed to be well over the six thousand mark at the present time, with several prospective extensions and new lines under construction. The fine Peking-Kalgan line had Chan-Tien-you, a Yale graduate, as chief engineer and was financed and built by Chinese. It is operated entirely by natives and has had a far reaching effect upon the entire railway situation in China. Railroads naturally lead the way to the introduction of the telegraph and postal systems of western countries. The first telegraph line in China was operated between Tientsin, the Taku fort and the Pei-ho River in 1879. The speed with which the system has been expended is almost "Japanese," because a report issued in 1913 showed over thirty-eight thousand miles of wire and over six hundred stations in operation. Down to the late years of the last Manchu dynasty, there was no postal system in the modern sense. Communications, chiefly official, were sent through the country by elaborate and extensive relays of couriers, so timed that when one arrived at a post station other men were in readiness to carry mail along towards destination without a moment's delay. But the railroads have brought a new era, and today there are regular postal routes that cover considerably over one hundred thousand miles, all under the control of the central government at Peking, although the first attempt at a western postal system dates only to 1878. Telephones were not in use in China until 1881, when a private service was installed by the British at Shanghai; which has been extended to the large cities, at least those frequented by foreigners.

These, and many other things, not only prove that China is awake, but also that there is a latent spark in the nation that responds to a quickening impulse from without. Pessimists have believed that art, for example, was dead. I asked several connoisseurs and collectors in various cities if they could tell me of one native Chinese who at the moment was devoting himself to painting or sculpture; and I always received the same negative answer, with the possible exception of Shanghai, where I was told of Chinese newspaper and magazine caricaturists and cartoonists, who are fashioning their work after Western models and doing comparatively nothing to prove that the art of Chinese traditions still lives. Yet, as the train passed a small town on the Hankow-Peking line, an art expert from America, who held commissions from various collectors and museums, told me an interesting story to prove that art is not dead in China, as many people believe; but that it may feel the quickening influence of the Western "contact" that is making itself felt in so many directions.

COOLIES, HANKOW

"It cost me just six hundred dollars to find out that art is not dead in China," he related, "or that is what it has cost me to date, and this is the town where it all happened." He pointed to the sign-board that hung over the entrance of a small station. "I have never been here before, but this town is the home of a young genius. In my search for curios and art works for America, I came across a splendid marble figure which was represented to me as being an antique. Now I know a thing or two about Chinese art, but I had never seen anything like this particular piece. I examined it closely, and the dealer, a Frenchman, resident in China, assured me that it was a rare specimen of the work of a certain period. I had some misgiving, but try as I would I was irresistibly drawn back to the piece when I attempted to ignore it. I thought perhaps none of the people I represented would care for it, so I decided to purchase it for myself. I bargained with the dealer, but I could not bring him to better terms, so I gave him six hundred dollars cash and congratulated myself on my bargain.

"There is a Chinese collector whose judgment I respect and with whom I have often discussed my purchases. So I took my marble to him that he might rejoice with me. 'It's not an antique,' he said at the first glance. 'I know the young sculptor; he lives in a little town on the Hankow-Peking railroad.' I told the collector that I had no reason to doubt his word, but if what he said was true it would be worth the young sculptor's time and inconvenience to come and see me. Immediately, I recalled several wealthy Chinese who had lamented that art was dead in their country. I would see the youth, I thought, have a talk with him, and then bring him to the attention of men who would be glad to send him abroad for study, for the glory of China and as proof that the artistic impulse has not departed.

"Well, he came to see me, an ignorant, sensitive and superstitious young man, who told me that he represented the youngest generation of a family which for many years had earned a meager living as stone-cutters. Their principal occupation, I believe, was making the big stone dogs, which the Chinese like to place at the entrances of their homes or gardens. The boy was suspicious of me and it was with considerable difficulty that I persuaded him to admit that he carved the marble which had come into my possession. He said that a figure in the local temple had been his only model, while his relatives, the stone-carvers, had been his only instructors. He had taken the block of marble and worked on it in his leisure moments, he said, and one day he sold it to the French dealer, who was well aware that it was his own work. He received only a few dollars in payment and was amazed when I told him that the piece had passed to me upon the payment of six hundred dollars.

"I told him that I would bring him to the attention of some Chinese gentlemen who would take an interest in his future. I had but one request to make of him and that was that he would accompany me to the French consulate and make affidavit of the fact that he had told the dealer the marble was his own work, because it had been misrepresented to me as an antique. He consented and we went to the consulate. Several questions were asked of him in a formal manner and he swore to the document and affixed his signature. He was very nervous during the proceedings, and my Chinese friend assured me afterwards that the youth became absolutely panic-stricken. As quickly as the legal formalities were over, he made a dash for the door and went directly to the railway station to take a train for this little town, his own home. Apparently he believed that he was becoming involved in some weird plot that would end in trouble, perhaps imprisonment. He vowed never again to touch his hand to anything more important than the stone dogs, the occupation of his honorable fore-fathers. I made one more effort to induce him to come and see me, but he sent back word that he never cared to leave his village again. He had been to the city once and considered that he made a fortunate escape, a belief which his family doubtless shared with him. Yes, it cost me six hundred dollars, but I found out that art still lives in China. And, what's more, I would not give up my specimen of modern Chinese sculpture if any one placed six hundred dollars in my hand."

The early part of the trip passed without undue excitement, but as the train entered the province of Ho-nan we observed that excited crowds—most of the men still wearing their queues—had assembled at every station. They were festooning the railway buildings with bolts of coarse white canvas and wreaths or garlands of fresh flowers, some of them great pieces of jasmine that sent forth an odor that could be detected before the train stopped. Under the artificial arbors were fifteen or twenty chairs—evidently for the chief dignitaries of the cities. At first we thought it must be local celebrations or festivals, for perpetually there is one of them on the calendar, as one finds out who attempts to transact any business at the banks, which always avail themselves of all holidays. Then we asked:

"Funeral train of President Yuan Shi-k'ai will pass here to-morrow; this his province, his old home. His body will be brought home for burial."

"But President Yuan died three weeks ago," we commented.

"Very true, but Chinese do not bury quickly," was the rejoinder, which we had reason to know two days later, because when we visited a temple in Peking there was a horrible odor that sent us out to the fresh air, although several Chinese were lounging around the place, visiting and smoking, apparently not disturbed by the air they were breathing.

"Too bad, very sorry," apologized our guide. "General Chong was killed at Shanghai two months ago. They sent his body here and it has not yet been buried. His eldest son comes here every day to worship at his father's bier. Chinese do not bury their dead too soon."

When we arrived at Peking, we found the big station, just outside the principal gate, festooned with straw matting and fresh flowers. Our information had been correct. Yuan was to be buried, or at least his funeral was to be held on the following day. His remains had lain in the Imperial Palace in the Forbidden City for three weeks. We wondered if we would be able to see the funeral; and a quick trip to the American legation assured us that it might be possible. In a short time we received passes to go to the old Tartar City wall, mount it, approach the ancient gateway and look down, seeing what we could see.

"And it will be a sight to remember," volunteered an attaché, making our anticipations mount higher and higher. "They hated President Yuan, while he was alive—perhaps none in the republic was so hated—but the Chinese seem to forget everything when they are in the presence of death. It is the great leveler. Conditions were much the same when the late Dowager Empress passed away. She had not been beloved by her people during her life; but her funeral—what a spectacle it was! And we understand that Yuan's funeral procession will be just as spectacular."

CHAPTER IX

BURYING A PRESIDENT

IT has been said that the Chinese think more of death than they do of life. The great to-do over Yuan Shih-k'ai, after he had stopped breathing, seemed to point to the truth of this statement. No doubt, Yuan was a monster. Sometimes in the news dispatches that reached us in America we were led to think of him as a progressive president of a great republic that was striving to forget the traditions of the old empire. We were asked to think of him as a noble personage who came to the aid of his country in time of stress. It was acknowledged, even by his bitterest enemies—and they seemed to be numbered by the tens of thousands—that he was a powerful man. He was thought to be the only man, after the Manchu dynasty had been overthrown, who should be president, because it was thought that he was the only man who could unite the various political factions. He held China together in a fashion, until vain ambition rose to the surface and the country beheld the real Yuan.

Still the country tolerated him in a fashion. It was no secret that his life story told a bloody history, because it was well known that his custom was to see to it that men who opposed him were assassinated. He was treacherous in a superlative degree. His greatest *coup*, before he became president, proved that. He was trusted by the Emperor, who was virtually a prisoner in his island home at the Summer Palace just beyond the walls of Peking, and he turned traitor to his liege lord, because he thought it better to play into the hands of the Dowager Empress. Yuan, became stronger than ever in the councils of the mighty, but the people forgot or passed lightly many of the things in his earlier career. At least they thought he would be able to weld together the broken strands. But Yuan was not satisfied. We had hints in America that he would proclaim himself emperor in a year and found a dynasty which would rule, after centuries of Manchu oppression. That was the great turning point. The South of China revolted. It was not for this that they had just passed through a revolution. But the South of China is always revolting at something, and the news was given out as if it was another of those periods of dissatisfaction with any government. As a matter of fact, Yuan was emperor. The American legation in Peking has received documents signed by him as emperor, using the name that he had taken for himself, and signed with the imperial signet. I have seen a photograph of the crown that he had made and expected to place on his own head when the time came.

President in name, he was ruling China as despotically as any of her foreign rulers had attempted to do in the past. By his followers he was acknowledged to be emperor, and it was supposed that the succession would pass to his eldest son, a paralytic, heartily disliked in Peking. The country was in flames. It is still a question whether or not he would have been able to stem the tide of opposition. But these things were not the whole truth concerning him. They made good material for speeches and editorials at home and abroad, but our writers seemed to overlook the fact that Yuan was a reactionary of the worst type. He did not believe in reform, and it was merely a pose when he claimed that he did. He hated Christians, and was a true Chinaman in his religious beliefs, as superstitious as the coolie of the country districts.

A member of his cabinet, whose name I am not at liberty to use, said when I asked for permission to visit the Imperial Palace: "It would have been impossible a month ago, because Yuan was more rigid in these matters than any of the deceased rulers of China. He did not want a foreigner within the palace gates. Now it is different."

Yuan was popularly supposed to have had fourteen wives. It is gossiped in Peking that two of his wives gave birth to sons on the same day. This is no particular scandal in China, however, because men' who can afford it have many wives, but it speaks much for his "modern ideas," of which such glowing accounts were sent through the press of the world.

Then Yuan died. Of course, everyone thought that he had been assassinated, because that is the way of things in China when any one in power is so cordially disliked. He had an official taster, who ate of his food before every meal since he came to the presidency. His life was one of perpetual terror, because he expected momentarily to be blown to death by bombs. But he died a natural death. It is said that Chinese physicians hastened the end by their practices, because at the last he did not follow the advice of his French physician and went back to "his kind" for aid, in response to the urgent pleadings of his wives. Suddenly, everything was changed. All of the military put on mourning and everything and everyone was sad—or pretended to be. The President of the republic was dead. China loves any sort of death and all of the accompanying ceremonies. So the country, particularly the capital city, went into mourning, while messages came from the South that hostile activities would cease, at least for the time being.

For twenty-one days the country wept over Yuan. One would have thought him a national hero, whereas a few weeks before it was difficult to find any one not absolutely in his employ who had a good word for him. The newspapers ran columns of eulogy and all seemed to be "forgotten."

The day on which I arrived, the day before the funeral, the capital seemed to be unusually dull; but I did not understand that it was looking forward to its holiday on the morrow. I read a two column story in a newspaper, showing the lineup for the parade, and after noting where the Honorable This and That "would bow profoundly before the casket along its route," according to precedent and station, I was amused to read that following the body the immediate family would walk from the Palace to the railroad station "weeping violently." And when the great day arrived the family lived up to the scheduled expectations.

The eldest son was propped up by two servants and seemed barely able to walk at all. With him was a numerous family that resembled a small crowd. Yuan had enough children to have filled all the public offices of the capital at some future time. He knew how to turn a trick that would make money. He was immensely wealthy when he was a provincial governor, and there are reports, exaggerated no doubt, that he counted his profits, as president, by the millions of taels.

"We have promised the Chinese government that nobody will be on the gate while the procession is passing," said an official of the American legation, when I presented myself at the Tartar City wall early in the morning on the day of the funeral. "That would be 'bad luck' and the Chinese do not care to take any chances. So please stand to one side of the middle archway."

I posted myself according to instructions, and without overstating the facts, I saw more people than I had ever seen at one time in my life. They thronged the capital highways and fought for places. The military was out stronger than we have been led to believe that China could exhibit in war time. Thousands of soldiers were in evidence, many of them mounted. They clubbed and whacked at the crowd in a merciless manner. People do not count for much in China, and the military does not spare the limits of its authority in such matters. Finally, we heard the drums from behind the Imperial Palace walls in the Forbidden City and we knew that Yuan had started on his last journey. Outriders, brilliantly costumed, galloped along the avenue, which was closely guarded by soldiers, standing shoulder to shoulder. Then came a big Chinese band, playing (in deference to European custom) Chopin's "Funeral March." Then dignitaries of the army and navy, each in full uniform and surrounded by their staffs. Then hundreds of the government officials in full evening dress, the diplomatic corps in full dress togs and plumes, then more Chinese officials in native costumes. There was another band playing Chopin, then hundreds of officials and the "parade" threatened to become tiresome, but finally an enormous Chinese band, dressed in yellow silk robes, came along, fairly shaking the stones of the wall with metal cymbals, drums (draped in black crepe), flutes that shrieked horribly, stringed instruments that sounded like the moaning of lost souls, and triangle metal affairs that resembled the tum-tum of bronze bells.

This was followed by men who carried great hampers of paper discs with holes punched through the center. The wind was blowing and they caught the breeze and fluttered over the heads of the crowd, eager to get them as souvenirs. It was "money" for Yuan's soul and it was a bribe to the evil spirits. They were obliged to pass through every hole of every piece of tissue before getting at Yuan's soul, so they lost out in the race. We could vouch for that, because millions of the discs were scattered between the palace ground and the station.

Immediately following this came the remains, reposing in a gigantic coffin, the size of an ordinary living-room in an American house, and painted vermillion. It was carried by eighty-two coolies dressed in vermillion silk robes. And directly behind was a great white silk canopy carried by coolies, under which marched the "family" of the late president "weeping violently."

Then followed great pieces of fresh flowers, the tributes of the nations, each carried by separate coolies in silk robes, huge biers upon which were stretched all of the clothing of the deceased, food for him in the next world, his tablet and his photograph.

The police held the crowd in check until the remains reached the station grounds, which were ornately decorated with new straw matting and flowers. Then bedlam broke loose. Every one scrambled for something or other. It was an indescribable sight from above the heads of the crowds. I looked in the papers the next morning to see some account of how many persons

THE LATE YUAN SHIH-K'AI

were wounded or killed in the crush, but Peking papers do not give many of such harrowing details. Life is so cheap, and so many people are born every minute, that a few deaths do not attract much attention.

Business was entirely suspended on the day of Yuan's funeral. All the banks were closed, and it was a national holiday in which everyone seemed to participate by going into the streets and becoming excited. Foreigners kept quite close to the legation quarters, where they belonged. Nobody knew what might happen, but everyone suspected that something was brewing. But on the following morning the banks opened, the shops took up their business as before and things seemed quiet in Peking again. For how long nobody dared to venture a guess, but the new president, Li Yuan-Hung, who had been vice-president, seemed to command the respect of the crowd. Even the agitators were quiet because they understood that not even President Li had been favorable to Yuan, when he was alive and in office. Perhaps better times were coming; at least there was a tendency to give the new man a chance. Li was acceptable to the South, and that was a great problem solved. The South has nothing in common with the North. The peoples of the two sections do not even speak the same language, and excepting when each speaks with the "mandarin" honorifics, they cannot understand one another anymore than if they belonged to different races.

China is full of the republican idea. It is through with emperors and imperial families. It is in a half-dazed condition and does not know exactly what it does want, but it wants some sort of government "by the people" and will doubtless work out its own destiny—at least that is the fairest opinion of men in close touch with the situation.

Although for reasons of state, he has not said anything that could be construed as an official utterance regarding the subject, it is believed that Li Yuan-Hung, President of China, is a Christian convert. Now, when a Christian practically occupies the Dragon Throne of Cathay it is time that the world took notice. It seems almost that China has become a republic in reality—instead of a gigantic nation without any real form of government acknowledged and respected throughout the wide domain. Probably it would not serve his own cause or the cause of Christianity best if he should make a bold proclamation in regard to his religion because it would necessarily antagonize the conservatives, who are believers in more ancient doctrines than those taught by Jesus Christ. This great element could not comprehend what it would mean to them to have a Christian ruler. Even if he were a supreme personality, and otherwise quite acceptable to them, the fact of

"Christianity" would immediately stir up troubles in the already trouble-burdened country. Probably it is better for General Li not to talk too much on this subject. But I have information from a gentleman who knows him well, and who is, indirectly, a member of his official family.

Next in importance to the new president's religion seems to be the fact that General Li did not covet his position; he did not dream of such an exalted station in life, and he was not particularly happy when the great time came and he found himself in the supreme position in China. In other countries- a ruler or president may have his enemies, but they are usually political; in China they are blood enemies. When a big question arises they seem to say: "Your life or mine."

When I was at Canton a Chinese school professor—one who had been a teacher in Manila and spoke English perfectly—and a group of his friends told me about a "mistake" that one of the leading politicians of Canton had made. They calmly explained to me that a man of such great responsibilities had no right to make "mistakes," or if he did, he must expect to pay for them, and pay dearly. His action to which they objected had been adjusted to their complete satisfaction, but they explained that it would be necessary for him to pay for his "mistake" with his life. This seemed bravado and I paid little attention to it at the time, but when I reached Hongkong I read that the official about whom we had talked was assassinated in his own house two days after our conversation. So it seemed to have been a well-known and well-established fact when the men were predicting it. The papers calmly reported that he had paid for his folly. It was as strange a news item as when the newspapers of China deliberately declared that So-and-So was elected to such and such an office yesterday, by the aid of the police and soldiers. Of course everyone knows that this is the condition of things, but it makes rather "frank" newspaper matter. And if all of these things be true of a minor official, they are a hundred times truer of the chief executive. Yuan Shih-k'ai made one "mistake," or at least one shone out beyond all of the others. He declared himself emperor. The people of China had mistrusted him previously, but it was merely mistrust. This "mistake" they would not forgive, although Yuan weakly pleaded that he had been badly advised and had believed that it was the will of the people. But the people knew that this was a lie. He had hoped to found a dynasty to follow the Manchus on the throne of China; all of his republican statements were merely veneer to cover his real desires. This "mistake" the people would not forgive, and it was probably a merciful providence that caused his natural death, because he was so set around by guards, so well fortified within the Forbidden City at Peking that it might have cost tens or hundreds of thousands of lives to have accomplished his death or abdication. And nothing else would have satisfied China. The country was almost unanimous in one thing, more so than it had been on a given point for many years. Yuan must pay for his "mistake" with his life. Natural disease, increased by worry and terror—and Chinese doctors—accomplished the desired end.

So perhaps it was obvious why General Li did not care to accept any of the political offices that were offered to him after the fall of the Manchus and the beginning of the republic. He was essentially a military man. That was his life, and his only great desire was to assist in bringing about a better army for China. He realized as well as any man that if the great swarm of China's male population could be brought under proper discipline, the country would be in a position to "dictate" terms to other nations instead of accepting the humiliating position of being dictated to by Japan and Russia. It was the work to which he had pledged his life.

Early in life Li went to Japan to receive most of his military education. His ambition—a rare thing in China—he wanted to do something for his country, but did not care for personal honors or "rewards." But his brilliant achievements soon attracted attention after he had returned home, and it was impossible for such a man to remain hidden in the background or unknown. At the time of the great revolution in 1911 he was selected by his own troops—a rare honor—as the one man who should lead them against the armies that were clamoring at their gates. That he proved himself a leader of men on this occasion is history. It was his first big chance to show his mettle, and thereafter Li Yuan-Hung was a person to be reckoned with, although he protested that he had acted merely as a military man should act and wished no further glory.

When Hankow and Hanyang were retaken by the imperial forces from the revolutionists many of the leaders of the uprising fled, but not Li Yuan-Hung. He stood his ground, and while doing so he conducted a brilliant and historical correspondence with Yuan Shih-k'ai, who had been recalled to Peking by the Manchus as the one man in the empire who could save them and their cause. General Li was largely instrumental in arranging the peace conference at Shanghai, in which Tang Shao-yi and Wu Ting-fang reached the agreement that changed the form of government in China from a monarchy to a republic. Events were moving rapidly and he was moving with them, although his friends say that he always vainly tried to keep in the background, aiming not to appear to be an important figure, although his was one of the important brains in all deliberations.

After the abdication of the Manchus, Yuan became president by his own strategy. "With Li it was a different matter. The people felt that under a republic they had certain "rights," so one of the first of them to be exercised was the demand that General Li be made vice-president, chief of general staff and Tutuh of Hupeh. It is said that he was never Yuan's friend, did not approve of his methods and policies, and never pretended to be friendly to him. But the people wanted him in the vice-presidential chair, so he accepted it and had practically five years of administrative work before he was called to the chief position of state at fifty-two years of age, by the death of Yuan. The country has had its "eye" on him for several years. When an independent government was established in May, 1916, he was elected president by the revolutionists. When the monarchial movement was at its height and Yuan's fate hung in the balance, he gave a fine exhibition of his character.

Yuan sent a group of monarchists, his henchmen men, to make a formal call upon Li and they tried to present their cause in a light that would win his approval, which Yuan felt would mean much to the cause. The men were ushered into the vice-president's reception room. After a few minutes the vice-president entered, a calm and dignified figure. He stood before them silently as they urged their monarchical cause. They even told him that he would receive the highest title that the new emperor could confer upon a subject, "The Brave Prince," and the emoluments of that rank, which were not to be despised by a "commoner." When they had finished with their "temptation," General Li made no reply, but bowed courteously and strode out of the room. And all of these things did not tend to make him "popular" with the coterie around Yuan, but they feared him, because they knew that the people believed in him. So it happened that there was no more general rejoicing at Yuan's death than over the fact that under the constitution General Li took his oath of office and moved into a palace of the Forbidden City to begin his rule. He did not go to Yuan's palace. There are so many palaces within this great wall that practically every high and mighty person may literally "take his choice." Yuan's palace was sealed with strips of paper after his body was taken out for its last journey to Honan, and it is commonly reported in Peking that his numerous family took so much loot and furnishings with them that the place would have been barely fit for the reception of a new president.

For a few days there was peace. Even the South seemed to be satisfied with Li. But it was the general belief that the South was merely waiting to see what would be his policies. I had the privilege of talking to several men in Peking who know China well, and I received various opinions and prophecies regarding the future. None doubted the good intentions of President Li, but most of them were doubtful concerning the future. The best informed men with whom I talked delivered themselves of two opinions:

The first: "China is naturally divided into two parts by the Yangtze-kiang River. It is two countries instead of one. The people speak different languages—and they are different people. What will be agreeable to one, will never suit the other. It was possible to keep them in check under the Manchu murderous and despotic rule, because it was a rule without toleration. It will not be possible, perhaps, under republican rule. The quicker the country is divided into two parts, with separate rulers and government, the quicker will come peace and prosperity for China."

The second: "There is but one way to establish permanent peace in China. The great nations of the world should appoint a joint commission to rule China for a period of ten or twenty years, solemnly vowing to return the reins of government to the Chinese at the end of a given period, when China is capable of running her own affairs. During that time, Western civilization might become well established, and at the end of that time China would have produced a man, or men, thoroughly capable of keeping order."

CHAPTER X

IMPERIAL PURPLE METROPOLIS

IN all the world there is no such city as Peking. In various parts of China there may be imitations of the capital, just as all the cities scattered along the banks of the Nile seem to be miniature Cairos. Many cities have been the capital during some period of history, and as tradition, convention or necessity seem to require the partial or total seclusion of the ruler most of them were and still are surrounded by massive walls, penetrated by ornate gates, usually painted in brilliant colors. Lesser rulers of kingdoms and provinces followed the imperial custom to a degree, and seemed to feel that there was not only greater safety, but also a dignity befitting their stations if their dwellings were set within great banks of masonry, and sometimes within walls that were entirely surrounded by higher walls. Yet none of the others approach the grandeur of what has often been called "Imperial Purple Peking." It is no longer imperial, because the empire no longer exists and within the massive walls of the Forbidden City a mighty stronghold well in the center of the "Tartar City" and "Chinese City," the dual city being surrounded by walls enclosing an area of twenty-five square miles and thirty miles in circumference, resides the President of the vast Flowery Republic. But just as one still thinks of this inner heart of China as the "Purple Forbidden Palace," so he thinks of Peking as the Imperial Purple City. It is the proud queen of the Orient, to many people the most wonderful city on earth, and even to the casual visitor one of those rare places of earth that quickly stamp themselves on the memory and never depart. To the Westerner, it may be a weird enclosure of mysteries, but the veils are being drawn aside with the passing of the years. Lucky is the curious traveler today! He may penetrate into the corners that were forbidden to the foreign kings who came this way in an earlier day. And while it may be human nature to care to pass beyond walls that have guarded their secrets jealously for centuries, there is a joy in seeing the Peking of the streets, the shops, restaurants and hotels that might not come from a similar visit to any other city.

It is popularly believed that one who has no connection with, the legations, or who is not fortified with powerful credentials from home, either of official or commercial significance, will not think much of the "society" or the social life of the capital, which is about as brilliant as that at any capital of the world. Foreign society in Peking is supposed to be very self-sufficient and "exclusive." Just as China has learned many lessons from its vast experiences, so Peking society has learned to be singularly cautious. The Chinese capital at one time and another seems to have been the most popular rendezvous in the world for the flotsam and jetsam of the European and American continents. Society has "taken up" this and that sprig of Russian nobility, the American "millionaire," German army officer or Spanish grandee only to find out a little later that he was an adventurer and outcast from his own country, a pretender to distinctions which he never enjoyed at home. Even the legations, themselves, have been deceived, until they have thrown out social barriers that are somewhat difficult to surmount. Peking, however, is counted an unusually attractive temporary residence, and travelers are coming to make it a city for an extended sojourn, like Paris, Berlin or Rome. Conditions have changed in the past few years, and while living expenses are greater that in Europe or America, if one is to enjoy "all the comforts of home" while living in the midst of "the Middle Ages of Europe made visible," it is now possible to find the conveniences of the West as regards food and lodging, at the same time partaking of the luxury of living in the Orient, which undeniably casts its spell. Over anyone who does not deny himself the enjoyment that comes from forgetting previously formed ideas and prejudices.

Quite apart from this social life, however, into which the usual traveler could not and does not care to enter, there is a crowning climax to the Chinese excursion in beautiful Peking. One's first impression may be that it is a county rather than a city. There are great vacant spaces within the walls necessarily passed in going to the principal points of interest from any given point, so that sight-seeing often becomes a lengthy journey from the hotel; but they will never be tedious journeys. The streets are always thronged with a colorful mass of human beings, every group of which will have its distinct and separate interest for the stranger. Some one seems always going to his bridal feast, or returning from a burial, preparing for the celebration of a festival, or paying honor to some departed saint or sinner,

BEYOND THE WALLS, PEKING

and always with prescribed processional and costumes. Peking streets, to the newly-arrived foreigner, seem to be the constant and kaleidoscopic breaking up or formation of a circus parade. Perhaps the foreign residents become accustomed to these things in time, and yet it is not unusual for the foreigner's telephone bell to ring a hasty call to all friends and acquaintances to assemble at a certain point to see some unusual and unexpected parade, ceremonial or celebration. The foreigner never understands the Pekingese. He dwells in their world perhaps, but he is not of it, and finally arrives at the point where he is surprised at nothing. It is always the unexpected that is happening, and it is happening so frequently and constantly that when nothing else calls for his time and attention the visitor may summon a motor or rikisha and fare forth almost certain to encounter something in human life that his eyes have never before beheld, something likely as not that he had never before believed existed in the Twentieth Century.

Little wonder then that many tourists and travelers who enter China from the North never care to venture far beyond the gates of Peking, and thus deceive themselves into believing that because they have seen so much they have seen China. Peking is not China, as so many capitals are fairly representative of a country; but Peking has an individual charm and fascination that is far-reaching. And they may become deceptive, because not even the most casual tourist should imagine that less than one million of China's vast population could be fairly representative of the remaining millions that dwell beyond the confines of the capital city. Peking may lure people from all the country, and it may be the most brilliant jewel in the great diadem of China, where statesmen, financiers and scholars are attempting to fuse the conflicting ideas of the East and the West and by quickening the heart action send renewed life and vigor to remote extremities, but, on the last analysis, it is merely one of the many capitals where this or similarly difficult experiments have been tried. Perhaps it is the most interesting of all of them, and perhaps a part of this fascination comes from the fact that it is the most recent capital, for here as recently as 1908 dwelt the Son of Heaven, the sacred personage who joined his ancestors in death, leaving the most ancient throne in the world, one that is not likely to be occupied again so long as time endures. One cannot look from his hotel window, or from a rikisha, toward the yellow wall of his late residence—at least one who has a drop of romance in his veins—and not thank the lucky stars that have guided him to the fantastic, almost unbelievable capital that surrounds the palace of the late Kuang-Hsu.

Chinese Priests at Prayer

The railway stations lie beyond the walls. Trains entering the city where the emperor dwelt was unthinkable at the time the railways were built, and that leading across country from Hankow originally came to a stop far beyond the city, but it has now stretched itself close to the great Cheng-yang-men Gate, through which one passes and quickly comes upon the Foreign Concessions that are scattered along the well paved and shaded avenue with the flags of the respective nations flying—great walled enclosures guarded by their own soldiers. This Legation Quarter, known to Chinese as the *Tung-Chiao-Min-Hsiang*, dates from 1689, when China signed a treaty with Russia, the first time that she had affixed her signature to such a document, indicating that she recognized it to be on an equal footing with herself, and when Russia stationed her representative in Peking, building for him what was long known as the "Russian House," Great Britain followed the example in 1861, closely followed by France, the United States, Italy, Germany, Holland, and other countries. The Legation Quarter of Peking figured as an important feature of the world news and interest when it was besieged by the Boxers in 1900, and its inhabitants narrowly escaped extermination through the timely arrival of the troops of the various powers. In accordance with the peace concluded after the suppression of the Boxers, the legation compounds were placed under heavy guards of their respective troops, the gate to each compound being guarded as if it were the approach to a royal palace.

Peking has changed materially during the last few years. A fine water system reaches to the principal sections and the roads that were notoriously the worst to be found in any large city in the world have been paved or are being paved. The common means of conveyance is the rikisha, but automobiles are gaining in favor and are convenient for the long trips across the city. Palanquins are available for going into the narrow, crowded streets. Natives are fond of riding in the Peking cart, a springless two-wheeled vehicle in which passengers sit on the floor and move towards destination at a snail's pace. These carts will carry ten passengers, and as they are usually drawn by a single small horse, not even the leisure-loving native would patronize them if occasion prompted him to hurry, which would be seldom if ever, unless he had an appointment with a foreigner.

Excepting for a comparatively short period, Peking has been the capital of China since the Thirteenth Century. The emperor, Yung-lo, noting its importance (1421) removed from Nanking, whence the first Ming emperors had taken the imperial seat; but under various names Peking dates to most

LAMA TEMPLE, PEKING

ancient times and was the residence of petty rulers before it became the capital of all China. Thus in 2000 B.C., it was known as Yu-chou, and in the Eighth Century B.C., it was Yen. In ancient days it was surrounded by a mud wall, but with the opening of the Grand Canal, which brought it into direct communication with the great rice districts of the interior, and with the prestige gained from having become the imperial residence, blocks of stone soon took the place of the mud fortification, and the gorgeous capital attracted the admiration of the world.

The day after Yuan's funeral I mapped out an itinerary for myself, which, no doubt, had been prompted by watching the spectacular procession that moved from the gates of the Forbidden City along the avenue over which I had taken a stand. As so frequently before, it had seemed to me that China was a country without a religion, yet in this cortege of the late executive were representatives of several religions. Yuan himself had said: "I am unequivocally a Confucianist, but nothing but Christian ethics can save China." But Christianity was not officially represented in the parade, while several other religions were there with banners, colors or costumes to distinguish them. In a way, they mingled as religions seem to mingle in many Chinese temples. Perhaps they all make "concessions" to ancestor worship, as did Christianity in an earlier day, although it declines to do so at the present time. Thus, one may enter a Confucian temple and see a figure of Buddha, or a Buddhist temple and come upon the sayings of the Chinese sage, or even the utterances of Lao-Tze, the founder of Taoism, or Meng-tse, known to the Western world in the Latinized form of Mencius, who taught a gospel of "benevolence, wisdom and propriety." All were there, the Confucianists and the Lamaists particularly prominent; and there seemed to be no argument as to the status of one or the other. In fact, nobody seemed to care. It was strangely demonstrative of what I had observed elsewhere, and what I had surmised was the case from previous reading, when striving to ascertain something about the "religion of China." China has had no great religious wars corresponding to the Crusades of the Western world, there have been no persecutions for religion's sake corresponding to those that followed the beginnings of Christianity in Europe, or which followed the Reformation. Probably there was nothing to fight for, no definitely held faith, so there was no fighting. But religion has played an important role in China as elsewhere. Arrived in the capital of the country, I resolved to find out something concerning its practice, even if in the most casual manner of the hurried observer and inquirer.

First, the guide took me to a Buddhist temple, then to one where Lamaism is practised, later, to a Confucian shrine, and finally, we penetrated to the great Temple of Heaven, seemingly the most remarkable place of worship in China, and later to the Temple of Agriculture. It was a full day spent amid holy places, and yet I came back to the hotel with feelings of admiration for the architecture, with a thought of gratitude to certain priests, who had not resented my presence in sacred incisures; but the day's pilgrimage was one very unlikely to inspire reverence for the places I had seen, or the persons with whom I had talked, most of whom seemed to be much more concerned with the collection of fees, which were exacted from "infidels," than with their holy office. In fact, one priest, who was seated at a desk in the temple, writing prayers on strips of paper, which the devout purchased and burned on the altar, or carried away to their homes, answered my inquiry in excellent English: "These are prayers which the peasants believe will bring them luck if they paste them on the doorposts of their homes. They believe it, but I don't."

One of the first things that impressed itself upon my mind was the similarity between the outward forms of the Roman Catholic ceremonial and that in a Buddhist or Lamaist temple; but this was noted not only by missionaries of the Christian Church, on their first visits to Thibet and China, but also by students of comparative religions who have given the matter serious study that has resulted in many volumes of controversy. Yet Sven Hedin, who noted this similarity during his journey into Thibet, was obliged to cite many references to prove his contentions. H. H. Wilson, the Sanskrit scholar, says: "They all agree in the resemblance between the religion of the Lamas and Christianity."

Dr. T. W. Rhys Davids, another authority, says: "Lamaism indeed with its shaven priests, its bells and rosaries, its images and holy water and gorgeous dresses; its services with double choirs and processions and creeds and mystic rites and incense, in which the laity are spectators only; its worship of the double virgin and of saints and angels, its images, its idols and its pictures; its huge monasteries and its gorgeous cathedrals, its powerful hierarchy, its cardinals, its Pope, bears outwardly at least a strong resemblance to Romanism, in spite of the essential difference of its teachings and its mode of thought."

The resemblance was noticed by the monks of the Middle Ages, and many Catholic missionaries have written exhaustively upon the subject, arguing that instead of proving that Christianity borrowed anything from the older religion it proves conclusively that Lamaism, a form of Buddhism, and Buddhism itself, recognized the superiority of Christianity and incorporated the forms of worship in a way that would barely be recognized.

Buddhists go much further than this, however, and note a strange similarity between the legends that surround the founder of their religion and the Christian gospels, according to Luke and John. For example, the stories regarding the mother of Buddha are strangely like the descriptions of the Virgin Mary in the Christian gospels. Wise men came to pay homage to both children soon after their birth, there was the presentation of both in the Temple, both fasted and went into the wilderness, both seemed more concerned with the salvation of the meek and lowly than of the rich, and both selected their disciples from among the humble classes. As to these "resemblances," however, most of them have been swept away by "higher criticism." Jesus Christ fasted, and so did Buddha; but so also did Moses (Exodus xxxiv: 28). Jesus was tempted by the Devil, and Buddha was tempted in similar fashion by Mara, who brought troops of beautiful women, who sang and danced and endeavored to cause him to break his vows of chastity; but other prophets were tempted, even before the Buddha was born. And as "higher criticism" disposes of these points in Western countries, so the "intellectuals" of China are coming to regard Buddhism as no faith at all, but rather as a system of philosophy. An hour's conversation with one who knows his subject well, is likely at least to have the effect of embarrassing the Westerner, who has thought of the people who follow the teachings of Buddha—one-third of the human race—as idolaters. One of them called my attention to the fact that the Buddha is a saint of the Roman Catholic Church, and referred me to Max Müller's "Chips from a German Workshop," if I doubted his word, or cared to inform myself further concerning the canonization ceremonies at Rome.

It is not correct, however, to speak of Buddha as if it were the name of the founder of the religion. As we speak of Jesus Christ, instead of Jesus the Christ, this form has come into common use. Buddha, however, is an official title, and it is correct to speak of him as Sakya-muni the Buddha.

The father of Buddha was the powerful Rajah Suddhodana, and his mother, the daughter of a neighboring chieftain, was forty years of age at the time of his birth. It is recorded that she died within a few days of this great event, that having given birth to such a sacred personage she should have no more children. The *Lalita-Vistara*, a Sanskrit work, has much to say regarding her qualities and perfection, and also describes Buddha as a young

WHITE JADE AND GOLD BUDDHA, PEKING

man. He had a "large skull. His forehead is broad, his eyes dark. His forty teeth are equal and beautifully white, his skin is fine and of the color of gold. His limbs are like those of Ainaya, the king of the gazelles. His head is well shaped; his hair black and curly."

It appears that he awakened to religious ideals when he was about thirty years of age, although there is no way of determining the exact date in regard to any of these things, as the oriental savants place his birth in 1027 B.C., and European scholars prefer the date 653 B.C. He was married and his wife gave birth to one child before he started away into the jungle. He took one glance at his offspring, declaring that he would not return until he had become a Buddha (Enlightened One) and left the palace, accompanied only by his chariot-driver, whom he later sent back to his father bearing everything of value in his possession. He went to Brahman teachers for a period and then into retirement in the Vindhya Mountains, where he followed the life of a strict ascetic for six years. When he returned to the region around Benares he was accompanied by fifty or sixty disciples and taught and preached. "Word came to his father of the son's return and the family went out to meet him, urging him to come back to the palace and resume his rightful station in life. But he preferred to beg for a living, and not even an appeal from his father to visit his abandoned wife and child seems to have had much effect, for although he did see his wife, she became a Buddhist nun, when the founder of the religion, somewhat against his will, established the order for females.

When he was eighty-two years of age Buddha started on a journey of over a hundred miles north of Benares. He appeared to be much fatigued during the journey and when he arrived at his destination he threw himself upon a couch and his disciples observed many supernatural signs that foretold the coming of some great event. During the night, when they visited his couch, to see how he was resting, he "had fallen into the profound ecstasy of the elect from which no man returns or is born again; no, not one." The disciples reported afterward that they heard music chanted by celestial choirs and saw forms floating in the air.

Not long after his death, missionaries carried his gospel into Thibet, where it was quickly received by multitudes. It seems not to have penetrated into China until the year 67 A.D. Shortly before, the Emperor, Ming-Ti, dispatched messengers to India with instructions to learn what they could of the religion of Buddha and to bring back Buddhist missionaries. They returned with the teachers and brought a horse-load of Scriptures. When the horse died, it was buried on the spot now marked by the "White Horse

Arch in Temple of Confucius, Peking

Temple," at Ho-nan City, the first temple erected to the worship of Buddha in the land of Confucius. Before long, the Sutras were translated into Chinese. India sent more missionaries and teachers, and the converts to Buddhism in China visited India for further instruction. The Emperor was a convert and a strong believer in the new doctrine, and with court favor the religion spread rapidly.

Lamaism, a form of Buddhism, came into China from Thibet in the Thirteenth Century, the great Kublai Khan making a Thibetan priest his chaplain. For a time, the corrupt form of the faith took precedence over purer Buddhism. It is difficult in a short time to gain even a superficial knowledge of the teachings of Buddhism, which has now divided itself into as many sects as Christian Protestantism. J. M. Kennedy, in "The Philosophies and Religions of the East," sums up briefly what may be taken as the fundamentals and basis of the religion:

1 Misery invariably accompanies existence.
2 Every type of existence, whether of man or of animals, results from passion or desire.
3 There is no freedom from existence but by the annihilation of desire.
4 Desire may be destroyed by following the eight paths leading to Nirvana.

In a few words, the "Eight Paths" are: right views, right feelings, right words, right behavior, right exertion, right obedience, right memory and right meditations.

Unlike Christianity, however, Buddhism has no Savior as a mediator; but teaches that man must depend upon himself alone to attain supreme moral perfection. And no claim is made that any of the writings of Buddha, or the words from him reported by his disciples, were divinely inspired. His message was from a leader of men to mankind, and when it reached China, Korea and Japan, it seems to have been the first message of a life existing after death.

Kung-fu-tze, whose name is better known to the Western world in its Latinized form of Confucius, seems to have been the fountain head of all the Chinese wisdom during the last two thousand years, and Confucianism has exercised a greater power for good upon the nation than any other system of philosophy. He was not the founder of a religion and doubtless never claimed to be, but he made a collection of the classical writings that served as an ethical code, and by the example of his own life won devoted followers, who have been numerous during all succeeding centuries. In fact, Yuan Shih-k'ai, the late president, was not only an ardent Confucianist, but the first republican regime is believed to have done everything in its power to renew the nation's interest in what is doubtless a system that has outgrown its usefulness. Confucius was born 551 B.C. and comparatively little authentic information has come to us concerning his youth, excepting that his father died when he was very young, that his mother was poor and that he was married when he was nineteen. When he was twenty-two or twenty-three years of age he became a teacher. In 510 B.C. he was governor of Chung-tu, where his teaching and personal conduct led to a great reformation among his immediate subjects. About 497 B.C. he gathered several disciples and started on long tours through the country, extending his teaching to peoples of other provinces. In 479 B.C. he died, and his followers compiled his sayings into books that became what has been considered the Chinese model system of morality. These books have been the basis of native scholarship and have been more available to the masses than the Buddhist canon which in Chinese is said to consist of nearly fifteen hundred works and over five thousand volumes, many of which have never been collated by European scholars. Nearly two centuries after Confucius, appeared Meng-tse, known to us as Mencius, who was an eloquent expounder of the Confucian system and whose message seems to have been that man should collect and utilize benevolence, wisdom and propriety. A temple was erected to Confucius at his native town of Chu-fou, and by imperial order similar temples were erected in most of the large cities of the country, where supreme homage was paid to his memory.

Taoism, another important system in China, usually dates back to Lao-tze, born at Honan in 604 B.C., although it seems likely that alchemists and geomancers formulated their own devices and ascribed them to the teachings of the famous man whose name gave them added prestige. Lao-tze seems to have taught that men should not strive, but should always pursue a course of inaction, because things will come to a successful conclusion without effort. "Never interfere and let things take their natural course" was his rather aristocratic echo of Confucian doctrine. But the Taoists began to claim to make "pills of immortality," and painted beautiful word pictures of the "Island in the Eastern Sea," where the elixir- of life might be found. One who had a full knowledge of Taoist mysteries, it was declared, might ascend bodily to heaven on the wings of a stork. The religion received an impetus from the superstitious emperor, Shih-huang-ti, in the Third Century,

B.C., who actually dispatched a commission to the "Eastern Sea" in search of the mythical island and its herb of immortality. This religion was popular with many succeeding rulers, Emperor Chen-tsung of Sung having caused the building of a colossal monastery, where twenty thousand Taoist priests were gathered for the practice of weird rites. But with the coming to China of Kublai Khan, the religion lost imperial favor, owing to the precedence of Lamaism, but it was later revived and remains today, although most of the ritual and ceremonial of the present has been borrowed from Buddhism.

Christianity was introduced into China as early as 625 A.D., by the Nestorian fathers, who seem to have gained considerable influence, judging from the inscriptions on a monument set up in 782 A.D. at Si-an, and excavated in modern times. But the date usually considered the one that marks the real beginning of Christian missionary work in China is 1580, when Matteo Ricci, an Italian Jesuit, preached throughout the region between Canton and Nanking, over a period of twenty years. When he went to Peking he was thoughtful enough to take along a set of astronomical instruments, by means of which he won the favor of the Emperor, who gave Ricci and other missionaries who had joined him a residence in the Inner City and ground on which to build a church, which became what is now known as "South Cathedral." In addition to their spiritual work, the Roman Catholic missionaries have performed many good works for China, such as map-making, and, despite periodical persecutions, they have held their own and are represented in most of the cities of the country. The introduction of Protestantism is usually dated to the arrival of the Englishman, Robert Morrison, who, after tremendous labor, published an Anglo-Chinese dictionary and was active in the work of translating the Bible into Chinese. American missionaries began to arrive about 1830, and today all sects and denominations are represented and they have had much to do with the present period of enlightenment that is evident in all parts of the country.

Christianity as taught in the Gospels, and religion as defined in the Old Testament, seem to be divided from Chinese religions by a chasm difficult to cross, and yet, as hinted, there is much in Buddhism that corresponds to Christian teaching, and there is a strange conformity of passages in the ancient Chinese sacred books with the Mosaic record. Emile Bard has compiled a collection of these in his "Chinese Life," from which the following are fair examples:

The Temple of Heaven, Peking

"There is life that did not receive life."—*Lie-tse*.

"He who is himself the beginning and the end, created heaven and earth."—*Tchuang-tse*.

"The inordinate desire for knowledge, caused the downfall of the human race."—*Ho-nan-tse*.

"Waters spread over the face of the earth covering all things."—*Confucius*.

Of all Peking places of worship, however, of all temples and shrines in China, and perhaps of the many that I have visited in various parts of the world, from the "High Place" of the Nabbatæeans in the Arabian Desert, to Philæ in Egypt and the Temple of Jupiter at Baalbek, or St. Peter's at Rome and the Mosque of Omar at Jerusalem, none have left such a vivid impression as the Temple of Heaven and the Altar of Heaven, where the "called of God an High Priest, after the order of Melchisedec" (Hebrews v: 10) the Son of Heaven paid homage to the Supreme Being at least once a year, so long as he occupied the Dragon Throne. The Mohammedans point to a little altar in the Church of the Holy Sepulcher at Jerusalem and say that it is the center of the universe. But even the smiling guides and priests admit that it is not so; such a place would be worthy of a more beautiful chapel, shrine or monument. The Chinese point to a circular slab of white marble in the center of the great Altar of Heaven, which has the blue dome of the sky for a canopy, and say not only that here is the center of the world, a matter that is open to debate, but also that in this spot the emperors of China, as earthly vice-regents, communed with the Supreme Being, a declaration that barely admits of argument. In these later days even the Chinese seemingly have neglected this Holy of Holies, to which no infidels were admitted in an earlier day. In his sublime egotism, but with a full knowledge of what is latent in the Chinese mind, the late Yuan Shih-k'ai promised his people that if they recognized him as emperor he would go to the Temple of Heaven and sacrifice. If there was anything in the world that would convince them that he was a true Chinaman, and anything that was likely to cause them to believe that the Supreme Being was reconciled to the latest seizure, of the Dragon Throne, it was this, and Yuan realized it. But often led to enthusiasm by similar "concessions" of usurpers, the people were unmoved by Yuan's appeals to their religious superstitions. The Manchu emperor, Kuang-hsu, had ascended to his imperial ancestors on the back of the Great Dragon and the Chinese seemed to doubt if the Supreme Being would receive the customary homage from the commoner from Honan, who had assumed the

Brazier at Altar of Heaven

vice-regency. At least, he was not given the opportunity to mount the great altar and assume the position of High Priest. President by his own cunning, strategy and by force of circumstances, yes; but Yuan was never a sacred personage, even in the eyes of his admirers.

So the weeds and shrubs crop through the marvelous white marble pavement and splendidly carved balustrades of the Altar of Heaven. A progressive executive may see to it that this splendid religious monument is repaired and preserved for future generations; but, likely as not, it has been the scene of the last great ceremonial, and, while devout Chinese may prostrate themselves before the tablet of the Supreme Divinity or the tablets of the emperors in the great blue-roofed pagoda-like Temple, the day of imperial sacrifice is over and worshipers will not follow the officiating officer, the High Priest, as they make their prostrations and recite prayers. The sheep, descendants of those formerly selected for sacrifice, graze at random through the great walled enclosure of three miles. The silk does not pass the gate, nor the rice, wine and food. The dancers and the numerous orchestra remain beyond the walls, and the great furnaces of green porcelain are cool, because no fire is kindled beneath their ovens. The vast cast-iron braziers, where prayers were burned, have no ashes to remind one of the last ceremonial. Hawk-like guardians stand at the Great Gate, through which the emperor passed when he came on his nocturnal mission from the Purple Palace, and fling open the portals when they see a rikisha deposit a visitor who carries a fee in his hand.

There is a long, paved avenue leading through an evergreen grove, as through a long city park. At times it is possible to see the cupola-like peak of blue tiles which pierces the skyline above the Temple of Heaven, but as there are many walls, buildings and bridges to be passed en route, and as everything remains about as it was when the great enclosure was created for the prayers of the Emperor to the Supreme God, in the Fifteenth Century, the reader will not only visit the numerous points of interest but will like to recall in passing something of the nature of the ceremonial which was discontinued in recent years. The time of the imperial visit was on the night of December 22, and on special occasions of drought or famine, when he made a special appeal for his suffering subjects. The emperor left the palace after sunset, and in olden times was drawn over the route in a cart pulled by elephants, a large herd of which was kept in the imperial stables, specially constructed to provide quarters for thirty or more. In later years, because the climate of Peking was not favorable to elephants, the Son of Heaven was carried in a litter, accompanied by about two thousand courtiers, two hundred and thirty-four musicians and the same number of dancers. A Taoist priest walked ahead of him, bearing an ancient copper image about fifteen inches in height, upon which he kept his eyes, until he reached the Temple Gate. Once arrived there, he inspected the sheep, deer—and, in early days, the horses—that were later to be sacrificed during the ceremony.

The first building visited was the temple called the "Hall of Fasting," where he sat for some time in contemplation and prayer, after which he took off the robes of his station as emperor and put on the robes of his office as the High Priest of China. He passed along the white marble paving to the magnificent temple where he paid homage to the tablet of Shang-ti (Supreme God) to the tablets of the emperors and to those of the gods of heaven and earth, wind, cloud, rain and lightning. Then he approached the Altar of Heaven, a triple terraced white marble elevation that is two hundred feet wide at the base and which rises about fifteen feet from the ground. The posts and balconies of each terrace are ornately carved and the upper surface is paved with marble blocks forming nine centric circles, the innermost consisting of nine blocks and that on the outside of eighty-one blocks. On the central stone, which is a perfect circle, and which the visitor is now invited to tap with his walking-stick or umbrella handle to hear the hollow echo from beneath, which our guide assured us was proof that beneath it was a well "that reaches to the center of the earth," the emperor knelt, surrounded by his numerous court. White and blue silk, pieces of blue jade, a symbol of heaven, and cups of rice wine were brought to the High Priest; the cup of wine was drunk (strangely in the manner of the Jewish Paschal sacrifice) and a piece of blue wood on which a prayer was written was placed before him and he chanted the words, whereupon he knocked his forehead on the stone and the choir of musicians struck up a hymn of thanksgiving and the dancers began to move about in slow, rhythmic posturings still characteristic of assistants at oriental ceremonials in the temple. The silk was burned, so was the blue prayer tablet, and the animals, which were slaughtered and placed in the oven, after their hides had been buried. The Son of Heaven, emperor and High Priest, stood erect on the altar with all his princes and officials and watched the sacred flames as they mounted to the midnight sky, while acolytes passed among the company burning incense.

This must have been one of the impressive religious spectacles of the world, one that was more mysterious than the gathering of the cardinals around the Pope in the Sistine chapel, the processions of the hierarchy in the presence of the Dalai Lama at Lhassa, or even the Mohammedan pilgrims making their circuit of the Kaaba at Mecca. One thinks of the Roman Coliseum lighted with flaming torches, as the audience looked into the vast arena to witness the games. It is true that features of the celebration were "heathenish," when viewed from the distance of our own time; but there was little to suggest the worship of carved images, as the entire Altar and Temple are singularly lacking in these and given more to blank walls and vast spaces. The image held before the eye of the emperor was not "worshiped," but was intended to direct his attention from all worldly things, inspiring him to contemplation of the Great Unseen and All Powerful.

It is a short rikisha ride beyond the walls of the Temple of Heaven to similar walls and a similar enclosure of about three hundred acres in which is the Temple of Agriculture. The park in the latter, however, unlike the other, is usually much occupied by natives, who like to make a recreation ground of any temple courtyard, and find the shade of the trees in the park a comfortable place to spend the afternoon with friends, drinking tea and smoking. As noted in an earlier chapter, however, my visit to the Temple of Agriculture was cut short by the terrible odor and the explanation of the guide that the remains of General Chong reposed in the building awaiting a propitious day for burial. But on the balcony of a tea-house within the grounds, I listened to a guide relate the interesting story of this temple, where, as at the other, the emperor was accustomed to come at stated intervals, performing ceremonies almost as complicated in form as when he presided at the Temple of Heaven as High Priest. Before the Son of Heaven set out on a journey he came here to offer sacrifice to the gods of the mountains, valleys, rivers and plains. On other occasions he made similar sacrifice to the gods of snow, wind and rain; and when there was desired rain, snow or wind, he made another trip to offer prayers of thanksgiving. Some of the ritualistic prayers delivered after a successful harvest were strangely similar to the annual proclamation of the President of the United States preceding Thanksgiving Day and declaring it a legal holiday. Here also, it was the custom for the emperor to take off his royal robes, assume the role of a peasant, follow an imperial-yellow plow, drawn by an ox draped in yellow and led by an official also dressed in yellow garments. He plowed nine furrows and the princes followed him and scattered the seed, while imperial choristers chanted anthems in praise of husbandry. It is said that this spectacular ceremony dates from the Emperor Shun, who flourished in 2200 B.C., and being a practical farmer, was particularly concerned with

The Altar of Heaven

agriculture, which has always held a place of importance and dignity in China. The example was followed by succeeding emperors. When they had plowed, it was the signal for all others to do likewise. The practice was not unlike that of the Empress of Japan feeding her silk worms, a matter of sufficient importance at the present time to be chronicled in the newspapers of the capital. If Her Majesty tends silk worms, then it is a dignified and popular pastime for other women, with the result that the country yields a larger quantity of silk than might have been the case without the illustrious encouragement. If the Son of Heaven could place his hands to the plow and turn the furrow, if the noble princes could walk behind him and scatter grain, why should not his subjects be willing to do likewise? And if they did, there would be food enough for all, one of the most important problems in all China for the officials to wrestle with two thousand years before the dawn of the Christian era, just as it is today.

CHAPTER XI

IN FORBIDDEN PALACES

THINGS have moved rapidly in China in the last few years, and thus were undergoing a great change during the days preceding my visit. The Empress Dowager, whom a diplomat once described as "the only man in China," is dead and lies in her tomb. The unfortunate young emperor is dead. The Manchus have been driven from the throne forever and Yuan Shih-k'ai, the President, lies with his ancestors in Honan. The present Manchu emperor, now about ten years of age, with a few members of his family, is caged up in a corner of the Forbidden City, and is little more than a state prisoner. General Li Yuan-Hung, an enlightened executive, shares few of the fears and superstitions of his predecessors, so my application to be permitted to visit the almost unknown precincts of the Forbidden City and the Imperial Summer Palace was quickly answered by receipt of the much envied document that opened doors usually so impassable to foreigners a few years ago.

So I spent a day at Wan-Shou-Shan, the wonderful pile that rises on the banks of the Kun-ming-hu, a clear fresh water lake about eleven miles to the west of Peking. It was the favorite residence of the late Dowager Empress, and by paying rather insignificant fees demanded by the wretched palace attendants, I was enabled to tread on what was "holy ground" only five or six years ago, and to go over the scenes of the principal events in the life of one of the most remarkable of women in the past century, old Hsi-Tai-Hou, the she-devil who sat on the Dragon Throne and conducted affairs with a high-handed authority, much of her own making, but rarely equaled elsewhere on earth.

Tsze Hsi An, or Hsi-Tai-Hou did not like the Forbidden City of Peking and she made any excuse to retire to her country palace, which was destroyed by the English as a "lesson" to the Chinese in 1860, thus giving her the opportunity to rebuild it in all the barbaric splendor that a whimsical old despot could conceive, one who reveled in power and money and seemed to live only to gratify her own desires.

An automobile called for me at an early hour in the morning. It seemed almost that I had been summoned to court, for the old Empress often held audiences at six o'clock in the morning, and her courtiers, or others to whom she gave audience, who spent the night in Peking, were obliged to leave their homes at two or three o'clock in the morning, in order to be present at the appointed time. But Hsi-Tai-Hou did not care about inconvenience to anyone else. She had made herself supreme by overcoming all obstacles. She remained supreme until the end. Every one acted exactly as she commanded. If they did not, they received from her the silken cord (an invitation to commit suicide) poison was placed in their food, or they were made aware of her displeasure by slapping them in the face, thus degrading and humiliating them. According to "backstairs" gossip, which I heard, she even went so far as to administer a good resounding slap in the face to her generals, if they displeased her. I was well-prepared for the visit, because the evening before I spent four hours with the husband of the Manchu Princess Der Ling, who was for two years first lady-in-waiting to Her Majesty, acknowledged to be a prime favorite at court, and the author of a fascinating volume on her experiences in the Forbidden City. But while assuredly Der Ling told the truth, she did not tell all of the truth. There were too many people still living when she wrote. She is said to be planning another volume that will be more "personal" than the first. She has a fund of unbelievable stories that are likely to cause the world to sit up and take notice when they are printed. Her husband gave me some first-hand information about affairs at the Chinese court under the Dowager Empress that sounded more like the romances of Dumas than modern fact, and they whetted my appetite to see at least the scenes in which this remarkable woman moved.

That the Empress liked to watch human beings undergoing torture is a well-known fact easily explained no doubt by the criminologists. Der Ling tells in her book that the Empress would have her coolies and eunuchs beaten and lashed for her own personal entertainment and satisfaction, but she omitted one important fact. One day when she was walking in the garden of the palace with the imperial lady, the Empress flew into a rage about something. She commanded a coolie to kneel before her, and with her own hands she pounded his head to a pulp with a bamboo and with a smile on her face watched her victim expire.

But the Empress is gone—otherwise I could not have passed the outside gates, although a few persons were permitted to do so on state occasions "for state reasons." The Empress is gone and the Manchu sun is set, there being not the slightest hope among the faithful that the Emperor will ever occupy the throne of his ancestors. He is a prisoner in the hands of politicians and his is a lost cause. And the magnificent Summer Palace, lately the scene of courtly revelry that almost equaled the splendors of the court of Louis XIV of France, is fast going to decay. There is none to keep it in repair for future generations, as France has done at Versailles. The Manchu dynasty left such a trail of horrors behind it that nobody seems to wish to recall them. I have never seen such absolute poverty amid such magnificent surroundings, and I doubt if similar scenes could be equaled elsewhere on earth. Doomsday has come for the Summer Palace and its once stately retinue.

Soon after I had passed the towering arch at the entrance and passed through various courtyards ornamented by magnificent bronze images set on white marble bases, after I had inspected the pavilion of the Empress with its magnificent treasures heaped into corners, as if ready for speedy departure, six rowers came up to the marble balcony and invited me to take a ride on the lake in the barge in which the Empress took such delight when she sat in state, surrounded by musicians, courtiers, fortune-tellers and the strange retinue with which she surrounded herself. They were eager to take me—just how eager I did not understand at the time. One does not receive such attentions ordinarily from the personal attendants of an empress. Yet these men, who doubtless served their mistress well—else they would not have lived until the present time—acted like a pack of hungry wolves. So I shall digress a bit in the story of my day among them, just as I did in reality. I shall postpone telling of the wonders of that barge-trip on the lake and quote a few of these men, who were as eager to talk as they were to row, because they saw an extra coin for their trouble.

It is believed at Peking that the Dowager Empress spent about fifty millions of dollars on this palace and the grounds surrounding it, money that was appropriated for the Chinese navy. The grim old lady had her little joke. If it was money for a navy, then she would build a boat with some of it, so she caused to be constructed the wonderful white marble pavilion that sits out into the lake in the form of a boat floating on the water. She maintained a numerous court, and this court required the services of a small army of men. It is said that she had over a thousand eunuchs, one of whom had more power than anyone else in the realm, save the old lady herself, and in many ways he was the real ruler of China during her later days, because of his influence over her. Everyone at court was waited upon by someone else. So the army grew and grew. The population of the palace was that of a small city.

Eunuchs were the privilege of the ruler and of certain members of the royal family. The first mention of them in China is back in 1100 B.C., under the Chu dynasty; but they had no official standing until about the Eleventh Century of our era, under the Emperor Ho-Ti, whose troops are supposed to have gone as far west as Judea. In ancient (and modern) times, the emperor of China was entitled to three thousand eunuchs, while princes and princesses were entitled to thirty each, nephews and young children of the Emperor to twenty each, and cousins of the Emperor to ten each. They were formerly provided for the palace by the Chinese princes, each of whom was expected to supply eight eunuchs for his imperial master every ten years. But it was customary for the Emperor to pay for his gifts at the rate of two hundred fifty taels each. Being the tribute of the princes, the latter were responsible for their behavior and it was necessary to know that they had been in service for a term of years before entering the palace gates. It was the custom of many families throughout the empire to sell their children for this purpose and a register for applicants was kept at the palace. About three hundred eunuchs usually made up a company of actors and givers of exhibitions for the amusement of the court, while several of them were lamas, whose duty it was to look after the spiritual needs of the royal family. The body of eunuchs was divided into forty-eight distinct classes, each with special duties and privileges. All of them, however, enjoyed permission to smoke opium.

Then, one day, the old lady died and the old order was quickly changed. The republic came and there was a multitude of men without jobs, men wholly unfitted for service elsewhere, yet men who had given practically their whole lives for their imperial mistress. The republican Chinese government decided to pension them, and in its desire to show its gratitude towards faithful public servants it voted them four dollars a month and a bag of rice each.

Many of the men were married and had families before they entered the government service. And even if they were unmarried, the pinch of living on one dollar a week was too much. Perhaps they made ends meet at first, but now they are literally starving. The palace is crumbling to decay, but men being less sturdy than yellow tiles and stones, are preceding it. One day, if they live long enough, the walls literally will fall over their poor, lean bodies and end their suffering; and the Chinese government will have "solved" the imperial servant problem in a way that China has of solving all similar problems.

One by one, I told them to put down their oars and come and sit beside me as they told their story, which was interpreted by a guide who fortunately spoke the "Mandarin" Chinese. Some of them looked like apes, with hair cropped so that it fell to the shoulders in a shaggy mane, decayed teeth, skin that seemed to cling to their bones, dirty bare feet and long fingernails, which one of them assured me proved that they are not "laborers," nor of a common class.

"I always hated the 'Old Buddha,' as we used to call her," said the first. "I hated her because she had us whipped so unmercifully. No, she never whipped me and she never ordered me to be whipped by others, but she had my best friend lashed with bamboo until he died, just because she became angry at something for which he was not at all at fault. She said it would be an example to the rest of us. See there!"

He pointed to a marble platform with carved steps of the same stone that came down near to the water's edge. "That is where she used to sit and fish. She did not order enough fish put into the lake, and I guess they were not hungry; anyway, they did not bite much and she did not catch many. When she would sit there and fish for a time without any results, she would call a servant and have him lashed with bamboo. That was the way of the 'Old Buddha.'"

"I liked her," said number two. "I liked her because while she was a wicked woman and whipped us, we were all well taken care of when she was alive, and we would have food enough today if she were alive. Sometimes on her birthday, she would send a dollar to each of us. We even received a bag of rice in addition to all."

"I never saw Hsi-Tai-Hou," said one cowering individual, who seemed to think that he was on the witness stand. "No, I was in her employ for fourteen years, but I never once laid eyes on her. They sent me over there on the island with the emperor and told me that she did not like to be seen, and that when I knew she was coming that way I must get out of sight. I had heard of her whippings, so I never disobeyed, and in all the fourteen years I never once looked up as she passed, for I usually concealed myself in the shrubbery and kept my head bowed and my eyes closed, when she came along."

Another told me that all the palace servants knew of several instances in which the old lady had commanded her high officials to come to her for what was a "show" occasion. They came in full uniform and knelt before her. Then she walked up to them and gave them a resounding slap across the cheek that almost floored them.

She sat when she ate her meals, but sat alone, and permitted nobody in the palace to eat a meal until after she had finished hers. The palace grounds are extensive and the old lady liked to exercise in the air. Sometimes she would walk, but oftener she preferred to be carried in a chair or litter. If it suited her fancy to stray away from her pavilion two or three miles and if she were suddenly overtaken by hunger her meals were prepared and carried in a procession behind her, by servants, being kept warm on charcoal braziers. Sometimes she would decide, when three miles away from home, that she would rather wear pearls than jade. The boxes of jewelry were also carted along behind, when she went for an airing, in case she wanted to alter her adornments. She was always eating and was particularly fond of pork. "When she knew that the ladies in her train did not relish any particular dish she would command them to eat it in her presence. She always liked to "nibble at" roasted watermelon seeds, so a servant carried a dish of these beside her as she walked or was carried. I heard thousands of these minor details, and then, glancing at my watch, I saw that it was time for lunch, and as we were in the neighborhood of the Marble Boat I had the rowers fetch me up beside this beautiful creation, and it pleased me to open the box that I had brought from the hotel at an inlaid teakwood and mother-of-pearl table where old Hsi-Tai-Hou had so often sat at her water-melon seeds and pork.

It was incongruous. But no more so than the fact that the old lady's servants, a few years ago the wearers of imperial livery, sat beneath me on the barge and eagerly snapped at the morsels from the bountiful box that I threw to them. My stock of cigarettes was low, and, feeling that I had only one that I cared to give away, I passed it to the man who appeared to be the head-rower. He lighted it, took one deep puff and passed it around to the others, all of whom received at least one coveted taste of tobacco, which seemed to be much appreciated.

Take a beautiful stretch of land, extending over hills for something like ten miles, enclose in its valley a placid lake, surround its shores with a yellow sand walk, with a four-foot white carved marble railing, erect magnificent white marble bridges at convenient intervals, where streams enter into the lake, erect palatial villas on the island in the lake, each with its own formal gardens, studded with priceless pieces of bronze and marble, and from the water's edge to the crest of the highest peak at one side erect

THE PAVILION, SUMMER PALACE

pavilions, palaces and temples, all connected by miles and miles of ornately painted and decorated covered walks, with mosaic tiling—and you have spent enough money to bankrupt an empire.

That is what Hsi-Tai-Hou did, in a way, when she built what is known as the Summer Palace. It is popularly supposed that she built it with the appropriation of fifty millions for the Chinese navy, but this seems to be rather conservative. This may have "started the ball rolling," but it took the income of an empire to keep it going. And the Dowager Empress did keep it going. Detested by her four hundred millions of subjects, the old woman nevertheless had the ability to withstand all opposition, and only death could conquer her. The nations of the world gave her a severe check when they combined against her, but even after the Boxer troubles she remained supreme, and with all the time, thought and craftiness that it must have taken to accomplish such marvels, she seems to have had most of her time to spend just as she pleased. She hated the palace at Peking, so she lived out in the suburbs, where she could spend her time as it suited her whim. Even in her fifty million dollar residence she had no provision made for heating, but she did not mind that. She piled on the clothing and told the court to follow her example. The winters are very cold around Peking, but she did not care. A woman's prize is her home, and Hsi-Tai-Hou liked hers; she insisted upon living in it.

Earlier in life, there were many things that bothered her. Her son died and then there was another empress. But she overcame little difficulties like that. When it came time for the emperor to rule, she put him on an island in the middle of the lake, visible from her palace, and made him a prisoner. She let him live through her "mercy" and "grace" but he was a dummy and never was emperor in fact.

He was not stupid, however, as the world was led to believe. Princess Der Ling reports that he asked her plainly to tell him if Europe and America did not consider him an idiot. Der Ling says he was merely an unfortunate man who should have sat upon the throne of China; but could not do so, because an old lady was there and declined to budge. He had plenty of time for reflection, and one day he devised a great scheme. He would send for the popular Yuan-Shih-k'ai, win him over, upset the throne by the aid of Yuan's army and be emperor in fact as well as in name. Crafty Yuan heard him out and ostensibly started for the South to collect his army. But he thought better of it, after he had left the Emperor's island dwelling. Perhaps his chances would not be so good with the Emperor as with the Empress, so he went to

The Lake, Summer Palace

the old lady, told her what her royal prisoner was planning to do and there was a great rumpus in the royal family of China. Hsi-Tai-Hou doubled her guard over the Emperor on his island. In future he was not to be permitted to speak, excepting in the presence of witnesses. When he received visitors, a verbatim report of the conversation was delivered to Her Majesty the following morning.

There is a magnificent white marble arch bridge that reaches out from the main land of the palace grounds to the island in the lake. It was guarded by the old lady's officers. The Emperor merely pined away in his palace, worshiped at his little temple—and waited. Probably he dreamed of the day when the "Old Buddha" would die and leave the throne to its rightful heir, but when Hsi-Tai-Hou realized that she was dying she gave instructions to poison the Emperor within twenty-four hours of her demise, or at least that is the version of his death believed at Peking. And her command was executed. They both passed to their ancestors on the same day.

I asked the rowers of the imperial barge to take me to the island palace of the Emperor, and I stepped ashore at one of the ends of the bridge. The pavilion is sealed up now, but the windows are of paper, and ruthless hands have poked peep-holes, so that it is possible to look inside. Splendid furniture is piled in heaps in the corners of the rooms. Beautiful bronzes are piled upon one another, like kettles in a junk store. Tapestries are rolled up and folded. The occupant of the palace is gone and his house looks as if his belongings were to follow him, although as a matter of fact they doubtless will be stolen, given away by bribery, or allowed to decay; that is the way in China. The palace sits on a little bluff of rock. I was rather liberal with the attendant who demanded twenty cents, if he showed me everything. I gave him fifty cents and he was almost ready to throw in something for a "souvenir." He lifted up a stone near the emperor's sleeping-room and motioned to me to follow him. He went down through a carved, rocky passage-way that led to the water's edge, but completely hidden from sight. I asked him if this was for the purpose of escaping across the lake when the time came, and he shrugged his shoulders, saying that he did not know about such matters. At best, it seemed to be no fitting residence for the Son of Heaven, the absolute ruler by right over four hundred millions of people.

Then the rowers poked the barge back through great fields of flowering lotus, under white marble arch bridges to the base of the big audience chamber. This, like all of the other buildings, was tiled with imperial yellow of the Mings. Most of the tiles were cast in ornamental designs, many of them having dragons or other animals upon them. I told one of the boys that I wanted an imperial dragon. He climbed up the side of the palace and was about to rip one from its moorings when a signal of distress went to him from the others of the crew. Three mandarins were seen coming down the walk some distance away. They might detect the thief and have him punished, and the poor fellow had such a scare that he did not speak again the whole day, partly showing his fright, partly his humiliation, because he knew that he had "lost face" before me—and partly because he expected a few cents reward, which he did not get.

Viewed from a distance, this audience chamber seems to rise to the crest of the hill. When one has passed it he goes through terraces all roofed in with the inevitable yellow tile, one entire building of bronze, various rest-houses of elaborate design, where the late dowager liked to stop on her travels upward, and so much hewing of rock and tiled splendor that it fairly becomes dizzying to the visitor, until one finally comes to the magnificent yellow temple that crowns the hill. From a distance it was one colossal building. In reality, it is perhaps thirty or forty of them. We came back through the long covered pathway ornamented with hundreds of paintings, setting forth the beauties of the Summer Palace and grounds and lake. Then to the theater.

Hsi-Tai-Hou was a liberal patron of the theater. She had one of the best playhouses in China constructed not far from her pavilion, and she did not stop at the theater. She knew that she could command the services of the best actors in China, so she actually had palatial quarters built for them in the courtyard. It is roofed with enameled planks, painted screens and bronze and marble. Here, says Der Ling, the old lady would order a performance for the afternoon. Arrived at the theater, the performance would begin and old Hsi-Tai-Hou would immediately fall asleep and sometimes slumber for hours, while the ladies of her retinue were obliged to stand—because they were not permitted to sit in her presence, asleep or awake.

I was sitting on the stage of her theater, taking in the rather grim and solemn spectacle of today and thinking of the days of old, when a youngster perhaps seven years of age came up to me with his pigtail flying in the air. He was the son of a palace servant. He turned somersaults, shouted to make echoes, and otherwise conducted himself in such an ambitious manner that I remarked to the guide that he was clever. This was communicated to the boy and immediately bore fruit.

"If I am clever," he said to me (as interpreted) "take me to America with you as a slave boy. Come, we will go and see my father about it now. Give him a little something for me and I am sure he will be glad to let me go."

"When could you be ready?" I inquired.

"I am ready right now," he replied. "Come, let us go and see my father"—and he tugged at my arm, really believing that he saw an escape from his palatial poverty.

As we came back to the outer gate of the palace, word had gone around apparently that a millionaire philanthropist was in the palace, for all the denizens of the palace had aroused from their slumber, which causes them to forget the gnawing of hunger. I had rarely seen so many palms extended for help, so many pleading faces, nor have I heard more genuine entreaties for aid. And yet they were in the Summer Palace! They belonged to it, as much as did the imperial tile, less than five years ago. But thus are they rewarded by a republican government. Perhaps I must admit to a liking for the theatrical. I like "scenes." I have no liking for those that are "set" and do not come up to expectations, but occasionally one sees a "thriller" that has not been rehearsed, a scene that will linger as long as does the mind. Such a scene was that when I left the magnificent gate of the courtyard of the Dowager Empress of China.

Fortunately, I had made an extensive collection of coppers the day before and they were still in my pockets. One of them is worth about one-half cent in American money. By careful distribution, I made them go around the crowd, and thus gave one-half cent to each person. Some of the recipients literally kowtowed to the ground, and all stood with the bowed heads of thankfulness. Here was a scene. When Hsi-Tai-Hou left her palace in the earlier day, all of her attendants kowtowed, because they were afraid of her. She had a fifty million dollar home and she was absolute ruler of four hundred millions of people. The gaudy costumes were gone, but otherwise the *mis-en-scène* was the same. And for a half-cent I received as deep kowtows as did ever the old Buddha of the Dragon Throne. So could I be blamed for asking myself: What is the use of being rich or mighty?

Coming back from the Summer Palace, it was late in the afternoon, but I learned that there would be time to pay a visit to the famous Five Towered Pagoda, known in English as the "Temple of the Five Towers." That, as before hinted, is one of the joys of going anywhere in Peking or environs; there is always something to be seen en route, an enumeration of which would seem to be merely a page from a guidebook. Although Peking stretches far, there

Marble Boat, Summer Palace

are pagodas, temples, shrines or palaces on the surrounding hills, all worthy of a visit from the hurried tourist, and each an interesting destination for a day's tour from the leisurely-going temporary resident.

Wu-ta-szu, as the five-towered temple is known to the natives, is much pictured in geographies, books of travel, works on architecture and upon souvenir postal cards. It is almost as distinct a sight as the great bronze Buddha at Kamakura, Japan. From the prominence given it in the past, I was led to expect it to be a jealously guarded treasure, one of those places that are so "holy," that it takes a substantial fee to unbar the gates for the admission of white men. The "fees" were forthcoming, as elsewhere in China, but they did not reach the palms of priests or officials. Arrived at a point in the road, almost a mile from where the five spires were visible among the trees, the chauffeur stopped his automobile and remarked: "this is as near as I can go, there is no road beyond here—only a path."

Immediately there appeared on the scene one of those suddenly assembled crowds which no Westerner can understand. Let anything out of the ordinary transpire, and the paving stones, or where there is no paving, the grains of sand, seem suddenly to assume human form. Men, women and children crowd the thoroughfare, and there is a medley of voices that cannot be adequately described, but, which heard, will never be forgotten. Presumably, the five-towered temple is not visited by all the tourists who go to Peking; at any rate, not by many of them, so that a white man in the region is something of a curiosity. As quickly as the automobile stopped, the road was filled with farmers, their wives, sons, daughters and relatives. Some of them brought along their forks and other agricultural implements; others left them in the field, and hastened into the roadway. Here was one of the great sights of China and a hundred natives, ranging in age from six to seventy offered their services as guides through the rice fields to the temple, every one of them not only telling of his own ability, but singing forth the fact that none of the others were so well-fitted for the commission. There is but one thing to do, under the circumstances, and experience had taught me to do it quickly. I engaged a "courier" and set out upon my way.

It was a circuitous route and we were obliged to walk single file along the banks of the little rice paddies and around the small fields of the farmers, many of whom accompanied us part way, but one by one resumed their work in the fields, which they had left suddenly when they saw the opportunity to gain a few pennies without manual labor. We went past small groups of houses, for the Chinese seem to be particularly fond of the idea of living in "communities" and we paused a few moments beside a small mud walled yard, where a young man was driving a blind-folded ox around a big flat stone, on which a young woman was scattering grain. Closer inspection showed that the ox was hitched to a cylindrical stone which was being dragged around over the grain; as primitive a method of grinding flour as one is likely to see beyond the interior of Africa, and yet this was within a few miles of the gates of Peking.

The temple is in a somewhat dilapidated condition and it seems to be abandoned by all, save the peasants and farmers of the vicinity, who look upon it as one of their inherited blessings, because they guide visitors through the rice fields to its entrance. It was built during the reign of the Emperor Yung-lo, at the beginning of the Fifteenth Century and is strictly in the Hindoo style of architecture. It consists of a square marble terrace fifty feet in height, which may be ascended by a stairway inside. From this terrace rise five spires, which are covered with Hindoo characters. It was erected to shelter five gilt images of Buddha and a model of the diamond throne, which were the gift of a rich Hindoo, who came from the neighborhood of the Ganges.

The side trip to the temple was not what one might have expected it to be, because it was another example of China's neglect of her great ruins that would delight succeeding generations; but it brought a beautiful golden day to a close, one that could not be forgotten, whatever might pass under one's observation at a later date.

Coming back within the walls of the city, my ears heard unearthly grumblings, as if they were the grunts of an alligator intensified by a megaphone. "Manchu bride is going to her husband's house," said the chauffeur, so I told him to stop his car and I alighted at the side of the road, if possible to catch a glimpse of the lady and the strange orchestra that was accompanying her. I was not rewarded by getting even a peep at the bride, however, because although it was very warm, she was seated in a small square box brilliantly decorated and so draped and festooned that it was impossible to realize how she obtained air enough to breathe. The box was in the middle of long bamboo poles, upon the shoulders of eight coolies, and as it bounded up and down, the men failing to keep step and apparently not being trained chair bearers, there was no doubt that the chair was occupied by a young lady who was taller, heavier and more plump than her Chinese sisters. Ahead of the chair and behind it, walked coolies who carried great horns fully five or six feet long. Behind each horn walked a virtuoso, who puffed his breath into the megaphone unceasingly, with the results noted.

"Probably she marry a very rich man," commented the chauffeur.

"No doubt, but why do you think so?"

"Because, instead of one horn, as you see, she have seven. Probably her husband have much money and want her very much. Maybe she is beautiful lady, but oh, it is very sorry we cannot see!"

Again the mystery of the Orient! Most beautiful ladies are hidden away in curtained boxes. Beautiful palaces are behind high walls. The best treasures of the temples are locked in altar chests. The most remarkable books are too precious to be brought into the daylight.

"Perhaps she is so ugly that her husband did not want anyone to see what sort of a wife he had bought," I remarked, feeling a momentary pique at being denied a glimpse at something else that was "forbidden."

This amused the chauffeur and he assured me that I was mistaken. "No Chinaman would have seven horns if wife with ugly face was coming to his house. No, she must be very beautiful and he must be very rich."

We had halted beside a fine pai-lou that stretched across the roadway from curb to curb. It was built of marble and bore a long inscription, which I asked the chauffeur to interpret for me. It is popularly known as the Kettler Pai-lou and was put up by the Chinese government by way of expiation for the murder of the German Minister, Baron Kettler, by the Boxers in 1900, and thus of greater interest to a Westerner than the other pai-lous which dot the China landscape and often enough extol the virtues of a distinguished citizen thus remembered by his neighbors. The inscription reads:

"The German Minister, Baron Kettler, since his arrival in China, faithfully discharged his diplomatic duties and won our confidence. After the outbreak of the Boxer troubles in the fifth month of the twenty-sixth year of Kuang-hsu, the said minister was killed on the twenty-fourth day of that month at this very spot, to our great grief. This monument is erected in order to proclaim his good name and to point out what is good as good and what is evil as evil. Let all our subjects learn lessons from the past occurrence and never forget them. We order this."

My excursion the following day to the "Purple Forbidden Palace," was much less satisfactory and less gratifying. Just as a theatrical celebrity may be over-exploited, just as a singer may be advertised until the performance is certain to be disappointing, so the anticipation of gaining entrance to the Forbidden City was so great that the actual experience could not possibly come up to expectations. The very name "Forbidden City" was enough to

Marble Bridge, Summer Palace

arouse curiosity, and any reference to it in literature of any kind has made it a place of mystery. It seemed to be more the abiding place of the Son of Heaven than any of the other palaces. Fabulous stories have circulated around the world in regard to it. Here were buildings the inside walls of which were a succession of cabinets or shelves, in and upon which reposed the most remarkable collection of art objects in the world, bronze, jade, ivory, gold, silver, and precious stones. It was a treasure heap, according to persons who claimed to have derived their information from persons who had seen what they described, or who had talked with others whose information had been gained from a "trustworthy source." Some accounts went so far as to picture the buildings in which there were vast accumulations of gold, similar to that which was offered for the ransom of the Inca of Peru.

Before I left the hotel I read in C. F. Gordon-Cumming's "Wanderings in China"—one of the best books of travel ever written on the country, and by a woman—that "within these sacred precincts no foreigners have ever been permitted to set foot, tho' they may gaze from beyond a wide canal, at the very ornamental archways and the double and triple curved roofs of many buildings, rising above the masses of cool dark foliage." There was further reference to the mysterious yellow-tiled roofs, upon which all visitors had gazed—but from beyond the walls. Probably the first place that nine out of ten newly arrived visitors in Peking have asked their guides to show them was either the forbidding walls around the palace, or the city walls, from which they thought they might have a peep into this garden of mystery that rivals the gardens of Persia, Arabia or India, as the locale for intrigues, plottings, poisonings and assassinations, and which has a glamour similar to that of Mecca, which last is said to be interesting principally because the majority of the human race is forbidden to enter the city on account of religious fanaticism.

The trip to the Purple Palace began as a dismal failure, and my temporary embarrassment was not at all that which one who was about to tread upon such holy ground had reason to expect. I was about to do something that every stranger who has visited China, for centuries, has wanted to do; I was to achieve what had been supposed to be the unattainable, but the start was undignified, at least for one who was about to enjoy such a privilege. As the palace entrance is only a short distance from the hotel I summoned a rikisha, instead of a more stately vehicle, knowing that I would be obliged to leave it at the gate and proceed on foot. The rikisha boy started off at a trot and proceeded about ten yards, whereupon his conveyance collapsed and I was

THE KETTLER PAI-LOU

thrown sprawling to the pavement. According to my instructions from the American legation officials, I was to be escorted beyond the walls of mystery by a Chinese colonel, who had been assigned for the purpose the preceding day. Our rendezvous at an appointed hour was not far from the palace gate, and as I endeavored to rearrange my clothing, after the accident to the ancient rikisha, I had mental visions of the worthy officer becoming weary with waiting for me. Perhaps, after all, I was not to enter the Forbidden City. It seemed that even the rikisha and rikisha coolie had conspired against me. But with a hasty brushing of hat and clothing with such equipment as the boy carried beneath the seat of the rikisha, usually used to scrape the mud from the foot-mat, I pressed along and reached the colonel on time, although it took him some time to recover from the shock that his dignity had suffered when he received the announcement that the foot passenger was the bearer of a permit to enter the Purple Palace, and not merely a servant or out-runner, who had been sent ahead to acquaint him with the imminent arrival of some badged, medaled and uniformed diplomat.

But misery does not shrink from company and while the colonel was rather cocky and superior during the first minutes of our acquaintanceship, he soon suffered humiliation that was greater than my own when I was attempting to rise from the pavement. Such a poor beginning to the morning's adventures established an almost equal footing for us and we became good friends as the hours passed and the "mysteries" were revealed to me. As we approached the first great gate in the wall, the guards asked to examine my permit. It said that I would be accompanied by the colonel, whose military duty on this particular day, it seemed, was to see to it that I carried away from the palace nothing more than its celebrated "secrets." So the colonel had dressed in civilian costume. There was nothing about him to prove that he was a colonel. A lively debate ensued between him and the guards. Was a colonel of the President's army to be treated in this manner by a common soldier? On the other hand, was the soldier to follow his instructions or not? The guard said something, which it appears from the apologies which followed was something like: "When you have your uniform on, I know that you are a colonel, but, when you do not wear it, how am I to know that you are the person referred to in this permit as the gentleman's escort. You cannot pass and he cannot pass, because he must be escorted by you."

It was a bitter little pill for the colonel to swallow, but he mastered his temper and told me that he would make a quick trip, if I would be good enough to wait for him at the gateway, and he came back uniformed as his subordinates demanded. It all seemed to be rather farcical; but it was another outcropping of the old China, which is so firmly and deeply rooted that it is difficult to remove its customs and prejudices in three or four years, or, perhaps, in a generation. The truth of the whole situation was that the guards at the palace gate did not care to permit a white man to pass. They had been obliged to see a French official enter the Forbidden City the same morning; but he was "official," resplendent and glittering in appearance and costume. It was different with the American. Perhaps they could not prevent his entering, but they could delay the hour, or if not the hour the minutes; and this is why they were unable to "recognize" the colonel until he had put on the trappings that proved his rank.

In less than an hour, however, we entered the great gate, and my feet were not only touching the sacred soil, but they carried me over miles of it, because instead of being a "palace," in the usual acceptance of the word, the Imperial Purple Palace is a city, and seems at a glance to be of greater dimensions than the Summer Palace, which stretches around the shores of a ten-mile lake. But the Summer Palace is in the country; the Winter Palace is in the heart of the capital city, occupying a position similar to Hyde Park in London or Central Park in New York. In the Forbidden City is a large lake, canals and lengthy roadways, but bordering all of them are dozens, perhaps hundreds of buildings, the merest enumeration of which, With a brief description, would fill pages with a rather tedious architectural record. There are many halls of vast proportions, just as an example of which may be mentioned: the *Tai-ho-tien*, where the Son of Heaven held court on New Year's Day; the *Kun-ning-kung*, which was the residential district of the late Dowager Empress; the *Yang-hsin-tien*, which was used as a residence by the late Manchu emperor and his number one wife; the *Chung-ho-tien*, used by the court for various religious services; the *Pac-ho-tien*, where the emperor held a banquet on New Year's Eve, in honor of the ambassadors of the tributary states; the *Chien-ching-kung*, where the emperor gave audiences to high officials of state; the *Chiao-tai-tien*, where the imperial seals were kept; and all of these are surrounded by residences of the court functionaries and government officials of various sorts and conditions and rank. Thus the Purple Palace is a crowded city in parts, and like beautiful villages elsewhere. In places, the banks of the canals are as thickly crowded with buildings, with connecting bridges, as a Venetian water route a short distance inland from the Grand Canal. There are so many huge buildings that when there is a desire for a change of location the change is made and there is ample room—all within the forbidden enclosure. Buildings that were used by one emperor as his residence were not desired by the next ruler, so he dwelt in another section of the city. It is all so vast and so unexpectedly crowded that a visitor of one day is bewildered by so much splendor and reaches the exit with the impression of having started at the Battery in New York and having walked to Central Park with a determination to "see" everything en route in two or three hours.

There is a sameness to most of the structures, as they have the curved yellow tile roofs, ornate carvings and panels that are visible in less secluded precincts of Peking and China. This sameness, however, makes it exceedingly difficult for one to recall any particular structure, unless it be identified with a personage. It is much as if all the national buildings at Washington were grouped within one walled enclosure, with residences for senators, congressmen, their secretaries and the vast army of government clerks, the President, his cabinet and all other functionaries of state.

The residence of the late Yuan Shih-k'ai will remain in memory, because I asked to see where this man, who proclaimed himself emperor, had elected to dwell, with all the imperial palaces at his disposal. The doors of his residence were sealed, after his body started in the funeral procession for Honan, his boyhood home. Big sheets of paper were pasted across the knobs, so that none might enter, but after considerable palaver between the colonel and the guards one of these was broken, and I was permitted to enter what might have been the comfortable city residence of an American merchant. The house was furnished in Western style. The chairs and sofas were covered with linen, in the French style, as if the occupant of the house had gone away on his summer holiday. There were several pieces of bronze, marble and pottery in the various rooms that indicated wealth and the good taste of the collector, but nothing more.

General Li, the president following Yuan, never cared to occupy this house, and therefore, caused another to become the executive mansion. The little emperor lives with his Manchu relatives in another corner of the Forbidden City, where they are waited upon by many of the late Empress Dowager's eunuchs, who doubtless fare much better than those servants who have been left behind at the Summer Palace. At the close of the morning's rambles the colonel assured me that we had not been "within miles" of where this little Son of Heaven is held a prisoner.

Excepting for a feast to the eyes, on account of a few beautiful souvenirs of the bygone, like the magnificent" Dragon Wall," and the knowledge

Residence of the Late Yuan Shih-k'ai

that it had been until the present an almost impossible experience for the foreigner, the Purple Palace was not as interesting as the imperial dwelling in the suburbs. It was too much like the crowded city streets of the commoner's Peking, and I understood, as it was impossible to understand before, why the Dowager Hsi-Tai-Hou liked to leave the place for the comparative quiet of her suburban retreat.

Probably by the time these words are in print, the Purple Palace and its "mysteries," will be a part of the itinerary of each visitor to Peking who makes application for permission to enter it and is vouched for by his nation's representatives in the Chinese capital. The new executive is in favor of a most liberal policy in these matters, as in all others. He has none of the terrors and fears of his late predecessor; and does not fancy that each foreigner armed with a camera is a prospective bomb-thrower and assassin. President Li would make his capital the great metropolis of the East, and a part of his wide-reaching policy is to attempt to dispel the "mystery" and establish a closer relationship between the East and the "West, which he believes would follow a better understanding of one and the other.

CHAPTER XII

ON ROYAL BYPATHS

A PART of the trip to the Great Wall of China and the Ming Tombs, which may be accomplished in two or three days from Peking, is as easy as the trip from New York to Atlantic City. Most of the books of travel relate weird and uncomfortable experiences in this section of the country, naturally and justly beloved by all travelers; but they were written in the days before the Peking-Kalgan railway, when it was still necessary to follow the rocky, winding road in the valley that leads to the Nankou Pass, that marks the great highway between China and the countries to the north. Sedan chairs, donkeys, carts or camels were the means of conveyance in the older day, and there were delays, camps by the roadside, possible encounter with unfriendly neighbors, and travelers usually seem to have arrived at their destination fatigued and quite unable to enjoy a full measure of the joys of the excursion.

It is different now. The train I took was equipped with first, second, third and fourth class accommodations. The fourth was the most popular because it was the cheapest. It permitted passengers to climb into open cars and squat on the floor, surrounded by their goods and chattels. The cars looked almost exactly like ore or coal gondolas on American railroads, but a hole was cut through one side which served as an entrance. The third class consisted of wooden benches on which passengers squatted usually with the windows closed tight so that not one breath of air might enter. The second class is only a little less comfortable than the first, but it is considerably cheaper, so the seats are usually crowded. First-class passengers pay an excess fare for the privilege of keeping the windows open and for the assurance that there will be plenty of room, even if they do not come to train two hours before starting time, which is the custom of the others.

At Nankou, I went to a Chinese inn, which had been "Europeanized"— at least so the manager assured me. He said that a Chinese inn was good enough in the old days, but now that so many "foreigners" are coming to the Ming Tombs and the Great Wall—he had entertained three that week—he decided to put in modern beds that "stood on legs," and his table was filled with all the canned stuffs that England and America afford, because he knew that "foreigners demand them."

The trip to the Ming Tombs and back is about twenty-six miles from the inn, and no Chinaman or foreigner has built a railroad. It is necessary to travel in a sedan chair on the shoulders of coolies; but here are coolies who should have a memorial erected to them. I am certain that they are more worthy of it than some of the emperors who are incased in imperial yellow porcelain in the royal mausoleum. The average Chinese coolie is a willing person. He merely wants his meager pay and then he will tug a heavy load an incredible distance. But I have come across plenty of them who would emit a grunt after they had toted my two hundred pounds a distance of five miles. Not the coolies of Nankou. The four of them lifted me to their shoulders as if I had been a feather-weight. They started off down a ravine from the hotel at a lively clip. "Wait five minutes," I whispered to myself, "and you will hear the signal of distress." But I did not hear it. They kept up the jogging gait for twenty-six miles in one day, and when we returned in the evening there was a rainstorm threatening, so they increased their gait to a trot and finished the last two miles at what amounted almost to a run. And the four of them demanded the sum of two dollars for their joint labors that day.

Just why the emperors of the Ming dynasty elected to be buried in this out of the way valley, shut in by hills on three sides, is something of a mystery. Perhaps they wanted to make it as inconvenient as possible for their surviving relatives and subjects to worship at their tombs. It is known that Emperor Yung-lo built his tomb in 1409, about fifteen years before his death. What it cost in money and labor it is not possible to calculate, but the toll of human life and dollars must have been almost incredible. His example was followed by the other Ming emperors, but they did not do such a colossal job. There are thirteen tombs altogether, but the distances are so vast that the casual tourist is likely to be satisfied with a glimpse of the others, while paying a visit to Yung-lo in his posthumous palace.

After we had cantered through several small villages, past great fields of vegetables and grain in which the Chinese peasants were working, we arrived at a magnificent carved stone gateway of five arches. Pilgrims were resting in the shade of its colossal framework, with their blankets spread out on the fine pavement of white marble slabs that extended in various directions over a high knoll.

"The tombs are exactly six miles from here," said the guide. That seemed a long distance, even taking him at his word, but it was the longest six miles I ever covered, yet it was one of the most interesting avenues through which I ever passed. The road, about four yards wide, splendidly graded, was paved with huge slabs of stone and marble the entire distance. In many places the roadway has crumbled, but in others, it is in as fine condition as the boulevard of any city. About two-thirds of a mile from the marble gate there is another gigantic gateway roofed with the imperial yellow tiles. Here is a notice to all officials to dismount from their horses or chairs to make the closer pilgrimage on foot. Then gigantic stone monuments of various kinds, met with only in China. One contains an essay by the fourth Ming emperor. There are clusters of great marble pylons and then finally the animals, elephants, camels, horses, goats and other creatures that seem to be a cross between dragons and zebras—all colossal stone images set up against the great paved roadway. Then stone effigies of officials, military and civil.

And barely a human habitation in sight, these being only the straw-thatched cottages of poor peasants! They cultivate the soil up to the curb of the "Great White Way" and to the bases of the pedestals on which the stone beasts repose. The great monuments mean nothing to them; neither do the tourists who come this way. Theirs is too hard a struggle for existence. Many of them must have been aware of my passage in the chair, but, although they were only a few feet away, they did not look up from their toil in the fields. Some of them were groaning or grunting native songs to while the time away. Some were merely dumb and silent. They probably thought "what a mad creature a foreigner must be to come so far to see these monuments!"

The coolies trotted on and on, and finally deposited me in front of a high stone wall surrounding an enclosure. This wall was capped by yellow tiles in fantastic designs and beneath the eaves were friezes of porcelain plaques of the same color.

I passed through the portal into the great paved enclosure. On into a tremendous building, the oratory, the high roof of which is supported by a forest of teakwood pillars. The ceilings are panels of highly decorated designs. In the center of the hall is the "tablet" of the emperor.

Through this oratory I passed on to other courtyards and other buildings, all ornately carved and decorated, every square inch being of priceless artistry. Finally, again into a spacious courtyard. A yellow tiled building is for the burning of prayers. In the center of the court is a great white marble carved altar, on which all the altar ornaments, censors and vases are of gigantic size and of carved white marble. Then on again, and to the tomb itself. Yung-lo reposes in the hillside with a magnificent temple-like structure over him. One approaches the tomb on inclined stone ways that lead to the top of the hill. Here is another tablet, setting forth his virtues.

And this is but a meager description of the magnificence of this tomb—which is but one of thirteen. And all practically hidden from human sight in the hills beyond Nankou.

It is said that the Ming princes come here once a year to worship, and even in the time of the Manchu Empress Dowager a royal pageant made the trip for similar purposes, for ancestor worship is still the leading "religion" of China and the noblest act one can perform is to do homage to one's predecessors.

Inside the walls of the tombs are a poor half-foolish crowd of hangers-on, who offer visitors warm drinks. I took one of the men aside. He was a strange, pig-tailed peasant, who looked as if he had lived in the time of Yung-lo himself.

"I don't want anything to drink," I told him, "but I would like one of the imperial plaques on the frieze of Yung-lo's tomb."

He threw up his hands in horror at the thought, and I respected his reverence for the departed emperor. Then, after a half hour, when I was preparing to leave, he beckoned me to one side. He had been out on a little foraging expedition, while the others begged for money. He placed in my hands the coveted plaque. I trembled, fearing his demands for his sacrilege.

"How much?" I asked.

"Ten cents," he replied, naming a Chinese coin equal to that amount.

"Not only ten cents, but ten times ten," I said to him, handing him a dollar and pleased at my bargain. Later I showed it to a Peking-New York antiquarian and asked him what it was worth.

"To me perhaps ten dollars," he smiled. "To a collector of antique pottery in America—well, I might charge him a thousand. He'd think more of Ming porcelain if I did."

"Better take one of the wooden benches from the veranda," chuckled the Chinese manager of the inn at Nankou, when he saw me getting ready to go to the railway station to catch the train that runs up through the old Nankou Pass to Ching-lung-chiao the next morning. Of course I did not understand, and this merely caused him to chuckle more.

STONE ANIMALS AT MING TOMBS

"When you go to the station, I'll send a coolie with a bench anyway," he added, "if you want it, you can take it; and if not, he can bring it back."

I did want it, really needed it. The Chinaman knew best. He had seen the train that runs each morning over the territory that I wanted to cover. In many ways it is one of the most remarkable trains that run anywhere. I looked it over carefully before going aboard. In fact, I was obliged to do so, for the purpose of picking out a convenient spot for my bench. Evidently this train does not live by its passenger traffic, so no accommodations are made for mere human beings. There were flat cars for bales of hides and pelts bound for Russia. There were box-cars (without roofs save for straw matting) filled with merchandise. And there was a little car at the front of the train, which served as a sort of caboose for the train crew. But train crews in China do not demand many modern comforts. They squat on the floor. One of the men was actually lying in the corner of the car asleep, with his head on a brick, when I entered. A tea-kettle was steaming over a charcoal brazier, but otherwise there were no "furnishings." About all the line did for passengers was to sell tickets, and these were sold with as much dignity as if the cashier had been handing out train deluxe coupons for a continental journey. But four Chinese who ran the train took me into their caboose, planted my bench from the hotel porch in the front doorway, and I sat down imagining that I had a special observation compartment.

In a few minutes we received a terrific bump, which proved that the engine was being coupled on, just as does on an excess fare train in America. The difference was the engine was attached to the rear of the train and pushed, instead of pulling it in regulation fashion. Trust to the Chinese to do everything in exactly the opposite manner from which Europeans do it! And almost before we were aware of it, we were off! I was bound for the great wall of China. The thought gave me a thrill. And so did the train. It slid along through the valley between towering hills and finally stopped at the little station of Ching-lung-chiao, which had a weird assortment of loiterers, many of whom looked as hoary and ancient as I expected to find the Great Wall itself.

From the station platform it was possible to see the wall in the distance, meandering over the hills and through the valleys, a magnificent engineering feat that seems almost incredible in these days when we call the Panama Canal "the greatest engineering work of man," and look upon the pyramids of Egypt as one of the "seven wonders of the world." This great work, which would crumble before modern guns, but which was a formidable barrier to encroachments from the north in its day, was begun two centuries before the birth of Christ. Yet today it stands in places as perfect almost as the day it was constructed. I have not the exact dimensions, but they are easily found in books of reference. The impressive fact is that it is so high that it could barely be scaled by the aid of ladders, it is wide enough at the top for two or three carts to pass, it is built of hewn stone and brick, and at frequent intervals there are towers, turrets, secret passageways and inclines to the inner base, and in addition to being a magnificent fortification across a tremendous territory, it is a thing of beauty that would be difficult for modern engineers to conceive or execute. I wanted to stand in its turrets, walk along the inclines of the top and look over into Mongolia. I wanted to see those turrets from which heaps of stones were hurled upon ancient enemies, the turrets where fire blazed and were flashed to other towers in the interior, warning China that the enemy was approaching.

So I engaged the services of an old man at the station, who had what I shall always believe is the ugliest donkey in the world. Probably the poor beast had brought produce to market at Ching-lung-chiao that morning and wanted his noon-day rest. But for a few cents the old fellow told me I could ride the animal—or attempt to do so—while he would walk along and act as guide.

The principal thing about the expedition seemed to be that the donkey didn't want to go to the Great Wall of China. It preferred to go in the other direction. Its owner pounded it with a club, which had no effect. It merely stood and waved its ears. Then he tried coaxing and petting. This availed nothing. Finally, the man started on ahead, thinking that the animal might follow its master. Even this had no effect until he had gone some distance, when the animal started off at a gait quite unlike that usually taken by Chinese donkeys, and quite disconcerting to the rider. But the scheme worked. The old man clattered off down the trail and the donkey and I followed. All went well until we came to a precipitous cliff over which there was a stone footbridge not more than twelve inches wide. Here the donkey halted again, as if considering whether or not to risk it with such a weight on its back. But it finally started out, when its master was about to disappear around a hill, and I felt as if I were suspended on a tight-rope over the gorge at Niagara Falls. But we reached the other side in safety, and as if encouraged by the experience, the donkey trotted along during the rest of the journey and deposited me safely at the triple, massive gateway in the wall that permits caravans to enter China from the north.

Dismounting, I was suddenly surrounded by a strange crowd of beggars. Blind men beating on cymbals and tooting little horns, legless men hopping around on their fists, men who looked strangely like lepers, and a strange riff-raff that evidently lives near the gateway in the ruins and survives from what it can beg of passing caravans. It was a strange aggregation and one of the most beseeching outfits that I ever encountered. They do not see a "white man" every day, and as all white men are supposed to be very rich they wanted to improve the opportunity.

One youngster immediately attached himself to me. He was a black little Mongol more ambitious than the others, because he insisted upon keeping a couple or three feet in front of me, turning somersaults, standing on his head, and otherwise "entertaining" me and showing that he was entitled to a present. I gave him a copper for his performance and hoped to be rid of him; but I did not know his kind. This merely encouraged him, and his antics became more strenuous by the aid of the monetary encouragement. He led the way to the towers of the wall. He flip-flopped along the great highway at the top of the wall, and after I had tramped around for a time on the great pile, he led me to a sort of secret stairway from the top to the Chinese base. Doubling himself up into a ball, by clasping his hands around his neck, he rolled down the great flight of stone steps and from the bottom looked up and grinned like an actor taking a curtain call.

A caravan arrived from the north as I sat on the gate. They were taking forty or fifty beautiful Mongolian horses into China. They looked up and saw me, chattered and each came up, staring in open-mouthed wonder as if they had never seen a man with white skin. The boy told them of my prodigal wealth, because I had given him the copper, and each of these stalwart men of the North came up and held out his palm for money, talking volubly and evidently explaining to me how difficult it was to get money or food in this part of the country. As chance would have it, I had twenty or thirty coppers in my pockets, as usual, because I had learned their value on similar occasions, so I gave each of them one—equal to a half-cent in American coin—and they started away as pleased as an Englishman can be when he inherits his uncle's fortune and estates.

After they had gone a little way they held a consultation. I wondered what was brewing because they came back again and the boldest of the crowd talked to me and slapped his hand to his head. I did not understand, but the boy came up and asked to take the broad-brimmed straw hat that I was wearing. They wanted to see it and to hold it. They looked at it carefully,

Boys at Great Wall

touched it and went away satisfied, waving a salute to me after they had gone far down the valley.

It was all an experience that prompted thought. Here I was, standing on one of the wonder-works of man. The brains that conceived the Great Wall of China were of a superior sort that must have represented one of the highest civilizations the world has ever known. But even the wall was a part of the great policy of isolation and conservation that in a couple of thousand years has brought the proudest nation of the earth to decay and close to ruin. While not at all typical of the Chinese of Shanghai and Peking, the men I saw were fair examples of China, the mass. Poor, half-starved men with brains just a little higher in the scale than the brains of animals. They seemed to have lived too long. There were the marks of world-weariness in the faces of the young men, while old men appeared to be ancient. They were born tainted with physical and mental decay and only a miracle can save them. And as I mused, I was confidently of the opinion that the name of that miracle is Japan. As I stood on the Great Wall and looked over at China, it seemed to me that there was nothing in all the world that offered such convincing proof of national disintegration. But, I looked off beyond the hills on the other side in the direction of Korea. I did not know it at the time, but soon was to come upon even greater evidences of the same thing. But Japan is in Korea, and has been there for some years, now being in absolute control of her ancient enemy. And out of the debris of a ruined nation Japan is causing miracles to be performed.

The Japanese object to being classed as of the same race as the Chinese or Koreans, but the blatant fact remains that all are yellow men. And there is further fact that yellow men respect and understand yellow men. Japan might redeem China. But the question is: "What would happen to the rest of the world if she succeeded in doing so and was permitted to follow her own designs in the work of redemption?"

THE GREAT WALL

CHAPTER XIII

AN ORIENTAL BERLIN

MY first impression of Tientsin was not favorable; but I was doing something that no traveler should ever permit himself to do, enter unknown territory and bring previously formed opinions and prejudices with him. My opinion of the city, as I quickly realized, had not been formed from the city itself, but from the environs. There had been severe rains, so that the land along the railway tracks had been flooded and as large areas seemed to be devoted to burying grounds the ground had been washed away, so that dozens of coffins were visible, some of them standing on end, and some upside down. I thought that I could not care much about a city, the people of which were so thoughtless of their dead. But, almost immediately, I forgot about the unpleasant sights and quickly realized that Tientsin is one of the most delightful cities in all China, corresponding to Shanghai and Hankow in commercial importance as a treaty port, and having a distinct fascination of its own, thoroughly oriental, but unlike any of the other cities. Tientsin is situated eighty-six miles from Peking by railroad and is the natural gateway from the ocean to the capital city. It was a walled city until 1900, when the Boxer uprising brought the armies of Japan, Great Britain, Russia, the United States, Germany and other countries to its gates, and the walls fell, giving place to an excellent tram line, which now runs along a fine road covering much the same territory.

Tientsin is credited with a population of close to one million, and there is a floating population estimated at fully thirty thousand, which dwells in the city at certain seasons of the year and then goes to the country for other seasons. The streets are wide and in the territory occupied by foreigners there are many fine residences and places of business that are well-shaded by mammoth trees of semi-tropical appearance, while there are parks and gardens that the traveler does not expect to find in the cities of China. About six thousand junks consider the city their "home" port and lie along the extensive waterways like the logs of a corduroy road. The harbor seems to be filled with ships from all foreign countries, the daily schedules of sailing sometimes filling the large bulletin boards in the hotels. One may not only select the line on which he cares to travel by water, but by waiting a few days it is usually possible to select the exact route preferred to all others, with reference to ports of call as well as destination. So many lines send their steamers here that while some of them do not accommodate more than eight or ten first-class passengers, on account of the ship being given over to freight, that Tientsin seems to be in direct communication with practically all the principal ports of the world.

The native streets are as "characteristic" of China as any elsewhere, but in a few minutes it is possible to pass beyond any of them and find a settlement of Europeans or Americans where there is little to suggest the exotic locale. Carriage and automobiles are common, there is a social life which foreign residents believe is second to none in China, and there are good hotels. The city is not beautiful in natural scenery and it has few of the sights that are catalogued for tourists; but it is a pleasant interlude in the tour from what has passed and what is to come, and many Westerners stay for an extended period and find the city enjoyable.

Perhaps no Chinaman has been so well known by name to Americans as the late Li Hung-chang, who paid us a sensational visit that attracted much newspaper comment, because he left his native country almost a discredited politician and from his popularity in America revived the interest of the Chinese masses, who felt that one of their countrymen who could attract so much attention in America must be a greater man than the Manchu court nobles admitted him to be. The famous Li spent some of his most active years at Tientsin and there is a fine temple with a beautiful lotus pond dedicated to his memory. Succeeding in becoming very popular as the result of helping to put down the Taiping rebellion, he was rewarded by being appointed viceroy of Chih-li province, and his yamen at Tientsin, a residence that was barely in keeping with the dignity of his office, became second in importance only to the palace at Peking. But Li was Chinese and the Manchus hated him, although he had been of great service to them and was known to exercise great influence with the people who trusted him. He was accused of being too "modern" and became the victim of court intrigues and plots that sought to discredit him. Back in 1887, Tientsin was almost a "boom" town, in the Western acceptance of the word, because it was a hive in which the concession-hunters of all nations were buzzing around the officials seeking for privileges. The city was very gay in those days, because it was not only the rendezvous of men who were seeking favors for important foreign interests in China, but likewise for high officials who assembled for the purpose of permitting themselves to be "entertained."

Li accomplished many things in the line of progress that would have been impossible to one of less influence with the natives. For example, when the Lady Li was ill he ordered that she be attended by a doctor from the West. The progress of her illness was watched with grave apprehension by the masses, who believed that help could come only from Chinese physicians. When she recovered, she founded a hospital and placed her Western physician in charge and her husband graciously ordered that a temple building should be devoted to the great humanitarian purpose, which gave an impetus to the "modern" tendencies that were beginning to invade China, and which have accomplished marvels since the death of the "Grand Old Man of China," who remained a Chinaman, but was enough of a prophet to realize what his country needed.

The natural position of Tientsin at the head of the Grand Canal, a railway connection between Europe, via Siberia, and the great republic and its port, visited by the steamers of the world, continues to make it an important city which will not diminish in importance with the passing of the years. Perhaps it is best known to the West as an important salt depot and for its beautiful rugs, which are famous around the world. The rugs are made from the great shag of camel's wool, and within memory, they could be purchased for eighteen cents the square foot; but in recent years the prices have gone soaring, and as the prices rose it is the opinion of collectors that the quality has fallen accordingly. An excursion for the purchase of a Tientsin rug, however, is counted as one of the interesting experiences of a visit to the city, and many times the inexperienced purchaser comes into possession of a souvenir that may be greatly in excess of former values, but greatly prized when home is reached.

We had expected to take the express train that leaves Tientsin twice or three times a week for Mukden, making connections with the Trans-Siberian at the Manchurian capital, often called "Little Peking," whence we expected to stop for a day and then proceed into the "Land of the Morning Calm," China's little sister, which has now entirely passed into the hands of the Japanese; but a chance hotel meeting with a German and his wife, long resident in China, changed our itinerary and delayed our Korean visit for several days. The Germans were much concerned over the war in Europe, but what seemed to concern them even more was the fact that Tsingtau, the German colony in China, was no longer ruled by Berlin, and had passed completely within the jurisdiction of Tokyo, something which they felt certain could never have happened excepting for the fact that the eyes of the world were upon what the nations considered more important events in Europe.

"Tsingtau was a paradise on earth," said the natives of Berlin. "I have seen many parts of the earth in my time," volunteered the husband, "but my choice of all was Tsingtau. It is not the same today as it was before the Japanese came; but even today it would be unfair to yourselves if you should leave China without seeing it. Go there, if but for two days, and I promise you that you will never regret it."

And much that this enthusiastic couple said was true and should be passed on to others with similar advice. See Tsingtau and you will never regret it. Perhaps it is not "paradise on earth," but it is a delightful spot on the earth's surface, and instead of becoming of lesser importance as time passes it is likely to assume great importance in world events of the future. Japanese statesmen declared at the time it was taken from the Germans that it would be restored to China at the conclusion of hostilities in Europe; but there is no reason to believe that this will be the case. Chinese statesmen believe that it is only another grip on the throat of the republic by the Nipponese government and discount the promises of Japanese officials by calling attention to the fact that when Tsingtau was taken the Japanese military violated the neutrality of China as the Germans did in Belgium. "One attracted the attention of the world," they say, "but the world was too much occupied to pay any attention to China's voice. It was futile for us to cry out and it is futile for us to expect Japan to keep her promises."

As a result of this chance meeting, we consulted the train schedules and within a few hours not only found ourselves on the railroad leading in the direction of Tsingtau, but actually arrived at the gates of Chin-an-fu, such an interesting old town that we made it the stopping-place for still another day that we had not originally included in our itinerary. It is not only a walled city, but has outer and inner walls and is supposed to shelter a population of three hundred thousand. It lies a little over two hundred miles south of Tientsin and has a hoary record as a city, having been a provincial capital for centuries before the Christian era began. Situated near the Huang-Ho River and Lake Taming-hu, which latter is as popular with loiterers and holiday-makers as West Lake at Hangchow, the city is not much frequented by foreigners, but taking its inspiration from the railway, it provides a good example of what is possible for a Chinese city to accomplish upon its own initiative when it once feels the desire to make advancement toward Western ideals. It was open to foreign trade in 1906, and although a popular means of locomotion is the wheel-barrow, there are many good roads in the vicinity; although certain districts are still musty with centuries-old filth, the city is lighted with electricity provided by the Chin-au Electric Light Company which has a paid up capital of $200,000. There is a good hotel in the European style and enough of interest to hold the tourist for several days. One of several interesting side-trips is to the Temple of a Thousand Buddhas, which lies on the slope of the Li-Shan mountains south of the city, usually visited by sedan chair. Here, against a natural stone wall, are one thousand Buddhas said to have been carved twelve hundred years ago. Another sight is the Dragon Spring Cave, whence there is a beautiful panoramic view of the city and its environs.

But we did not go to the mountains, and the morning following our arrival we boarded a train on the Shantung railway, work for the building of which was started in the presence of Prince Henry of Prussia, whose name and fame is much the same in this region as the Prince of Wales in Canada, following his similar visit before he ascended the throne of Great Britain.

Probably there are few examples of such almost miraculous speed in city construction in all history as Tsingtau. The shores of Kao-chou Bay passed to Germany in 1898, in the form of a ninety-nine year lease, and almost immediately there sprang up on the hitherto lonesome bay, a city that usually prompts the remark of "Little Berlin" from the visitor who has also visited the German capital. Few colonial possessions have had such a liberal home government, it being estimated that fully $60,000,000 of German money has gone towards the making of the important port. Too far away from our continent to have attracted more than casual notice, it is one of the most brilliant results of German "efficiency." Here, before the war in Europe, were about three thousand Germans, with schools that were beginning to attract attention throughout the Far East, magnificent granite piers that stretched far out into the harbor that had been dredged to accommodate any ship that floats, hospitals, churches, various laboratories, beautiful avenues and boulevards, remarkable hygienic safeguards to health, and finally, the sum of one hundred thousand marks had been appropriated for the purpose of planting trees on the barren hillsides. The Germans, realizing the attractiveness of this city, were making it one of the great summer resorts of the Chinese coast. There is not only one of the best bathing beaches of the whole coast-line here, but the surroundings and hotel accommodations were so much superior to anything in the region that Tsingtau was coming to be a popular summer resort and its praises were being sung to the world by all who paid it one visit.

But great events had transpired before we arrived. The Germans who remained in the colony were women, children and old men. The others were in Japan as "prisoners of war," and although plenty of signs bore German lettering and words, it was plain in the drive from the station to the hotel that Tsing-tau is occupied by aliens, and nobody with whom I talked gave me the least hint that the Japanese expect to withdraw at the conclusion of hostilities in Europe, or at any other time. A Japanese flag flies over what was the splendid Prinz Heinrich hotel and part of it has become the quarters of the Japanese officers in command of the port.

But at the time of our visit the principal points of interest were the destroyed fortifications, which with field guns and every possible "trophy of war" the German residents of Tsingtau blew up with nitroglycerine and dynamite before surrendering their "paradise" to the enemy, whom Germany theretofore considered a friend. Count von Rex, the German ambassador at Tokyo, is said to have been as surprised as anyone else when he received an official communication from the Emperor of Japan which said: "It is with profound regret that we, in spite of our ardent devotion to peace, are compelled to declare war, especially at this early period of our reign and while we are still in mourning for our Lamented Mother."

But the mourning for the Emperor's mother did not dampen the military spirits of Tokyo statesmen, who loudly and unblushingly proclaimed to the people that it was the opportunity of a nation's life-time to strike the blow that would further the ambitions of the empire.

"Japan, by attacking Tsingtau," said Chen Kuo Hsiang, a member of the Chinese Council of State, as reported by Jefferson Jones in his excellent account of the fall of Tsingtau, "is following out a continental policy cherished for at least twenty years. Its purpose is to seize Tsinanfu and northern sections of the Tientsin-Pukow railways."

Although the railways were beyond the territory of the German lease, Japan served notice upon China to clear the region of all military, and it required positive action at Peking to maintain order among the native troops who were incensed by this invasion of Chinese territory. Almost immediately, the Japanese soldiers began to pour into the territory. One large company marched on Tsimo, which was garrisoned by ten Germans, who defended themselves as long as possible in a mock battle which gave a Chinese city of thirty thousand inhabitants to the Japanese. A Nipponese aeroplane flew over Tsingtau and dropped bombs on the city. From the beginning it was a lost cause and the Germans knew it. As nearly as can be ascertained at the present time, irrespective of the naval operations, the invading force consisted of twenty thousand Japanese, nine hundred British regulars and three hundred Sikhs, while the Germans numbered something over four thousand, seven hundred of whom were sick or wounded and many of whom were mere boys. The Germans fought bravely, but the white flag went up, and Germany in Asia had ceased to exist. But, as before noted, there was nothing left in the beautiful little city that could be called a "trophy of war." Even the postage stamps, bearing the colony seal, were destroyed before the surrender. So also were all military papers and maps. Canned food from Germany was opened in store-houses and destroyed. In many ways, it was a small victory for Japan; but it was a tremendous victory, as her statesmen declared when they were defending the action before the masses of their countrymen, because they had improved the opportunity to gain a foothold on Chinese soil. They had avenged the "insult" of Berlin, which had demanded that they give up part of the spoils of the victory in the war with Russia. They had done their part in crushing a great military and commercial power of Europe.

We left Tsingtau and retraced our wanderings to Tientsin, where we made connections with the train bound for Mukden. Several interesting places were passed en route; Tang-shan, which is important on account of the rich coal fields in the neighborhood, Which, yield about nine thousand tons of coal a day, from which Japan is said to take six hundred thousand tons annually, Pei-tai-ho (usually pronounced Peterho) which is one of the popular summer resorts of China for Europeans, many of whom own villas; and Shan-hai-kuan, which is located about midway between the Manchurian and the Chinese capitals, notable principally because it is the eastern extremity of the Great Wall of China, which dips down to the sea. The last named place was famous in an earlier day, on account of its great barrier gate and castle, which was constructed in the Seventeenth Century and became the stopping place for the Manchu emperors, whose capital was in Peking but who made pilgrimages to Mukden to worship at the tombs of their ancestors. Shan-hai-kuan was occupied by foreign troops at the time of the Boxer disturbances in 1900 and again in 1911, on account of the

Street Scene, Tientsin

revolution. Many of the foreign troops remain and are quartered in the forts which are connected with the railway station by a tram. A sight of the great wall at Nankou is preferable, but the visitor who fails to make the side trip from Peking, should stop over here for a day, although few travelers will care to stop for a longer period.

Manchuria was so named from the Tartar tribes originally dwelling in the country, best known to the West for their conquest of China and the fact that a Manchu occupied the throne at Peking from 1644 until the beginning of the republic in 1912. The country is almost as large as France and Germany combined, has a rich soil and is supposed to have about twenty million inhabitants scattered over about two hundred and eighty thousand square miles. Perhaps the most famous Manchu was Noor-chachu, who was born in 1559 at a time when the country was a wild place and most of the people were living in tents or caves, without fixed towns or cities of consequence. At the time of his birth he inherited the prospects of becoming chieftain over six hamlets; but by 1616 he had conquered all the neighboring tribes and founded a kingdom. Noor-chachu, like the prince of Denmark, had a great aim in life, but in addition to avenging the murder of his father, also the murder of his grandfather by the Chinese, he spent his entire life in the pursuit of the revenge which gave the throne of the mightiest empire in the world to his successors. It is written in Manchurian history that he wrote "Seven Hates" upon a tablet and addressed them to the emperor of China. Instead of sending the tablet to the emperor, however, he went before the tombs of his ancestors and addressed his vow to heaven, performing sacrificial rites and permitting altar flames to consume his "Hates" and bear them upward on the waves of incense'. He retired to Mukden and made it his capital, and is said to have died in 1626, but he had so inspired his people with the fighting spirit and desire for conquest that his grandson ascended the throne of China in 1644 and Noor-chachu's spirit doubtless found peace, because his vow to heaven had been fulfilled.

The city of Mukden is credited with a population of nearly two hundred thousand at the present time. It is an important vortex for the caravans from all directions and a railway connection between China, Europe and Japan for passengers and the rich stock of furs and beans, which, with silk, form the principal products of Manchuria. Its street crowds are a strange and varied collection, representing many nationalities. The full-blood Manchus seem to be in the minority, while perhaps sixty per cent, of the pedestrians encountered are Chinese, Russians and Japanese. A rather forlorn suggestion of the Russian ambitions in Manchuria lingers about Mukden, as in several of the other towns and cities; but about the capital was fought the culminating battle in the Russo-Japanese war and the Japanese, who became supreme at that time, seem to retain that supremacy everywhere, although in not the acknowledged manner of the rule in Korea, which is now as much a part of the Japanese empire as Tokyo itself. Mukden has the glamour of the Orient, but as compared to the cities further south it is gray, cold and uninviting to the stranger. Perhaps few tourists would go far out of their way to visit it; but one passing through it should stop over a day or two—there is a comfortable European style hotel operated by Japanese—and interesting excursions may be made to the old Imperial palace, the examination halls, and the tombs where the ancestors of the last emperors of China are buried. It is a fascinating repository of many souvenirs of a brilliant past; and in its modern structures and the newer business methods that are being introduced there is much that is prophetic of a brilliant future. But the Great Wall of China was built to shut out from the Celestial Empire all connection with this alien country to the north, which excepting for its military exploits, and its conquest of the Dragon Throne, might never have seemed to be of great importance to the West.

Manchuria and its capital seem worthy of attention principally because the tourist or visitor in China—who should not think of visiting the Far East without at least a peep at one of the most wonderful little countries on earth, Korea—passes by rail through these northern provinces, which seem but the frontiers of that attractive yellow land to the south and only a dull reflection of its warmth and ancient attractiveness. It is practically the difference between the fertile area of Africa known as the Soudan, and the Nile Valley. When the Soudanese were wandering tribes of nomads, Egyptians were rearing immortal temples and monuments; when the Manchus were living in caves, China had a history thousands of years old. Culture is preferable to barbarism, even when viewed by the tourist of later centuries.

CHAPTER XIV

CHINA'S LITTLE SISTER

KOREA, again known as *Chosen* under Japanese rule, claims to date its history as a nation from the year 2333 B.C., which is about sixteen hundred years before the founding of Rome. Scientific historians are inclined to doubt this date, because the Eastern scholars are of the opinion that about this time the Son of the Creator of Heaven came to earth, accompanied by heavenly spirits, and being so taken with the natural beauties of Korea that he preferred the place to his previous abode, he alighted on a mountain-top and proclaimed himself lord of all the world. And, of course, he became the imperial ancestor of the rulers of the country, who now find themselves virtual prisoners of the Japanese, whose imperial ancestors were of much the same origin, according to native writers. Interesting as legends of a fancifully minded people, these stories are not of a kind that carry weight with Western scholars; but most of the latter seem to be of the belief that authentic history should begin from fully a thousand years before the dawn of the Christian era, which gives Korea an uninterrupted history of three thousand years, in all of which she possessed sovereign rights which have now passed away.

Even more successfully than China or Japan, Korea made of herself a hermit nation and until a comparatively recent date in history remained unknown to Europe. It is written that it was little short of treason for a Korean to as much as speak the name of another country, so self-sufficient did the nation consider itself. Presumably, the Arab geographer, Khordadbeh, who flourished in the Ninth Century, was the first to introduce it to "Western lands, and he wrote of it as "an unknown land beyond the frontiers of Kantu." A Jesuit priest was in the country in the Sixteenth Century, but the first authentic account of the nature of the country came from a Dutch sailor named Hendrik Hamel, who was shipwrecked on the coast and obliged to remain for thirteen years before he escaped to Japan and thence to his home.

Those ancient days, when the Land of the Morning Calm was so isolated that the outside world was barely aware of its existence, were in reality the golden days of its history; but Korea became out of joint with time in this seclusion and the manners and customs that grew up during the centuries finally sent her to her doom. Always a lover of peace, and rarely the aggressor, the time came when it was necessary for her to strike back in self defense, and her striking power was gone. She was impotent, and when her bigger neighbor had reached much the same comatose condition and from much the same causes, her alert and envious island neighbor, which had cherished the ambition for centuries, struck the blow and became master of the "Land of Gold," concerning which the Empress Jingo of Japan dreamed before she attempted its conquest and gave birth to her son, who is still worshiped as a Japanese god of war.

The old-time Korean society was divided into two classes: the oppressors and the oppressed—the *Yang-ban* (nobles) and the *Ha-in* (commoners). Theoretically, at least, the *Yang-ban* were the sons or the descendants of kings born of concubines. According to the custom, every son of a *Yang-ban* inherited his father's status, and this idle class, which not only claimed descent from royalty but, like the kings of Korea, claimed ancestors from heaven itself, became so numerous that at the time of the Japanese annexation it was said to include one-fifth of the entire native population. They could do no work on account of their elevated station in the social scale, so, naturally, laws and customs were evolved that permitted them to exist at the expense of the workers and the limits to which the privileged class extended their tyranny is almost incredible today. In a way, it corresponded to the social position of the *Samurai* in ancient Japan, men who tried a new sword's edge by hacking off the head of a commoner at a single blow, if the latter so much as raised his eyes as the military lords were passing them in the streets; but the *Samurai* were the courageous protectors of Nippon, while the *Yang-ban* were not even of this intrinsic value to Korea. They could ignore all debts, illegal but customary, their houses were inviolate against the law, they could demand the best accommodations at inns, for which they offered no payment, and arrest was impossible, except for treason, which left them free to do about as they pleased, and they pleased to do everything in their power to make the lives of the Korean people intolerable, and to drive the country into the hands of its enemies.

The king's person was so sacred, that all subjects were forbidden to mention his name during his lifetime, and his portrait could not be painted until after death. No male subject could touch him, nor could metal—which was directly responsible for the death of several monarchs, who might have lived if relieved by surgical operations. If, through an accident, the imperial person touched a male, the place where he did so became sacred and was distinguished by a red ribbon afterwards. When the ruler died, the entire nation was plunged into mourning for three years, during the first five months of which there could be no marriages in the country, no public or private entertainments, no slaughtering of animals, no execution of criminals, and all subjects were obliged to put on coats of unbleached hemp.

Even among Eastern countries the subjection of women reached its climax in Korea. The Mongol or Chinese princesses sometimes accompanied their fathers or brothers to the battlefield and their superiority to animals was recognized; but not so in the land of the *Yang-ban*. A girl was the slave of her brothers and father until her marriage, in which she had no voice, and thereafter she was the slave of her husband and sons. Custom did not permit her to speak to her husband on the bridal day. Perhaps he would tantalize or plead with her, but her lips must remain sealed, and spying female servants in her new home were glad to report to her friends if she so forgot herself as to speak to her husband before she had been his wife for twenty-four hours. Her "inferiority" not only followed her through life, but also after death, because the widower mourned for her only a few months, whereas if the husband died, his widow was supposed to wear mourning the remainder of her life and, although she might remarry, it was much as if her second husband had taken a new slave into his house and her children were considered illegitimate.

The Koreans, however, rigidly maintained their national isolation until the last quarter of the Nineteenth Century. The country has a total area of about eighty-four thousand square miles, with a coast line thought to be about seventeen hundred miles in length. Its waters teem with fish, but the Japanese and Chinese fishermen reaped many of the benefits therefrom, even in an early day, when all that Korea asked was that foreigners never land on her soil. The land, however, was always a temptation to the Japanese fishermen, who often became pirates and then carried home exaggerated tales of the Land of Gold. Hideyoshi, the "Napoleon of Japan," the commoner who humbled all feudal lords of his own country, invaded Korea and terrible bloodshed and plunder resulted. Even in the distant days the rulers of Japan were determined to annex this territory of the continent of Asia to their own island possessions, an ambition that

YANG-BAN, SEOUL

was not realized for many centuries, but which has now come to its fullest flower.

Korea is recognized by the visitor entering it from Manchuria, because it is a country of hills and mountains, which the early missionaries described as "very like the waves of the sea in a storm." The train runs along through valleys and around hills, much as it does in the mountain regions of Pennsylvania. Almost immediately the character of the land changes after the border is crossed, and even a view of the country from a car window is a pleasure that the foreigner should not deny himself.

Roughly speaking, Korea is as large as the British Isles, and it occupies a place in Asia similar to the peninsula of Florida in the United States. The population figures are given at about fourteen million, but there are already over three hundred thousand Japanese in the land, and their number is being augmented with the passing of each steamer from the Japanese ports.

More than "Paris is France," Seoul, the capital city, is Korea. From it, and its environs, it is possible for the visitor to obtain an impression of the country that will enable him to form an opinion of what the entire country is like, because it is the great meeting place for all classes and conditions of men, and life in and around Seoul is typical of what exists in all parts of the country. Arriving in Seoul, I had the good fortune to fall in with a guide who seemed at first glance to be something of a "shrinking violet," after the rather confident and bold Chinese who served in a similar capacity in the big neighboring republic. But he proved to be a most competent guide, and from the officials I saw, the Koreans who were still left in office, as well as by comparison to the gentlemen I met in the streets, he seemed to rise head and shoulders above the crowd, and in reply to my questions he soon assured me that he had not lost his "ambition," but that it was "too late" for him. The most he could hope for—perhaps he was thirty years of age—was that his children would fare better than he.

"The Japanese are here and perhaps they will bring about great reforms," he said. "I hope so, and so do all Koreans, for we realize that we had nothing to hope for from our own rulers. It was a case of falling to the Chinese, the Russians or to the Japanese. Perhaps it is better as it is. But you cannot change a people's way of thinking in one generation, even if you do enforce foreign laws, widen streets, clean up centuries of filth, stop graft in low and high places and put the house in order. These things may have a bearing on the next generation, but they cannot redeem this one. Take my case, for example. I learned English at a mission school and I was fairly

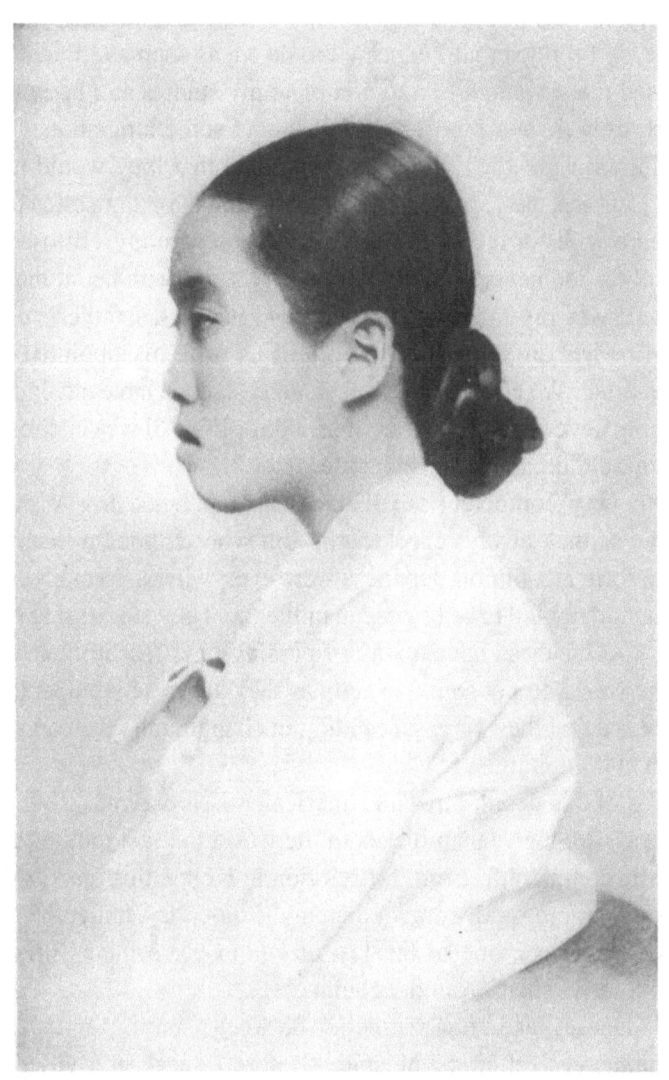

A KOREAN BEAUTY

well educated in the classics of my own country and China. I had hoped, despite everything, that I might have a future. Everything went well until my education was 'completed,' as my father put it. He said that the time had come for me to marry. Now, every Korean considers it necessary to marry at some time, so I replied that I expected to do so, as soon as I found someone who pleased me. I wanted first to complete my studies and be in a position to support my wife and family. My father said something about 'European ways' being all right for Europeans, but added that they would not do for Koreans. You see, he reserved the right to think for himself. He said he had picked a wife for me, so I might as well prepare myself to be married immediately. I had never seen my wife until I stood with her at the wedding ceremony. It was my father's command and it was her father's command. Neither of us had anything to say. Both of us were disappointed when we saw one another. We could not like each other and we have never done so—and probably never will, but we are married for life. All we can look forward to is that our children may have happier fates."

So with very competent "explanations," I pursued my leisurely way through the capital, always checking myself when I thought that it was not yet time to form an opinion. Japanese were everywhere. So many of them in authority could not fail to be having an influence. They are passing most rigid laws—for the Japanese have a way of passing laws that in their translated form to the world do not sound exactly as they are in active operation—but I could not see that they were succeeding in changing the Korean's methods of thought and thinking.

Apropos of this detail, I met an American missionary who told me of his experiences. Although Japan blazes to the world the fact that under its rule there will be complete freedom for religion in Korea, this man said that the lines are much more rigidly drawn than in the older day, under the miserable rule of Korean kings, one of the last of whom persecuted Christians and attempted to drive them from the country.

"The Japanese make a fine distinction between a 'permit' and 'permission' in these matters of religion," he said. "Before I speak in a village, I must report to the authorities what I am going to say. If it passes muster, they give me a 'permit' to speak. But I may arrive at the village and find that my 'permit' does not give me 'permission' to open my mouth. I have a private school, supported entirely from funds received from home. But I am not permitted to mention religion in the school, because the Japanese will not permit it."

A General View of Seoul

Yet Korea is a country that has been receiving the Christian message since 1594, when Gregorio de Cespedes, a Jesuit missionary, was in the country. And Christian institutions have flourished for centuries, bearing very apparent fruits for good. But Christianity had a difficult field in which to work. The Korean intellect has reached a very low plane, after centuries of dissipation that went unchecked, and at least one avowed "Christian" to whom I talked could not tell me the difference between Christianity and Buddhism. He was a "Christian," just as many men in America are republicans or democrats—he did not know why, or at least could not explain why.

I wandered about Seoul streets and visited its principal sights and places of interest, including the old North Palace, where the queen was murdered only a few years ago, and finally came to the East Palace, where the king and queen reside. Here I had "reached the throne" of the country. To be sure, the throne was vacant, because the man who occupied it is in "retirement." And the vacant throne, the shabby furniture of the palace itself, the rusty "official," who showed me through—all at the heart of Korea—proved at last what I had at first surmised. Japan had annexed Korea; she had swallowed the country. Even the name has been changed, for Korea is now "Chosen" in the geographies and guidebooks. Japan is rapidly changing the names of the cities to conform with Japanese nomenclature. Seoul (pronounced in every way from Sole to Sow-ohl) has become *Keijo,* and most of the other cities are merely awaiting the edict that will make them Japanese in name as well as in fact.

Observers told me before I reached Korea that I would there find Japan in her full administrative flower. Formosa is too far away. People do not go there, unless they have business—tea or camphor. It is different in Korea, for around-the-world tourists usually pass through the country. As a power with colonies, Japan stands before the gaze of the world, and she is well aware of it; so things have been arranged as they are in Japan, to contribute to the traveler's comfort and interest.

So Japanese rule in Korea is a triumphant success, for all the stranger sees. Schools for experiments in all sorts of agricultural pursuits have been established at various cities. The Japanese have tried to introduce foreign farming implements to make work easier. They have tried to improve the silk industry. They have pulled down whole neighborhoods of unhygienic buildings to make way for boulevards and wide avenues, where there were alleys before they came. They have brought about a healthier people by cleaning up the foul cesspools. But the people feel that they have lost their "liberty." Of course they never had any real liberty, and almost any kind of an administration would be better for the country than the one which passed with the entrance of Japan; but the people know that their nation has ceased to exist. Koreans of the next generation will be Japanese.

To visit the famous East Palace one makes application at his consulate and the desired permit is readily granted, usually within a few hours. The document names the hour when the visitor is expected and an attendant is in waiting at the palace gate, to act as an escort for whoever is recommended by his national representative. The man who greeted me as my rikisha paused in front of the ornate gate was barely a person one would expect to be a palace attendant. In fact, he was a Korean who held his position by the grace of the Mikado's government in Chosen. The Japanese have not taken all of the positions, although they seem to be in the majority where the position counts for anything.

My attendant had a growth of beard which proved that he had not shaved for at least a week. Probably he thought he was dressed in the European manner, because he had on a rusty coat that was probably given to him by some visitor of the long ago. His collar was dirty and his necktie was frayed. In America he would have been classed as a tramp, if met in the streets. But he was the guardian of the palace, a beautiful series of structures enclosed within high walls, guarded by the oriental gate, at which Korean and Japanese soldiers stand at attention when there is an arrival by rikisha or carriage. As he stepped forward to examine my credentials it seemed like some grim joke; but I had been several days in Seoul, so I realized that it was no joke and acknowledged his bows of greeting.

Perhaps he thought he would receive a good "tip"—and he did, because I gave him fifty cents, which is a good deal of money in Korea—so he showed me the palace from cellar to roof. He told me many tales, which he assured me few strangers are permitted to hear, because "walls have good ears" and the Japanese are good listeners. It is not discreet to talk too much and the Korean does not "understand English" when questions are asked in regard to the Japanese administration of his country's affairs.

"Have you a card?" asked the palace attendant, after he had deposited the yen in his pocket. I handed him the requested piece of paper, and he wrapped it carefully in a big handkerchief as he said: "Each evening His Majesty asks me to tell him who has visited the palace and who has approached his throne. I shall be pleased to hand him your card."

It was a pathetic climax to my observations in the palace, and I came away thinking that old Korea is dead. Prom the ashes a new Korea will rise, but the world will know it as Chosen, and it will be merely a province of the central government at Tokyo!

The government railways have erected at Seoul what is popularly known as "the best hotel in the Far East." Tourists do not stop long at the inns and hotels in other cities; they form their opinion of Korea—and of Japan in Korea—while stopping at the Chosen Hotel. It is an institution that will compare favorably with any hotel in America, completely rivaling any in America or Europe in the very important matter of service. Private bathrooms are attached to each sleeping apartment in the place, and "Hot Water" on the spigot means hot water. And everything else about the place means exactly what is claimed for it, everything that might contribute to the traveler's comfort or peace of mind.

On arrival, one's luggage is taken to his room and deposited. Then, if wanted, a hot or cold bath is quickly prepared by an attendant, after which the guest may leave his apartment, absolutely confident, if the keys are deposited in the hands of the room-boy, that every article of clothing will be taken out of trunks and bags, carefully brushed or pressed and hung on racks in a closet or deposited in drawers. Perhaps the guest will dress for dinner. A word to the room-boy, and when one returns he finds everything in readiness, for this personage seems to know instinctively exactly what the "honorable mister" will care to wear, even to the particular collar and necktie. At night the guest goes to his room and finds as he opens the door that a small electric bulb has been left lighted near the head of the bed. A fine kimono and sandals are nearby on a chair, because the guest may care to read a little before retiring. Enter the room at any time of night and a servant usually taps at the door a minute later, asking if anything is wanted.

"Do you care to be called in the morning?"

"No."

"What time will you be awake?"

"Perhaps seven o'clock."

And as the hands of the clock reach that exact minute the next morning the Japanese boy enters with a tray on which are a pot of tea, two slices of toast, an orange or other fresh fruit, which he places on a stand at the head of the bed, while he goes to the bathroom and prepares the bath.

And this doglike faithfulness is amply rewarded at the end of the week by a fifty-cent "tip."

KOREAN FARMERS

"Leaving at noon today," says the guest. He may stay outside his room until eleven o'clock and come back to find every article packed in trunks and bags, much better than he could have arranged them himself. Porters take all checking and handling of baggage in charge—for it would not be "correct" to permit a white man to carry any sort of a parcel or handbag. An automobile with a uniformed chauffeur and footman waits at the front door of the hotel to take guests to the railway station, where another hotel attendant attends to tickets, and usually lifts his cap with "good-by" after he has seen to it that hotel guests have a comfortable seat in a railway carriage.

The stranger leaves Seoul after having been carried around on a bed of roses. Such wonderful service is remarkable in any country, and the traveler is pleased. He feels that Japan is accomplishing wonders in Korea, where travel was formerly such an inconvenience.

The food at the Chosen hotel in Seoul would compare favorably with that in a New York hotel or restaurant of the best class. The rooms and equipment would compare with any hotel in America. Japan knows how to please the weary foreigner.

The Koreans are an "unlovely race" at present, and one can understand in a measure how the Japanese looks upon them with contempt, just as he does upon the Chinese, and much as an Englishman looks upon the "natives" of Hongkong, or the American upon the Filipino. It is "contempt for an inferior race." Once I saw an American military officer who had been long in the East, plowing his way along a crowded market street, pushing aside women and children with his swagger stick. (Oh, yes, our Yankee soldier in the East soon acquires the swagger stick and wrist-watch habit!) We had been walking together, so when I stepped into the street and avoided the crowd I remonstrated with him for having literally to push his way through the crowd.

"I can't see that it is a mark of decent behavior, nor even a convenience," I remarked to him. "This is their country; we are the 'foreigners.' They are as good as we are."

"Perhaps you like to think that you are no better than they are," he sneered, "but that is because you are a stranger out here. I know blankety-blank well that they are not as good as I am, and they've got to get out of my way."

This is the attitude of "superior races" in the East, and perhaps elsewhere. Japan now knows that she is a "superior yellow nation," because her scientists have established to their own satisfaction that the Japanese people are of Southern Malay origin, and that they are only distantly related to their Mongolian brethren.

The typical Korean gentleman looks like a scare-crow, when he is "dressed" for a promenade in the streets—at least by comparison to the Japanese. He wears a long and loose grass-cloth white coat that looks like a Mother Hubbard, being tied by strings around his arm pits. On his head is perched a little black net "plug" hat that is tied with black strings under his chin. His baggy trousers are tied with a string or ribbon about the ankles, and he often has white tape wound around his feet for hosiery, which is set off by clumsy shoes about three sizes too large. An American man would look like a side-show freak in such a costume, so little may be expected from the Korean, who usually has a beard of hairs that could be counted in three minutes, and a mustache that cannot number more than fifty hirsute strands. He often has negroid features and oriental eyes that are merely slits in his face, and usually seem to be closed.

The national costume for the women consists of absurd balloon skirts and little short jackets that leave the breasts exposed—although the Japanese have endeavored to alter the national costume and have been successful in a measure, so that one so attired is popularly supposed to belong to the "lower classes." A Korean woman never puts her arms in the sleeves of her coat. The sleeves are there, but she drapes the collar of her coat over her head and permits the sleeves to dangle over her ears. It is said that the origin of the custom was something as follows: women were told in the early days that they must be ready to go away at a moment's notice in times of danger, not even waiting long enough to put their arms in the sleeves of their coats, because their lords and masters, the men, must not be kept waiting. Often they go bare-headed, save for the cloak, but one also sees them about the streets with head-gear of straw as large as two bushel hampers, which they hold in place with their hands. These, also, the Japanese are making it known, are worn only by the "lower classes," but plenty of the women care more for the Korean tradition than they do for the Japanese "class distinctions."

When the father of a Korean gentleman dies, the son goes into mourning by putting on a gigantic mushroom straw hat, which reaches far out over his shoulders and which he should wear for three years. A glance into the highways of Seoul causes one to think that the father of about every man in twenty has died within the time limit, because about that percentage of the male population seems to be in "mourning." And one does not "mourn," at least officially or outwardly, for a wife, sister or mother.

It is a question whether the male or female of Korea is costumed the more ridiculously. They are rarely seen together, however, for the Korean gentleman would not so far forget his "superiority" and dignity as to be seen publicly with a woman. So he struts around alone, or with his pals. And, apparently, they are never at home until well into the wee hours of the morning. My guide explained, when I remarked that all male Seoul seemed to be in the streets at night, in the restaurants, or at the theater: "They do not like to stay at home, where they must see their wives. Like mine, they were all chosen for them by their relatives and they do not care to look at them when it is unnecessary."

A Korean theater is a rather tame institution, where performances are given on the stage, but where the principal object seems to be to provide agreeable feminine companionship for the men. "Women, as a rule, never venture into the playhouses, and if they do, they sit off in a part of the house specially reserved for them, as in Chinese theaters. Sing-song girls cavort in a rather unseemly and dull manner in "national dances," and play instruments that are not pleasing to occidental ears, but seem to help the oriental to "forget." And that is what the average native of the Land of the Morning Calm seems to be doing most of the time; trying to forget to what depths his nation has fallen. He is not to blame, perhaps, for his father's father and grandfather paved the way for him. The reckoning was certain to come some day, and it is already here. Japan is his traditional and hereditary enemy; but Japan has won out in the race and is his master. Japan has her reward for much waiting, wrested from Russia after a bloody fight—but it is not just the land of gold that it was thought to be, worth more from a military point of view than from the treasures in the hills. But Japan is satisfied, and Russia seems to be; it being very apparent to the casual observer that the two nations which were at one another's throats a few years ago have come to an "understanding" in regard to the distribution of much of the territory of the earth's surface. Poor old Korea! There could have been little more than the national skeleton to pick at when Japan arrived. Perhaps there was never a better example of a nation passing into complete decay. Even old China is a lusty and healthy nation compared to her little sister to the north, because although temples have faded and become moss-covered, although temple courts are often enough the repositories of stagnant water and filth, although the religion of the people has passed and they have lost most of their interest in the arts, in agriculture and in commercial pursuits that bind a nation, the Chinese have not materially deteriorated physically, and it is

A Typical Korean Gentleman

still a question whether they have deteriorated mentally. The Korean whom one meets in the streets of the cities and the poor creature who drudges from dawn until sunset in the rice-fields in the valleys of this land of hills seems to be a dejected and unfortunate human being and his poor side-partner, wife, sister and mother, are only at his level, because they, too, have suffered from the miserable reign of debauchery that has held the country in its grip for centuries.

Seoul lies in a valley surrounded by pointed hills, almost as if it were in the tremendous crater of a volcano; but it does not convey the impression of being smothered by nature's great fortifications, which is so frequently the case in valley cities. Seoul ranges over a large territory within the city walls, and there is considerable area beyond that lies within the great basin, yet when one ascends any of the encircling hills and looks over the city it seems to fill the valley with red roofs, light buildings and green foliage. Such a view may be obtained from the top of the three-peaked mountain, which is known to visitors as the Cock's Comb. The ride in this direction is one of the many pleasant jaunts for foreign visitors to the capital city. But an hour's ride in any direction beyond the walls takes one into the country, where the conditions are almost as primitive as they are in remote parts of the country. The Korean peasant dwells in his little mud or straw-thatched cottage and tills his small fields that reach sheer to the walls of the metropolis, which are so crumbling in places that much vegetation has rooted itself in them and gives the big artificial mound the appearance of a natural ridge when viewed from a distance. The country people about Seoul are usually meek and gentle folk, who do not resent the staring eyes of the stranger, but seem to welcome his interest in their humble life.

The city wall is one of the sights of the capital that is likely to be a never-ending delight to the visitor. It is a structure that dates from the reign of Yi Taijo, who located his capital in the valley and is said to have requisitioned the services of two hundred thousand of his subjects when he put up the fortification, which was assuredly modeled after the Great Wall of China. It is fourteen miles in circumference, from twenty-five to forty feet in height, and is pierced by eight gates and numerous arches, which span the streams that here, as elsewhere in Korea, go rushing from the hills towards the sea. The Big Bell, which hangs in an ornate kiosk, has a direct connection with the walls and the gates. It is ten feet high and eight feet wide, and its booming is easily heard in all parts of the valley. For at least five centuries the bell sounded the signal for the closing of the city gates at night and the

Man in Mourning, Korea

opening of the gates in the morning. It also sounded a curfew in the evening, which was a signal for all men to go inside some building and the women of Seoul to take to the streets for air and exercise—a custom that departed after the city became popular with foreigners, but one that was rigidly enforced by imperial decree in the earlier day. It is related that when the bell was cast in 1396, the metals failed to fuse into the desired bronze until a living child was thrown into the molten mass; and the wails of the child are heard by the Koreans whenever the bell is rung.

The Legation Quarter seems to be almost in the country, although well within the city limits. Residences are surrounded by beautiful gardens, as are many of the homes of missionaries, about seventy-five per cent, of whom are Americans. About six miles distant are the buildings of the old Pook Han monastery, once a favorite rendezvous for the kings who had left their thrones, the priests of Buddha and the literati. A few priests remain, but the place is sadly neglected at the present time, although it is an alluring climax to a day's excursion from the Seoul hotel, and it is a popular camping ground for the missionaries during their summer holidays. A more pretentious collection of buildings—about fifty shrines and monasteries—are assembled on Diamond Mountain, about one hundred miles from Seoul. Arrangements for the traveler to visit these will be made upon application at the hotel, where guide and equipment will be provided; but it is a trip that will appeal to the more adventurous tourists, while the casual visitor will be satisfied with the more easily accessible points of interest in the neighborhood that will enable him to return to the hotel at night.

As before noted, the properly identified visitor will be admitted to the East Palace, and without identification or guide he may enter the grounds of the old North Palace; but the principal joy of the Korean visit is likely to be not in the palaces, which are rather tawdry imitations of the royal dwellings of China or Japan, but the street life, mingling with the people of the capital and the people of its environs. While the curio or souvenir hunter may not find so much to interest him as in the streets of the Chinese capital, there are a few things in the shops that he will not have encountered elsewhere, and hunting them out in uninviting little junk-shops and second-hand stores—the possessions of a Korean gentleman are frequently sold following his death—will make an appeal to many Americans and provide many interesting jaunts in the quest of articles that sometimes prove to be valuable specimens of native manufacture. Brass articles, bowls, candlesticks and teapots, are frequently as beautiful as any to be found in Damascus or other Syrian

A Gateway in Seoul

cities noted for similar wares. Chests of all kinds, from those manufactured from chestnut or the wood of the Chinese pagoda tree to beautiful rosewood chests trimmed with brass, will provide a veritable happy hunting ground for the lover of beautiful furniture, but alas, some of these things do not well survive the winters of an American steam-heated house, which is likely to diminish the joy of the lucky purchaser.

The North Palace consists of many brilliantly painted and intricately carved buildings, which are unoccupied, but which the Japanese government is taking steps to preserve for future generations; because they have played an important part in the Korean national history and they are likely to be treasured possessions to residents and visitors of the future. As it was said of a French novelist: "He is too young to be a classic and too old to be popular," so the events that have transpired within these palace walls are too recent to be viewed in the light of "history." The generation still survives that knew the oppression, maladministration, assassinations and horrors that emanated from these buildings, and they are viewed as the locale of one of the bloodiest dramas that was ever enacted in any country much as the modern Chinese view the palaces of the Manchus, who threatened to bring the country to ruin, but were unable to do so because of the vitality of the natives, who could not be crushed by the invading foreigner, although he remained for centuries. One of the most attractive buildings is the *Keikairo,* which is popularly known as the Summer Pavilion, the Hall of Congratulations and Audience Hall. It is a vast pavilion, the roof of which is supported by eight rows of large granite columns—rarely used in Far Eastern architecture—and it looks out upon a beautiful lotus pond, the banks of which are evergreen, with mounds of pine and fir trees. Here the concubine-loving monarchs of Korea spent their summer afternoons with the ladies of the court, and royal barges floated on the pond, which is now deserted, save by water fowls. This building seems to have been modeled after the celebrated floating palaces of India, and for a long period it was the scene of courtly revels that are depicted by the novelists, whose imagination could not picture more weird intrigues and plots than actually transpired on the shores of the lotus pond.

One of the latest of these startling events dates only to 1895, when the assassination of the queen precipitated most of the events in Korea's doom, as the assassination of the Austrian heir precipitated the Great War in Europe. The Queen, like Draga of Servia, had been influential in placing many members of her family in high positions. This and other things aroused jealousies, and she became the victim of the plottings of powerful men at

THE *KEIKAIRO*, NORTH PALACE

court, who had the aid of Japanese ruffians in the accomplishments of their black designs. Before dawn, they forced an entrance to the queen's pavilion, abused her ladies and compelled them to divulge her hiding-place. Flying from the assassins, she was stabbed and fell to the pavement, whereupon someone thrust a sword through and through her body. Still unsatisfied, the blood-thirsty mob carried the corpse to a pine wood nearby, soaked her garments with kerosene, set fire to them and piled on wooden fagots until only a few bones were recovered, when the authorities quelled the disorder the following day. The king fled in terror to the Russian legation, where he received protection and where he remained for an extended period. He had granted various concessions to Russian capitalists and finally reached the point where he was acting in open defiance of the law by exploiting the natural resources of Korea for the benefit of Russian syndicates in which the imperial family of Russia were financially interested. When Russian laborers, guarded by a Russian military guard, entered Korea for the purpose of felling the trees to obtain construction material for a railway the bomb exploded. The war with Japan followed, Russia was defeated and the country's affairs passed gradually, but certainly, to the control of Tokyo, culminating in the decree of annexation.

At the time of annexation the Mikado pardoned nearly two thousand Korean criminals, granted special gifts to over twelve thousand members of the aristocracy and literati, rewarded over three thousand "faithful women" and distributed bounties to the rural districts. Immediately a far-reaching school system was organized with special courses to advance the interests of all native industries. Nothing more fortunate for the people of Korea had happened since the Son of the Creator of Heaven began his earthly rule from a Korean mountain-top. The reign of terror was over. Of course Korea was paralyzed by the shock. A liberal and wise administration in her country was something so rare and unexpected that she has been staggered by the blow. She is passing through her transition period and will again assume her rightful place in the world; but, when she does, she will be a province of Nippon. Korea as a kingdom has passed forever, and perhaps for her people and the rest of the world it were better so.

One day I took the train that follows a serpentine trail from Seoul to Fusan, the enterprising city on the hillside from which the steamers make twice-daily sailings for Shimonoseki, Japan, whence a leisurely or rapid journey may be made by rail to Yokohama, the principal point of departure from the Far East for America. I went up to the captain's bridge and looked back at the Yon-sen Mountains, the barrier that separated me from China, where I had spent happy days, weeks and months. There came that feeling of sadness that one experiences when parting from old friends; but it passed with the next thought. It might be a long time before I would see China again. One thing I could do, however, I could recommend her unqualifiedly as a fascinating companion to all who seek a delightful excursion in a foreign country.

BIBLIOGRAPHY

There is a Manual of Chinese Bibliography by Moellendorff, which contains the titles of over four thousand books and articles on China, and the "Bibliotheca Sinica" by Henri Cordier contains hundreds of references of similar nature, while Wylie's "Notes on Chinese Literature" will be a valuable reference book to the student or specialist. These volumes, however, may not be easily accessible for casual reference, and the following condensed list is likely to be sufficient to provide desired information in regard to the general subject of the Tour of China:

BALL, CHARLES J.: Things Chinese.
BISHOP, ISABELLE L. B.: Korea and Her Neighbors.
——Yangtze Valley and Beyond, The.
BLAND, JOHN and EDMUND BACKHOUSE: China Under the Empress Dowager.
CARL: With the Empress Dowager of China.
Christianisme en China, Le.
CLARKE: Ten Great Religions.
DER LING: Two Years in the Forbidden City.
DENBY, CHARLES: China and Her People.
DOUGLAS, ROBERT K.: Society in China.
EDWARDS, OWEN M.: The Story of China.
FALKE: Buddha, Mahammed, Christus.
FEER, HENRI L.: Etudes Bouddhique.
GALE, JAMES S.: Korean Sketches.
GIFFORD, DANIEL L.: Korea: Every Day Life In.
GILES, HERBERT A.: Sayings of Confucius.
GILES, HERBERT A.: A History of Chinese Literature.
GORDON-CUMMING: Wanderings in China.
HAMILTON, ANGUS: Korea.

Hardy, Edward J.: John Chinaman at Home.
Hatch, Ernest F. G.: Far Eastern Impressions.
Holcombe, Chester: The Real Chinaman.
Jernigan, Thomas R.: China's Business Methods and Policy.
Jones: Tsingtau, The Fall of.
Kemp, E. G.: Manchuria, Korea and Russian Turkestan.
Kennedy: Religions and Philosophies of Far East.
Koeppen, Carl F.: Religion des Buddha, Die.
Lee Yan Phou: When I was a Boy in China.
Legge, James: Confucius' Life and Teaching.
Little: The Far East.
Longford, Joseph H.: The Story of Korea.
Martin, William A. P.: Awakening of China, The.
McCormick, Frederick: The Flowery Republic.
Meadows, Thomas T.: Chinese and Their Rebellions.
Millard, Thomas F.: The New Far East.
Miln, Louise J.: Quaint Korea.
Official Guide to Eastern Asia, Tokyo.
Parker, Edward H.: John Chinaman and a Few Others.
Parsons, William B.: American Engineer in China, An.
Saint Hilaire: Bouddha et sa Religion.
Schreiber: Buddha und die Frauen.
Scidmore, Eliza R.: China, The Long Lived Empire.
Simon, Thomas: Cite Chinoise, La.
Smith, Arthur H.: Chinese Characteristics.
Terry, Thomas P.: Japanese Empire.
Tokyo: Official Guide to Eastern Asia.
Vladimir: China-Japan War, The.
Von Plath, Johann H.: Confucius und seine Schueler.
Weale: Manchu and Muscovite.
Westergaard, Niels L.: Ueber Buddha's Todesjahr.
Wilson, James H.: The Ever-Victorious Army.
Wurm: Buddha, Der

INDEX

Abbé Huc, 47, 122
actors, 60, 63, 66, 67, 68, 70, 71, 72, 74, 75, 76, 174, 181
Ah Cum, 32
Amoy, 52, 110
ancestor worship, 154, 198
An-king, 118
art, 59, 74, 86, 106, 119, 132, 134, 135, 188

Bakst, 70
Bard, 162
Barker, 70
Benares, 158
bird fanciers, 56
Bogue, 17
Boxers, 152, 186
Brethren of the Pear Orchard, 71
Buddha, 77, 154, 156, 158, 160, 175, 180, 182, 184, 185, 234

Camoëns, 48
camphor, 224
Canton, 6, 16, 17, 18, 20, 21, 22, 24, 26, 28, 30, 33, 36, 37, 39, 42, 77, 110, 143, 162; City of the Dead, 24; Five-storied Pagoda, 18; Trade Guilds of, 24
Capital Punishment, 85, 86
Cats, as food, 18, 30
Cha Pih-yung, 71, 72, 74, 75, 76
Chang Shih-cheng, 92
Chan-Tien-you, 132
Chaplin, Charlie, 62

Chen-tsung, 162
Chien Liu, 90
Chih-li, 207
Chin-an-fu, 209
Ching-lung-chiao, 198, 200, 201
Chin-kiang, 110, 112
Chop Suey, 14
Chosen (Korea), 216, 224, 225, 226
Christian, 39, 40, 44, 103, 110, 111, 114, 122, 142, 154, 155, 156, 160, 162, 170, 209, 216, 224
Chu-fou, 161
Chung-tu, 161
City of Heaven (Hangchow), 78, 82, 88, 89, 90, 92, 94, 97, 98, 99, 102, 103, 111, 119, 209
Cockroaches, as food, 24
Confucius, 78, 106, 160, 164
Copper, 121
Craig, Gordon, 64

Dalai Lama, 168
Daruma, 124
Davids, Dr. T. W. Rhys (quoted on Lamaism), 155
Diaghileff, Serge de, 70
Diamond Mountain, 234
Dogs, as food, 18, 30
Dowager Empress, 85, 136, 137, 171, 172, 178, 181, 191, 192, 198

"Elder Brother of Jesus Christ.", 111
Empress Jingo, 217
"Ever Victorious Army,", 112

Index 243

Eunuchs, 172, 173, 174, 192

Foo-chow, 52
Formosa, 131, 224
Friar Odoric, 88
Funeral, 20, 28, 75, 136, 139, 142, 154, 192
Funeral Boats, 20
Fusan, 238

Gambling, 39, 44, 46, 47, 49
Gordon-Cumming, C. F. ("Wanderings in China" quoted), 188
Grand Canal, 78, 86, 110, 113, 154, 191, 208
Great Prince Chien,", 90
Great Wall of China, 195, 200, 201, 204, 212, 215, 232

"Hair Rebels", 111, 112
Han Hsin, 113
Hangchow, 78, 82, 88, 89, 90, 92, 94, 97, 98, 99, 100, 102, 103, 111, 119, 209; "Queen City of the Orient", 89; "Tour of the Lake.", 103; Tour of the Lake, 100; West Lake, 97, 98, 99, 100, 103, 209
Hangchow:, 88
Hankow, 4, 105, 107, 121, 122, 123, 124, 126, 128, 129, 132, 134, 144, 152, 206; "Chicago of China,", 121
Hankow-Peking Railroad, 126, 128, 132
Han-shui, 122
Han-wang, 113
Han-yang, 122, 123
Head-chopping, 63
"Heavenly Prince", 111, 114
Hedin, Sven, 155
Heung-Kong (Hongkong), 6
Heung-Shan (Macao), 39
Ho-nam, 20, 33, 34, 37, 38
Honan, 161, 164, 171, 192
Honan City, 145
Hongkong, 2, 4, 5, 6, 8, 9, 10, 12, 14, 16, 17, 21, 39, 48, 52, 110, 143, 228; "Fragrant Streams,", 6; "Gibraltar of the Orient,", 4; "The Peak", 6, 9, 12; Compared to Riviera, 5
Hotels, 3, 4, 8, 10, 14, 15, 21, 33, 52, 54, 58, 77, 79, 80, 94, 96, 115, 123, 148, 207, 226
Huang-Ho, 209
Huang-Ti, 121
Hu-kow, 119
Hung Hsin-chuan, 111, 112
Hupeh, 145
Hu-tsen, 56
Hwai-yin, 113
Hwang-chow, 121
Hwang-shih-kang, 108, 120

Ichang, 121
India, 123; floating palaces of, 236
Iron Ore, 108

Japan (in China), 2, 5, 8, 12, 14, 15, 26, 52, 67, 98, 100, 106, 107, 108, 110, 120, 131, 204, 209, 211
"Japanese Gardens,", 98, 99
Jesus Christ, 142, 156
Jones, Jefferson (quoted), 211

Kaiping Coal Mines, 131
Kao-chou Bay, 210
Kao-tsu, 113
Keijo (Seoul), 224
Kennedy, J. M. ("The Philosophies and Religions of the East"), 160
"Kingdom of Great Peace,", 111
King-teh-chen, 119
Kiu-kiang, 119, 121
Kowloon, 8
Kuang-Hsu, 150, 164, 186
Kublai Khan, 160, 162
Kung-fu-tze (Confucius), 160
Kun-ming-hu Lake, 171, 178
Kwang-si, 111
Kwang-tung (Canton), 20

Lake Po-yang, 119, 120
Lamaism, 155, 156, 160, 162
Lao-tze, 161
Lhassa, 168
Li Hung-chang, 14, 55, 112, 207
Li Yuan-hung, 123
Libraries, 89, 103, 111
Lion-li-ho, 130
Li-Shan mountains, 210
"Little Orphan Island,", 118

Macao, 6, 39, 40, 42, 46, 47, 48; "The Monte Carlo of the Orient,", 39, 44; Camoëns' grotto, 48
Manchuria, 208, 212, 214, 215, 220
Manchus, 68, 85, 143, 144, 145, 171, 207, 214, 215, 236
Marco Polo, 16, 26, 88, 89, 90, 92, 98, 110, 111, 119
Mencius (Meng-tse), 154, 161
Meng-tse (Mencius), 154, 161
Military, 28, 102, 113, 128, 139, 140, 144, 190, 197, 209, 211, 212, 215, 217, 228, 230, 238
Ming Emperors, 114, 116, 127, 152, 196, 197
Ming Tombs, 70, 195, 196, 198
Ming-Ti, 158
Mongolia, 201
Morrison, Robert, 162
Motion Pictures, 58, 59, 60, 63
Mo-tsou-hu, 116
Mukden, 68, 208, 212, 214
Müller, Max ("Chips from a German Workshop"), 156

Nanking, 43, 112, 114, 116, 152, 162
Nankou, 116, 195, 196, 198, 214
Nankou Pass, 198
Nestorian Christianity, 103, 162
Ningpo, 110
Noor-chachu, 214

Opium, 1, 6, 40, 42, 43, 44, 48, 52, 174

Pantomime, 66
Pao-ting-fou, 130
Pawn-shops, 18
Pearl River, 17, 20
Pei-ho, 132
Pei-tai-ho, 212
Peking, 8, 22, 44, 54, 75, 77, 86, 108, 111, 114, 116, 123, 126, 127, 128, 132, 134, 136, 137, 138, 142, 144, 145, 146, 147, 148, 150, 152, 162, 164, 166, 171, 172, 173, 178, 180, 182, 184, 185, 188, 192, 194, 195, 198, 204, 206, 207, 208, 211, 212, 214; Baron von Kettler's memorial arch, 186; Cheng-yang-men Gate, 152; Five Towered Pagoda, 182, 184, 185; Forbidden City in, 136, 140, 144, 145, 147, 154, 171, 172, 186, 190, 191, 192; Legation Quarters, 142, 152; Summer Palace at, 137, 171, 173, 178, 181, 182, 191, 192; Temple of Agriculture, 155, 168; Temple of Heaven, 155, 164, 166, 168
Peking-Kalgan Railway, 132, 195, 198, 200
Phonograph, 121
Pig, as pet, 86
Pirates, 17, 18, 21, 22, 33, 90, 218
Pi-tan, 116
Pook Han Monastery, 234
Postal System, 132
Princess Der Ling, 68, 172, 178, 181

Queue, 84, 85, 86, 128, 135

Railways, 94, 120, 126, 128, 131, 132, 152, 195, 198, 206, 208, 210, 211, 214, 226
Rats, as food, 18, 85
Reinhardt, Max, 66
Religion, 106, 142, 143, 154, 155, 156, 158, 160, 161, 162, 198, 222, 230
Revolving Stage, 67

Index

Ricci, Matteo (first missionary), 162
Russian Ballet, 70

Sen-tsen (Shanghai), 56
Seoul, 220, 224, 225, 226, 228, 229, 230, 232, 234, 238; "Best hotel in the East", 226; Called Keijo, 224; East Palace, 224, 225, 234; Keikairo, 236; Legation Quarters, 234; North Palace, 224, 234, 236; Pronunciation of, 224; Walls of, 225, 232
Shameen, 21, 22, 24, 33, 38
Shanghai, 4, 50, 51, 52, 54, 55, 56, 58, 60, 62, 64, 68, 77, 78, 80, 81, 82, 84, 85, 94, 104, 105, 107, 110, 114, 120, 122, 131, 132, 136, 144, 204, 206; "Paris of the Orient,", 220; Bird market, 55, 56; Mandarin's Tea House, 55, 58
Shanghai-Hangchow Railway, 94
Shan-hai-kuan, 212
Shantung Railroad, 210
Shih-huang-ti, 161
Shimonoseki, 238
Shun (Emperor), 168
Si-an, 162
Sino-Japanese War, 131
Slavery, 36, 66, 76, 124, 126, 218
Snakes, as food, 18, 30, 85
Soldier of China, 102, 139, 140, 143, 190
Standard Oil Company, 107
Suicide, 70, 72, 86, 172
Su-Tung-po, 121
Swatow, 52

Taiping Rebellion, 111
Tai-ping-hsien, 116
Taku Fort, 132
Taming-hu Lake, 209
Tang Shao-yi, 144
Taoism, 121, 154, 161, 162, 167
Ta-tung, 118
Tayeh Mines, 108, 120

Tea, 8, 15, 34, 36, 38, 55, 58, 71, 75, 81, 100, 119, 123, 124, 126, 127, 129, 168, 200, 224, 226
Telegraph, 132
Telephone, 132
Theater, 10, 28, 58, 60, 62, 64, 66, 67, 70, 71, 74, 75, 86, 181, 230; Flowery Way, 66, 70, 71
Thibet, 52, 105, 120, 128, 155, 158, 160
Tientsin, 4, 132, 206, 207, 208, 209, 212
Tientsin-Pukow Railway, 211
Trans-Siberian Railway, 208
Trench Warfare, 102
Tschoue-tcheon, 130
Tsimo, 212
Tsingtau, 209, 210, 211, 212
Tsung-ming, 106, 110
Tsze Hsi An (Dowager Empress), 171

Victoria, 5, 6
Virgin Mary, 156

Wang-ton-sien, 130
Wan-Shou-Shan (Summer Palace), 171
Wa-ti, 20
Whangpoo-Kiang, 52, 110
Widowhood, 32, 33, 34, 35, 36, 37, 38, 218
Wilson, H. H. (quoted), 155
Women, 6, 20, 28, 37, 42, 43, 44, 46, 48, 54, 56, 74, 86, 111, 156, 170, 171, 184, 211, 218, 228, 229, 234, 238; inferiority of, 74
Wu Ting-fang, 144
Wu-chang, 122, 123
Wu-hu, 116
Wu-sueh, 120
Wu-sung, 106, 131
Wu-ta-szu (Five-Towered Pagoda), 184

Yangchow, 112
Yangtze-Kiang, 4, 52, 105, 106, 107, 108, 110, 115, 118, 119, 120, 121, 122, 146; "Child of the Sea XE

"Yangtze-Kiang: "River of Fragrant Tea Fields"", 105; "River of Fragrant Tea Fields", 105; "Son of the Ocean", 121; gorges of, 121
Yellow Sea, 106
Yen (Peking), 154
Yi Taijo, 232

Yokohama, 8, 123, 238
Yon-sen Mountains, 239
Yuan Shih-k'ai, 137, 143, 144, 161, 164, 171, 192
Yu-chou (Peking), 154
Yung-lo, 114, 152, 185, 196, 198

www.ingramcontent.com/pod-product-compliance
Lightning Source LLC
Chambersburg PA
CBHW020327170426
43200CB00006B/300